THE SEARCH FOR THE
ORIGINS OF CHRISTIAN WORSHIP

Paul Bradshaw is Professor of Liturgy at the University of Notre Dame, Indiana, USA, but currently serving as Director of Undergraduate Studies at the University's London centre. He is also a priest-vicar of Westminster Abbey, an honorary canon of the Episcopal Diocese of Northern Indiana, a member of the Church of England Liturgical Commission, and chief editor of the international journal, *Studia Liturgica*. He is a former President of Societas Liturgica and of the North American Academy of Liturgy. Before he began to teach at Notre Dame in 1985, he was successively Director of Studies at Chichester Theological College, Course Director of the St Albans' Diocese Ministerial Training Scheme, and Vice-Principal of Ripon College, Cuddesdon, Oxford.

Dr Bradshaw has written or edited over twenty books and contributed more than seventy articles or essays. His major publications include *Daily Prayer in the Early Church* (SPCK, London 1981/Oxford University Press, New York 1982) and *Ordination Rites of the Ancient Churches of East and West* (Pueblo, New York 1990). Together with the Jewish scholar Lawrence Hoffman, he has edited a series of books on Jewish and Christian liturgy, entitled Two Liturgical Traditions (University of Notre Dame Press, 1991–9), and he was one of the editors of the revised edition of *The Study of Liturgy* (SPCK, London/Oxford University Press, New York 1992). The first edition of *The Search for the Origins of Christian Worship* was translated into French in 1995.

To my students, past and present

The Search for the Origins of Christian Worship

Sources and Methods for the Study of Early Liturgy

Second Edition

PAUL F. BRADSHAW

Carmelite Monastery
89 Hiddenbrooke Dr.
Beacon, NY 12508

OXFORD
UNIVERSITY PRESS

2002

OXFORD

UNIVERSITY PRESS

Oxford   New York
Athens   Auckland   Bangkok   Bogotá   Buenos Aires   Cape Town
Chennai   Dar es Salaam   Delhi   Florence   Hong Kong   Istanbul   Karachi
Kolkata   Kuala Lumpur   Madrid   Melbourne   Mexico City   Mumbai   Nairobi
Paris   São Paulo   Shanghai   Singapore   Taipei   Tokyo   Toronto   Warsaw

and associated companies in
Berlin   Ibadan

Published by Oxford University Press, Inc.
198 Madison Avenue, New York, NY 10016
www.oup.com

Published in Great Britain by SPCK
Holy Trinity Church, Marylebone Road
London, NW1 4DU

Library of Congress Cataloging-in-Publication Data
Bradshaw, Paul F.
   The search for the origins of Christian worship : sources and methods for the
study of early liturgy / Paul F. Bradshaw.– 2nd ed.
      p. cm.
Includes bibliographical references and indexes.
   ISBN 0-19-521732-2 (pbk. : alk. paper)
      1. Liturgies, Early Christian. I. Title.
BV185 B734 2002
264′.009′015–dc21

                                                            2001058098

1 3 5 7 9 8 6 4 2
Printed in Great Britain

Contents

Abbreviations

ACC	Alcuin Club Collection
A/GLS	Alcuin/GROW Liturgical Study, Nottingham
ALW	*Archiv für Liturgiewissenschaft*
BCE	Before the Common Era
BEL	Bibliotheca 'Ephemerides Liturgicae' Subsidia, Rome
BJS	Brown Judaic Studies
CE	Common Era
EL	*Ephemerides Liturgicae*
EO	*Ecclesia Orans*
ET	English translation
GLS	Grove Liturgical Study, Nottingham
JBL	*Journal of Biblical Literature*
JEH	*Journal of Ecclesiastical History*
JJS	*Journal of Jewish Studies*
JQR	*Jewish Quarterly Review*
JTS	*Journal of Theological Studies*
NTS	*New Testament Studies*
NovT	*Novum Testamentum*
OCA	Orientalia Christiana Analecta, Rome
OCP	*Orientalia Christiana Periodica*
PO	Patrologia Orientalis, Paris
QL	*Questions liturgiques*
QLP	*Questions liturgiques et paroissiales*
RevSR	*Revue des sciences religieuses*
SC	Sources chrétiennes, Paris
SJT	*Scottish Journal of Theology*
SL	*Studia Liturgica*
SP	*Studia Patristica*
TU	Texte und Untersuchungen, Berlin
VC	*Vigiliae Christianae*
ZKTh	*Zeitschrift für katholische Theologie*
ZNW	*Zeitschrift für die neutestamentliche Wissenschaft*

Preface

In the ten years since I completed the first edition of this book so much has transpired in the field of early Christian liturgical study that a second edition seemed to be warranted. Not only have I taken the opportunity to incorporate the fruits of the latest research and to update the bibliographical material, but what was originally Chapter 3 and entitled 'Ten Principles for Interpreting Early Christian Liturgical Evidence' has been entirely rewritten and moved to the beginning of the book to form Chapter 1 with a new title. Similarly, new chapters have been added on 'Ministry and Ordination' and on 'The Effects of the Coming of Christendom in the Fourth Century', the latter being a revised version of an essay that appeared in Alan Kreider, ed., *The Origins of Christendom in the West* (Edinburgh 2001), pp. 271–88, and I am grateful for permission to incorporate material from it here. Other additional material has been drawn from my essay, 'Continuity and Change in Early Eucharistic Practice: Shifting Scholarly Perspectives', published in R. N. Swanson, ed., *Continuity and Change in Christian Worship* (Studies in Church History 35; Woodbridge 1999), pp. 1–17, and once again I am grateful to the Ecclesiastical History Society for allowing me to use it here.

In the Preface to the first edition I referred to an article entitled 'Quest for the Mother Tongue' in *The Atlantic Monthly*, April 1991, by Robert Wright, who maintained that 'there are two kinds of people. In different fields they go by different names. In comparative linguistics they are known as the lumpers and the splitters. The lumpers like to put many languages into few families. The splitters like to inspect the resulting lumps and find fault lines' (p. 68). And I went on to say that in the field of early Christian liturgical study, I was a self-confessed splitter in an arena traditionally dominated by lumpers, who have tried to arrange the evidence so as to suggest that a single coherent line of liturgical evolution can be traced from the apostolic age to the fourth century. My book, therefore, was an attempt to present the case for the splitters' view of primitive Christian worship. That continues to be true, but in the intervening period I believe that I can detect growing support for the splitters' cause, not only from those who have followed my lead but also from those pursuing research independently of me. It would perhaps be premature to say that a scholarly consensus is emerging, but certainly a growing number of us would now share the following conclusions:

1   That we know much, much less about the liturgical practices of the first three centuries of Christianity than we once thought that we did. A great deal more is shrouded in the mists of time than we formerly imagined, and many of our previous confident assertions about 'what the early Church did' now seem more like wishful thinking or the unconscious projections back into ancient times of later practices.

2   That what we *do* know about patterns of worship in that primitive period points towards considerable variety more often than towards rigid uniformity. Nowadays, when we talk about 'what the early Church did', we need to specify *where* the practice in question is encountered (Syria, Egypt, North Africa, Rome, or some other region) and *when* (first, second, third, or fourth century, for each of these might be very different indeed from one another) and *whether* it is the only form found in that place at that time, for variant traditions could have coexisted alongside each other.

3   That the 'classical shape of Christian liturgy' that we have so often described is to a very large degree the result of a deliberate assimilation of different Christian traditions to one another during the fourth century rather than the survival of *the* one pattern of Christian worship from the earliest apostolic times, perhaps even from Jesus himself.

4   That what emerges in this post-Nicene era is frequently a liturgical compromise, a practice that includes a bit from here with a bit from there modified by a custom from somewhere else, rather than the triumph of one way of doing things over all the others, although this latter phenomenon is not unknown in some instances. This means that what then becomes the mainstream liturgical tradition of the Church in East and West is often quite unlike what any single Christian group was doing prior to the fourth century. A real mutation had taken place at that time, and many primitive customs had either disappeared or had been greatly altered from their former appearance.

The rest of this book will thus try to trace the history of scholarship that has led up to the adoption of these conclusions and to show what impact they are having on our understanding of various aspects of early Christian worship. As in the first edition, the whole volume may be seen as an annotated bibliography of primary and secondary literature pertaining to Christian worship in the first four centuries, and hence no separate bibliography is provided at the end, but readers should easily be able to locate the sources relevant to their interests by use of the indices, as full bibliographical details are given in the notes at the first mention of a text or study.

I would also like to reiterate my thanks to those who assisted me in enabling the first edition to come to birth, and especially to Roger Brooks, Professor of Judaism at Connecticut College, and Lawrence Hoffman, Professor of Liturgy at the Hebrew Union College–Jewish Institute of Religion, New York, for their helpful comments and insights on material in the chapter on the Jewish background to Christian worship; and to Harold Attridge, Professor of New Testament at Yale Divinity School, and Gregory Sterling, Associate Professor of New Testament at the University of Notre Dame, for their willingness to examine critically what I wrote about worship in the New Testament. But once again, my gratitude is due above all to my students, both past and present, to whom the book is dedicated and whose needs, questions, and own contributions to scholarship have challenged and stimulated me in my writing.

PAUL F. BRADSHAW, 2001

1

Shifting Scholarly Perspectives

It seems strange that, while conscious reflection on the methodologies appropriate to the discipline has constituted a significant element in scholarly research in such areas as biblical studies and ecclesiastical history in the course of recent decades, the same has not really been true in the field of liturgical history. There has been very little critical discussion of the particular methods which are applicable to this subject and few serious attempts to formulate principles for the interpretation of primary sources which ought to guide ongoing research. This chapter, then, attempts to do something towards filling that gap with regard to the early centuries of Christian worship.[1]

The Philological Method

The majority of scholars in the eighteenth, nineteenth, and even early twentieth centuries were generally quite confident that they had a clear picture of the pattern of worship practised in the first few centuries of the Church's history, and especially of the eucharistic rite. They began from the usually unspoken presupposition that in a matter as important as this, Jesus himself – or at the very least the apostles – would have left clear directives which all Christian communities would have followed. One had only to look, therefore, at the texts of rites known to us from later centuries, determine what was common to them all, and those elements would be the very ones that had persisted through the earlier centuries for which evidence was so limited, and would ultimately go back to apostolic times.

Thus, the earliest pioneers of liturgical scholarship were generally agreed that the variety of eucharistic rites found in the ancient Church must all be ultimately derived from a single apostolic model, and after an ancient church

---

1 For an earlier attempt, in a different format, see Paul F. Bradshaw, 'Ten Principles for Interpreting Early Christian Liturgical Evidence', in Paul F. Bradshaw and Lawrence A. Hoffman, eds, *The Making of Jewish and Christian Worship* (Notre Dame 1991), pp. 3–21.

order describing itself as *The Apostolic Constitutions* was discovered in the late seventeenth century, it seemed to many that the archetype had at last been found.[2] As Ronald Jasper indicated in his interesting survey of the work of British scholars on the origins of the eucharistic liturgy, this view was particularly held by Anglicans, and especially the Nonjurors of the early eighteenth century.[3] But it was by no means confined to them. It was also put forward, for example, by the French liturgist, Pierre Lebrun (1661–1729),[4] and it has been said of the German scholar, Ferdinand Probst (1816–1899), that he

> devoted immense erudition through a long lifetime to attempting to establish an impossible theory – namely that the College of Apostles, before they separated from Jerusalem, had elaborated, agreed upon, and enacted a comprehensive Liturgy for the celebration of the Holy Eucharist, from which all historic rites are descended; and that this archetype . . . was to be identified with the liturgy set forth in the eighth book of the fourth-century compilation known as the *Apostolic Constitutions*.[5]

That this text was of greater length than many of those which were considered to have been derived from it was not seen as presenting an insuperable objection to the theory. Until the twentieth century, as John Fenwick has pointed out,[6] ideas concerning the development of the Eucharist were haunted by a short tract *On the Transmission of the Divine Liturgy* attributed to Proclus, Bishop of Constantinople from 434 to 446.[7] This alleged that the earliest apostolic liturgies had been very lengthy, but that they were deliberately abridged in later centuries so as to retain the attention of less fervent generations of Christians. However, not only has its testimony long since been discredited,[8] but it has become a well-established canon of scholarship that

---

2 For this document, see below, pp. 84–6.
3 *The Search for an Apostolic Liturgy* (Alcuin Club Pamphlet 18; London 1963), pp. 3–5. See also W. Jardine Grisbrooke, *Anglican Liturgies in the Seventeenth and Eighteenth Centuries* (ACC 40; London 1958), passim.
4 *Explication littérale historique et dogmatique des prières et cérémonies de la messe* (Paris 1716–26 = Paris 1949), pp. xxxix–xl.
5 Bayard H. Jones, 'The Quest for the Origins of Christian Liturgies', *Anglican Theological Review* 46 (1964), p. 6. Probst's theory is set forth chiefly in two works, *Liturgie der drei ersten christlichen Jahrhunderte* (Tübingen 1870 = Darmstadt 1968) and *Liturgie des vierten Jahrhunderts und deren Reform* (Münster 1893).
6 John R. K. Fenwick, *Fourth Century Anaphoral Construction Techniques* (GLS 45, 1986), p. 4.
7 J. P. Migne, *Patrologia Graeca* 65:49B–852B; ET in F. E. Warren, *The Liturgy and Ritual of the Ante-Nicene Church* (London/New York 1897), pp. 197–9.
8 F. J. Leroy, 'Proclus, "De Traditione Divinae Missae": un faux de C. Paleocappa', *OCP* 28 (1962), pp. 288–99, argued that the tract was in any case the work of a sixteenth-century forger.

development in early Christian liturgy normally (although not invariably) proceeds from brevity to prolixity.[9]

Not even the eventual acceptance at the end of the nineteenth century that the rite of *Apostolic Constitutions* 8 was not in fact genuinely apostolic put an end to the quest for *the* original form of the Eucharist. Thus the leading German Lutheran scholar Paul Drews (1858–1912), although acknowledging the church order to be a fourth-century compilation, nevertheless defended a revised version of Probst's theory, by claiming, after a comparison of its liturgy with *1 Clement* and Justin Martyr, that it had managed to preserve the substance of the early 'official' celebration of the Eucharist.[10] This thesis was adopted by a number of scholars, including Anton Baumstark.[11]

As well as professing a strong belief in continuity in Christian worship traditions, such scholars, and those who came after them, were in effect employing philological rather than historical methods in their work, which is not surprising since most of them had been educated in classical literature rather than as professional historians. They were treating liturgical texts like other ancient manuscripts, comparing variant readings and trying to arrive at the original that lay beneath them all. As we shall see in the next chapter, a similar methodology was also employed by Jewish scholars in their search for the roots of their liturgy. However, the method has severe limitations for the study of the earliest centuries of Christian liturgical practice, for two main reasons.

First, as is also the case with Jewish liturgy, extant liturgical manuscripts as such from the Christian tradition are nearly all of a much later date, beginning around the eighth century CE. It is true that within early Christian literature there is a group of documents that look very like real, authoritative liturgical texts, containing both directions for the conduct of worship and also the words of prayers and other formularies. Since they claim in one way or another to be apostolic, they have generally been referred to as apostolic church orders. But they are not what they seem, as we shall see in somewhat greater detail in Chapter 4. Not only is their claim to apostolic authorship spurious – a judgement that has been universally accepted since at least the

---

9 This was one of Anton Baumstark's 'liturgical laws', though Baumstark regarded *Apostolic Constitutions* 8 as an exception to the rule, as it was not a true liturgical text, and in any case he was himself still somewhat under the shadow of (Pseudo-)Proclus: see below, p. 11, n. 28.

10 *Zur Entstehungsgeschichte des Kanons* (Tübingen 1902), and *Untersuchungen über die sogennante Clementinische Liturgie* (Tübingen 1906). For Drews' distinction between 'official' and 'private' celebrations of the Eucharist, see below, pp. 120–1.

11 *Vom geschichtlichen Werden der Liturgie* (Freiburg 1923), pp. 7ff. Fernand Cabrol, *Les origines liturgiques* (Paris 1906), p. 329, thought that the primitive character of the liturgy in the *Apostolic Constitutions*, 'quoique assez probable, n'est pas absolument indiscutable'.

beginning of the twentieth century – but they are not even the official liturgical manuals of some third- or fourth-century local church, masquerading in apostolic dress to lend themselves added authority – a judgement that is still not always fully appreciated by all contemporary scholars. Thus it is dangerous to treat them in the same way as authentic liturgical texts.

Apart from some fragments of what do seem to be the texts of individual prayers, therefore, sources for a knowledge of the practice of worship prior to the eighth century consist chiefly of brief, and often partial, descriptions of rites in letters and sermons; of even briefer, and less easily interpreted, allusions that appear in writings dealing with some quite different subject; and of pieces of legislation affecting liturgical matters that occur among the canons produced by various councils and synods; all of which we shall consider in greater detail later in the book. The philological method does not function nearly as well with such material as it does with parallel texts that can be compared with one another.

Second, liturgical manuscripts are in any case more prone to emendation than literary manuscripts. F. L. Cross once observed that:

> Liturgical and literary texts, as they have come down to us, have a specious similarity. They are written in similar scripts and on similar writing materials. They are now shelved shoulder to shoulder in our libraries and classified within the same system of shelfmarking ... But these similarities mask a radical difference. In the first place, unlike literary manuscripts, liturgical manuscripts were not written to satisfy an historical interest. They were written to serve a severely practical end. Their primary purpose was the needs of the services of the Church. Like timetables and other books for use, liturgical texts were compiled with the immediate future in view. Their intent was not to make an accurate reproduction of an existing model.[12]

In other words, copyists or translators of ancient material dealing with liturgical matters did not normally expend considerable time and energy on their work merely out of a general desire to preserve antiquity for its own sake but because they believed that the document legitimized as traditional the worship practices of their own day. What were they to do, then, when they encountered in a text something which did not correspond with their own experience – for instance, injunctions which advocated practices contrary to those of their own tradition, or the omission of some element which they regarded as important or essential? They could only conclude that the text before them really ought to accord with that with which they were familiar,

12 F. L. Cross, 'Early Western Liturgical Manuscripts', *JTS* 16 (1965), pp. 63–4.

that the traditions of their own church must be those which had been prescribed in ancient times and had simply been omitted by accident from the
document or had fallen out in the course of its transmission. It was then only
the work of a few moments to restore what they thought was the original
reading and bring it into line with current practice.

Liturgical manuscripts are not unique in this respect. They belong to a
genre which may be called 'living literature'.[13] This is material which circu-
lates within a community and forms a part of its heritage and tradition but
which is constantly subject to revision and rewriting to reflect changing historical and cultural circumstances. It would include such diverse specimens as
folk tales, the pseudo-apostolic church orders, and even some scriptural
material, all characterized by the existence of multiple recensions, sometimes
exhibiting quantitive differences (i.e., longer and shorter versions) and
sometimes qualitive differences (i.e., various ways of saying the same thing,
often with no clear reflection of a single *Urtext*), and sometimes both.[14]

This is a very different situation from, say, the copying of the works of
Augustine or some other patristic writer, when the desire was precisely to
preserve antiquity and make an accurate reproduction of the original.
Although such literary manuscripts might also be subject to occasional
attempts to correct what were perceived as lapses from doctrinal orthodoxy
in the text, these emendations are relatively rare and much easier to detect
than in liturgical manuscripts, where the risk of a passage being updated and
modified to fit a changed situation is far greater. Hence one should not easily
assume that the received version of any liturgical document necessarily represents what the author originally wrote, especially when it has been
subsequently translated from one language to another. The careful disentan-
gling of the various strata present in such texts can often not only point to a
very different reading in the original but also tell a fascinating story of how
later liturgical practice evolved.

On the other hand, we must also note that liturgical texts can go on being
copied long after they have ceased to be used. This principle serves as an
important counter-balance to the previous one, in that we should be cautious
about concluding that everything which appears in an ancient source must
have been in active use in the communities through which that document is
thought to have passed. We are all doubtless familiar in our own experience
with certain prayer-texts, or hymns, or complete orders of service that go on
appearing in successive editions of an official book of liturgies for years and

13 An expression used in reference to the *Didache* by Stanislas Giet, *L'Énigme de la
Didachè* (Paris 1970), p. 257. For the *Didache*, see below, pp. 77–8.
14 See further Paul F. Bradshaw, 'Liturgy and "Living Literature"', in Paul F. Bradshaw and
Bryan Spinks, eds, *Liturgy in Dialogue: Essays in Memory of Ronald Jasper* (London
1994), pp. 138–53 = (Collegeville 1995), pp. 139–54.

years without ever being used by anyone. They were appropriate or fashion-able in some earlier generation, perhaps at a particularly sensitive point in the history of that religious tradition, but have since become out of date. Yet nobody has the courage to say, 'Let's drop this from our formularies', since to do so would appear to be somehow a betrayal of our heritage, a reneging on our ancestors in the faith, or a wanton disregard for tradition. So it goes on appearing in the book, and everyone knows that when you reach it in the order of worship, you simply turn the page and pass over it to the next prayer or whatever.

Thus, while it is true that liturgical manuscripts were generally copied in order to be used, Christians of earlier generations were quite as capable as we are of carrying some excess liturgical baggage along with them, of copying out primitive and venerable texts into later collections of material just because they were primitive and venerable and not because of any real intention of putting them into practice. The problem is that they knew which of their texts were to be used and which passed over, while we are left to guess at it with whatever assistance other sources can give us. So, for example, while all who have studied the matter are agreed that in book 7 of the *Apostolic Constitutions* a number of the prayers have a strongly Jewish character, nobody can be sure what conclusions should be drawn from it.[15] Does it mean that Judaism was still exercising a strong influence on Christian worship at this late date, or is it just another piece of what the leading liturgical scholar Robert Taft has called 'liturgical debris', carried down by the tide of tradition from former times?

All of this is not to say that the philological method has no part at all to play in the study of early liturgical history, but only that its role is more limited than previous generations of scholars tended to assume. For we are not dealing here with the history of manuscripts in isolation but as tools employed within actual worshipping communities and so subject to all the forces operative in those particular historical contexts.

The 'Structural' Approach

In his well-known work, *The Shape of the Liturgy*, first published in 1945, Gregory Dix (1901–52) was one of the severest critics of attempts to find a single original apostolic eucharistic rite.[16] However, he did not really abandon the theory, but merely revised it. In his view, the various forms of the Christian Eucharist did have a common origin, but this was to be sought in the structure or shape of the rite rather than in the wording of the prayers:

15 See below, p. 92, n. 65.
16 pp. 209ff.

The outline of the rite – the Shape of the Liturgy – is everywhere most remarkably the same, after 300 years of independent existence in the widely scattered churches ... The outline – the Shape – of the Liturgy is still everywhere the same in all our sources, right back into the earliest period of which we can as yet speak with certainty, the earlier half of the second century. There is even good reason to think that this outline – the Shape – of the Liturgy is of genuinely apostolic tradition.[17]

In the years since the publication of his book Dix's influence has become all-pervasive and his methodology widely followed, even if some of the details of his conclusions would now be challenged. Although he applied his argument principally to the Eucharist, others have extended it to cover other early Christian rites. He has thus enabled both the traditional theory of a single liturgical archetype, albeit in a modified form, and also the basic presuppositions of the philological method, to retain a position of pre-eminence down to the present day, and for that reason his position warrants careful examination.

As the quotation above shows, chief among his assumptions, and those of his disciples, has been that the many varied liturgical forms found in different geographical regions in later centuries can all be traced back to a single common root in their institution by Jesus; and that variety tended to increase in the course of time as the Church developed and these practices were subject to differing local influences and emphases. Thus, what was common to most or all of these later forms must represent the very earliest stratum of Christian worship, while what was found in just a few instances, or merely one, was a later development.

Such views cannot really be sustained any longer in the light of recent scholarship. Those propounding the theory always have had considerable difficulty in demonstrating how such very diverse later practices could all have arisen from a single source, and in the course of their defence frequently had to resort to eliminating from consideration in one way or another awkward pieces of evidence which did not fit the theory, as, for example, the 'eucharistic' rite of *Didache* 9–10 or the apparent absence of 'confirmation' from the early Syrian tradition.[18] Now, however, there are the added complications, which we shall examine in the next two chapters, that first-century Jewish liturgy from which Christian worship took its departure was not nearly so fixed or uniform as was once supposed, and that New Testament Christianity was itself essentially pluriform in doctrine and practice.

Thus, it does not necessarily follow that what is common in later Christian liturgical practice is what is most primitive. It certainly *may* be so, but it is also

17 ibid., p, 5.
18 See below, pp. 119–21 and 146–9.

equally possible that resemblances that exist between customs in different parts of the ancient world are the result of a conscious movement towards conformity. Similarly, what is unusual or unique is not necessarily a late development. Once again it *may* be so, but it is equally possible that the phenomenon is in fact the vestige of what was once a much greater variety of forms of worship than we can now see in the surviving evidence. It may be an ancient local custom that somehow managed to escape – or at least avoid the full effect of – a later process that caused liturgical diversity to contract its horizons.

For, as we shall see in later chapters, the true story of the development of Christian worship seems to have been a movement from considerable differences over quite fundamental elements to an increasing amalgamation and standardization of local customs. The beginnings of this trend can already be seen in the second century CE, but it gathered much greater momentum in the fourth, as the Church expanded, as communication – and hence awareness of differences – between different regional centres increased, and above all as orthodox Christianity tried to define itself over against what were perceived as heretical movements; for in such a situation any tendency to persist in what appeared to be idiosyncratic liturgical observances was likely to have been interpreted as a mark of heterodoxy. As Robert Taft has written:

> This is the period of the unification of rites, when worship, like church government, not only evolved new forms, but also let the weaker variants of the species die out, as the Church developed, via the creation of intermediate unities, into a federation of federations of local churches, with ever-increasing unity of practice within each federation, and ever-increasing diversity of practice from federation to federation. In other words what was once one loose collection of individual local churches each with its own liturgical uses, evolved into a series of intermediate structures or federations (later called patriarchates) grouped around certain major sees. This process stimulated a corresponding unification and standardizing of church practice, liturgical and otherwise. Hence, the process of formation of rites is not one of diversification, as is usually held, but of unification. And what one finds in extant rites today is not a synthesis of all that went before, but rather the result of a selective evolution: the survival of the fittest – of the fittest, not necessarily of the best.[19]

19 'How Liturgies Grow: The Evolution of the Byzantine Divine Liturgy', *OCP* 43 (1977), p. 355, reproduced in his collected essays, *Beyond East and West* (Washington, DC 1984), p. 167 (2nd edn, Rome 1997), pp. 203–4.

The 'Organic' Approach

Over sixty years ago, in what became a classic work in the field, *Liturgie comparée*,[20] Anton Baumstark (1872–1948) attempted to define an appropriate methodology for the study of liturgical history by applying to the discipline an approach which was widely used in the latter half of the nineteenth century for the study of culture – the comparative method. Although it is commonly assumed that his work was inspired by the comparative study of language (and indeed Bernard Botte makes this assertion in his Foreword to the third edition of Baumstark's book), Fritz West has shown that the ultimate source of all the comparative sciences was nineteenth-century biological thought, as articulated in the *Naturphilosophen* of Germany, the comparative anatomy of Georges Cuvier, and the evolutionary theory of Charles Darwin.[21] From here comparative linguists and the other practitioners of the comparative sciences of culture derived both a model and a method. The model was the living organism. The method was systematic comparison and consequent classification on the basis of a supposed line of descent from the origin of the species.

The basic flaw in this approach was a failure to recognize the essential difference between nature and culture: whereas nature is generated genetically, culture is transmitted socially. As the French anthropologist Claude Lévi-Strauss has observed, 'the historical validity of the naturalist's reconstruction is guaranteed, in the final analysis, by the biological link of reproduction. An axe, on the contrary, does not generate an axe.'[22] Since the cultural objects of study were not truly 'organic', they were not in reality subject to the same laws of development as other organisms, and hence the exact analysis and predictive power of the natural sciences was simply not possible in these cases. Even so, since the evolutionary theory of the period maintained that development always progressed from simplicity to complexity, the same pattern was imposed upon the cultural data: the simple must be primitive; the complex must belong to a later period of time. Moreover, while in the study of language continuing structure provided the parameters to the field of comparison and made it possible to discern patterns of evolution, other aspects of culture exhibited no such evident structure. As a result, fields of cultural comparison tended to be defined on the basis of some *a priori* presumed 'essence' linking together the diverse phenomena, which the subsequent classification of 'genus' and 'species' merely served to reinforce.

20 Chevetogne, Belgium 1940; 3rd edn, rev. Bernard Botte, 1953; ET = *Comparative Liturgy* (London/Westminster, MD 1958).
21 Fritz West, *The Comparative Liturgy of Anton Baumstark* (A/GLS 31, 1995).
22 *Structural Anthropology* (New York 1963), p. 4.

Baumstark was not the first liturgical scholar to utilize analogies from the world of science, nor even the first to make use of the term 'comparative liturgy'. John Mason Neale (1818–66) seems to have coined the expression the 'science of Comparative Liturgiology', deriving it from 'comparative anatomy' and categorizing liturgies into species, each of which had its sub-species or genus and particular classes.[23] Later Edmund Bishop (1846–1917) likened the rigour of the methods of the physical sciences to those of the litur-gical historian;[24] and Fernand Cabrol (1855–1937) viewed the relationship of *the* liturgy to the various liturgical families as resembling that of a genus to its various species, and conceptualized the processes operative in liturgical history in terms of laws.[25] Nor have Baumstark and his disciples been the only scholars to seek to apply alleged universal principles to the study of early liturgy. There was, for example, the 'myth and ritual' school strongly repre-sented in Britain and Scandinavia in the first half of the twentieth century, which abstracted the concept of divine kingship from ancient Mesopotamian sources and applied it in blanket fashion as the archetypal pattern to religions throughout the Middle East, including Judaism and Christianity.[26] But Baumstark went further than any of these, both in his use of the comparative method as a tool of analysis and in his conviction that its conclusions could rival the certainty thought to be attainable by the exact sciences:

It is the forms of liturgical action and the liturgical texts of a given age which by their structure and rubrics can best teach us how their histor-ical development came about, just as geology draws its conclusions from the observable stratifications of the earth's crust . . . It is this abundance of forms which makes possible a comparative study of Liturgies, by using methods similar to those employed in comparative linguistics and comparative biology . . . In its method, then, the Com-parative Study of Liturgies approximates to that of the natural sciences. This method, as we know, is of necessity an empirical one; for it is only by setting out from exact results and precise observations that right conclusions will be reached.[27]

---

23 *Essays on Liturgiology and Church History* (London 1863), pp. 123–4. See Martin D. Stringer, 'Style against Structure: The Legacy of John Mason Neale for Liturgical Schol-arship', *SL* 27 (1997), pp. 235–45.
24 'History and Apologetics', in *Proceedings of the Rota* (London 1900), pp. 1–7 = Thomas Michael Loome, *Liberal Catholicism, Reform Catholicism, Modernism* (Mainz 1979), pp. 373–81.
25 *Les origines liturgiques*, pp. 23–44.
26 See S. H. Hooke, ed., *Myth and Ritual: Essays on the Myth and Ritual of the Hebrews in Relation to the Culture Pattern of the Ancient East* (London 1933).
27 *Comparative Liturgy*, pp. 2–3.

Adopting the linear and unidirectional understanding of historical development which was a common characteristic of the comparative sciences of culture, Baumstark maintained that the direction of liturgical evolution ran, both, from earlier variety to later uniformity, and also from austerity or simplicity and brevity to richness and prolixity. Yet he was forced by the realities of the historical data to qualify both these claims by acknowledging the existence of a 'retrograde movement' in each case: the movement towards uniformity was constantly being interrupted by a tendency towards local variation; that towards prolixity by a tendency towards abbreviation.[28]

To these fundamental principles, Baumstark added two basic 'laws' that he believed governed the process of the historical evolution of liturgy. The first was 'the Law of Organic Development', by which new additions to the liturgy at first took their place alongside more primitive elements, but in the course of time caused them to be abbreviated or even disappear completely.[29] The second law was 'that primitive conditions are maintained with greater tenacity in the more sacred seasons of the Liturgical Year',[30] in other words, that liturgical communities tend to preserve ancient customs on more solemn and significant occasions even though they may have disappeared from use at other times.

Later in the book he enunciated further, more specific laws, three of which had been formulated by his students. Fritz Hamm claimed both that 'the older a text is the less is it influenced by the Bible' and that 'the more recent a text is the more symmetrical it is'; Hieronymus Engberding proposed that 'the later it is, the more liturgical prose becomes charged with doctrinal elements'; while Baumstark himself added that 'certain actions which are purely utilitarian by nature may receive a symbolic meaning either from their function in the Liturgy as such or from factors in the liturgical texts which accompany them'.[31] In recent studies of Baumstark's work, Robert Taft has added two further 'laws' which he has detected there: that liturgical prose becomes increasingly oratorical and governed by rhetoric, and that the development of the liturgy is but a series of individual developments.[32]

---

28 ibid., pp. 15–22. The latter he explained as being a consequence of 'the decline in religious zeal of which the sermons of the great Patristic age often offer us abundant testimony' (p. 23). We can observe here the continuing influence of (Pseudo-)Proclus, *On the Transmission of the Divine Liturgy*: see above, p. 2.

29 ibid., pp. 23ff.

30 ibid., pp. 27ff. He had acknowledged in an earlier article, 'Das Gesetz der Erhaltung des Alten in liturgisch hochwertiger Zeit', *Jahrbuch für Liturgiewissenschaft* 7 (1927), p. 8, that this law arose from an observation by Adrian Fortescue, *The Mass* (London/New York 1912), p. 270, concerning 'the constant tendency of the greatest days to keep older arrangements'.

31 *Comparative Liturgy*, pp. 59–60, 130.

32 'Comparative Liturgy Fifty Years after Anton Baumstark (d. 1948): A Reply to Recent Critics', *Worship* 73 (1999), pp. 521–40, esp. pp. 524–7; and idem, 'Anton Baumstark's

Taft has rightly insisted that Baumstark's 'laws' were not formulated prior to nor as a surrogate for the facts of liturgical history themselves, but as attempts to explain the already determined facts. Nevertheless, by calling them 'laws' and at least appearing to elevate them to a status on a par with scientific laws,[33] Baumstark opened the way for others to interpret them as having an absolute character, and therefore being capable of predictive powers, rather than as merely observable tendencies in much liturgical history, which may or may not prove to be true in any given case. Baumstark himself implicitly admitted their limitation as laws when he acknowledged that the movement towards liturgical uniformity was constantly being interrupted by a tendency towards local variation and that towards prolixity by a tendency towards abbreviation, even though he wanted to label these tendencies as 'secondary' and 'retrograde'. We cannot judge a liturgical phenomenon 'primitive' simply because it exhibits variety, nor 'late' simply because it exhibits prolixity, since each of these may in fact be an instance of the alleged 'retrograde movement'. Similarly, although he adopted the premise that variety was a characteristic of early liturgy, he also asserted that uniformity was a sign of antiquity:

> Moreover, we shall have to regard as primitive [those] phenomena which are found with the same meaning, the same function, and in the same area, in all Christian Rites, or at least in a sufficiently large number of such Rites, and especially so if they have parallels in the Liturgy of the Synagogue. We shall pronounce the same verdict where anything has a Jewish parallel, even when it is limited to a few Christian Rites or it may be only to one. On the other hand, we shall consider as recent all phenomena peculiar to a single Rite or to a few Rites, but without parallel of any kind in the Synagogue. The same verdict must be pronounced on those which, although absolutely or almost universal, change their meaning, place or function from one Rite to another.[34]

Comparative Liturgy Revisited', in Gabriele Winkler and Robert F. Taft, eds, *Comparative Liturgy Fifty Years after Anton Baumstark* (OCA 265, 2001). The first can be found in *Comparative Liturgy*, pp. 61–70, the second (which is also derived from Hamm) in Baumstark's earlier monograph, *Vom geschichtlichen Werden der Liturgie.*

33 As in such statements as, 'by the law which *requires* that liturgical evolution *should* proceed from the simpler to the more complex, we shall deem the more austere the more primitive' (*Comparative Liturgy*, p. 31; emphasis added).

34 ibid., pp. 31–2.

Both of Baumstark's students in fact disassociated themselves from the absolute character attributed to the laws,[35] and his editor, Bernard Botte, also entered a number of caveats in his Foreword to the third edition. Although he believed that Baumstark's ideas were 'fundamentally right, even if he sometimes gave them too rigid a form and occasionally made unwarranted use of them', Botte warned of a number of pitfalls to be avoided:

> The first is that of being duped by words. While it is legitimate to inves-
> tigate the tendencies which have guided the evolution of the liturgy
> and even to give these tendencies the name of laws, it must also be
> remembered that this method is only a convenient device. The analogy
> with the natural sciences must not deceive us. These last set out from
> the postulate that phenomena are wholly determined, a presumption
> apart from which such sciences would not be possible. But when we
> pass to linguistics, this determinism is already mitigated . . . When we
> pass to history in which free-will plays an even greater part, the
> element of determinism is still weaker, and here we need much circum-
> spection if we are not to give the word 'law' too narrow a sense. There
> is a risk of confining what happens in history within an artificial
> framework which does violence to the facts. The first duty of the
> historian is always to respect the factual *datum* even when no place for
> it can be found in the scheme of a preconceived theory.
>   The second danger . . . is to take a logical construction as though it
> were a historic reality. The sciences do not always end in certainty.
> Induction may sometimes, indeed, lead to certain conclusions, but it
> often leads only to probabilities or even to provisional hypotheses . . .
> And so it is with history. When documents are wanting or too fragmen-
> tary, we must guard against too absolute conclusions. And it is here that
> we meet with the chief limitation of Baumstark. He did not always see
> where to draw the line between his hypotheses and historical reality.
> Hence it will be no matter for surprise if parts of his work must be
> abandoned. While some of his constructions were interesting and sug-
> gestive and have done good duty as working hypotheses, it would be a
> mistake to take them for historic truths scientifically demonstrated.[36]

---

35 Fritz Hamm, *Die liturgischen Einsetzungsberichte im Sinne vergleichender Liturgie-Forschung Untersucht* (Münster 1928), p. 97; Hieronymus Engberding, 'Neues Licht über die Geschichte des Textes der Ägyptischen Markusliturgie', *Oriens Christianus* 40 (1956), p. 46, n. 32.
36 *Comparative Liturgy*, pp. viii–ix.

The Comparative Method

All this is not to deny the value of the comparative approach advocated by Baumstark in helping us reconstruct liturgical history. Indeed, some form of comparison must necessarily be a part of any attempt to bridge the gaps in our knowledge; and a whole school of comparative liturgists has subsequently emerged from the pioneering work of Baumstark which includes in its number such leading scholars as Engberding himself, Juan Mateos, Taft,[37] and Gabriele Winkler. Their work, however, is much more cautious and sophisticated in its methodology: Taft, for example, insists on the importance of 'a constant dialectic between structural analysis and historical research'.[38] It proceeds from a close comparison of the similarities *and differences* between liturgical practices in different geographical regions, temporal periods, or ecclesiastical traditions to a hypothesis which attempts to account satisfactorily for the origin and development of those practices both in the light of the tendencies already observed in the evolution of other liturgical phenomena and within the context of their known historical circumstances. Obviously, such a process works better for periods when historical data is more plentiful, and especially after the emergence of actual liturgical texts, than it does in the less clearly defined world of the first three or four centuries of Christian history.

For this earlier time what we most need are not so much laws which tell us how the liturgy itself must have developed, nor even the observable tendencies in liturgical evolution which Baumstark's so-called laws actually offer us – useful though they are – but rather some guidelines to assist us in our efforts to interpret the fragmentary and often confusing primary sources on which any attempted reconstruction of primitive liturgical practice has to be based.

The Hermeneutics of Suspicion

Historians of early liturgy have traditionally tended to show a greater degree of naiveté in relation to their primary sources than have their counterparts in biblical studies. The latter have usually been much more ready to suspect that the documents before them were not always what they seemed, and might have less reliable historical data and more layers of interpretative strata than

---

37 See his important methodological studies, 'How Liturgies Grow: The Evolution of the Byzantine Divine Liturgy', *OCP* 43 (1977), pp. 355–78; 'The Structural Analysis of Liturgical Units: An Essay in Methodology', *Worship* 52 (1978), pp. 314–29 (both articles reproduced in *Beyond East and West*, pp. 151–92; 2nd edn, pp. 187–232); 'Reconstructing the History of the Byzantine Communion Ritual: Principles, Methods, Results', *EO* 11 (1994), pp. 355–77, esp. 356–64.
38 'The Structural Analysis of Liturgical Units', p. 316 = *Beyond East and West*, p. 153.

they purported to contain. Many liturgical historians, on the other hand, have often had a propensity to treat the sources that they use as simply offering raw factual data, and have failed to consider such matters as the particular character of the text, the author's aims and intentions in its composition, and the context in which it was written. Yet the answers to these questions are vital for a proper interpretation of any source, and the temptation to 'proof-text' must be resisted as much here as in biblical study. Thus Karl Gerlach has recently done a valuable service in criticizing the common failure to take into account the rhetorical purpose of the sources of our knowledge of the ante-Nicene Pascha and so assuming, for example, that claims made there that certain Christian groups were celebrating 'with the Jews' are always simple statements of Quartodeciman observance, when in reality they may well have been attempts to demonize some practice that was perceived as deviant by using the accusation that it was not truly Christian.[39]

Moreover, it is dangerous to read any ancient source as though it was a verbatim account of a liturgical act. This is obviously so in the case of the brief allusions to Christian worship that crop up in writings dealing with some quite different topic. We cannot there expect the authors to be describing in exact and full detail all the aspects of the custom to which they are referring, for they are naturally only choosing to mention what is germane to the point they are making. It is important to remember, however, that the same is also true of other early sources. Usually only particularly significant, novel, or contro-verted practices will tend to be mentioned, and others will probably be passed over in silence. Even the fourth-century sets of homilies delivered to new converts to Christianity and intended to instruct them in the meaning of the liturgies of baptism and the Eucharist cannot be presumed to be mentioning everything that was said or done in those services. The authors will have high-lighted those parts of the liturgy which seemed to them especially significant, or containing something they judged it important for the neophytes to know, but they probably will have passed over other parts which they thought less significant or lacking a relevant lesson. (Moreover, we cannot even assume that when they are apparently alluding to real liturgical texts, they are always citing them word for word: they may well be introducing their own interpreta-tion as a gloss on the text rather than quoting the actual form in use.[40])

---

39 Karl Gerlach, *The Ante-Nicene Pascha: A Rhetorical History* (Leuven 1998).
40 For example, the *Mystagogical Catecheses* attributed to Cyril of Jerusalem state that God is asked to send his Holy Spirit upon the eucharistic offering 'to make the bread the body of Christ and the wine the blood of Christ. For whatever the Holy Spirit touches is hallowed and changed' (5.7). But how much of this language existed in the prayer itself, and how much was merely the author's own belief as to what less explicit wording really meant? A similar question also arises in the case of the actual eucharistic prayer known to Theodore of Mopsuestia. For both, see below, pp. 113–15 and 109–10.

Similar selectivity can be expected even in sets of directions for the conduct of worship, such as we find in the ancient church orders, in conciliar decrees, or in early monastic rules. At first sight, they may look like a complete list of instructions, but one has only to consider for a moment the twentieth-century equivalents of these texts to realize how much is always left unsaid because it is presumed to be familiar to the readers. Indeed, many amusing stories can be told of groups attempting to replicate solely on the basis of the printed rubrics liturgical rites which they have never seen, for even the clearest of instructions always contain an element of ambiguity for those unfamiliar with the tradition. Thus, directions do not generally deal with accepted and customary things, but only with new, uncertain, or controverted points: everything else will tend either to be passed over in silence or to receive the briefest of allusions. This leads to the infuriating situation for the liturgical scholar of passages which give the reader an instruction like 'Say the customary psalms' or 'Do what is usual everywhere on this day', since it is precisely those things that were known to everyone of the period and so were never written down that are consequently unknown to us and of greatest interest in our efforts to comprehend the shape and character of early Christian worship.

On the other hand, we ought not to rush to draw the opposite conclusion and assume that the first time something is mentioned was the first time it had ever occurred. As Joachim Jeremias has said, 'In investigating a form of address used in prayer we must not limit ourselves to dating the prayers in which it occurs; we must also take into account the fact that forms of address in prayer stand in a liturgical tradition and can therefore be older than the particular prayer in which they appear.'[41] Yet, whether or not it is significant that something is mentioned or omitted from a text will again depend to a considerable extent upon the type of material with which one is dealing: the same treatment of a subject cannot be expected in, say, a catechetic lecture as in monastic directions for reciting the divine office.

All this naturally makes the task more difficult. We cannot assume that just because something is not mentioned it was not being practised. Equally, arguments from silence are notoriously unreliable. Earlier generations of liturgical scholars frequently attempted to reconstruct the worship of the first and second centuries by reading back customs which were described for the first time only in the fourth century, especially if they bore the slightest resemblance to Jewish customs which were, rightly or wrongly, thought to have been current in the first century CE, for it was concluded that the one was directly descended from the other and so must have been practised by Christians in unbroken continuity in the intervening years. In many cases, more recent investigation of either the Christian or the Jewish custom has often

41 *The Prayers of Jesus* (London 1967), p. 26.

shown such conclusions to be mistaken. Whenever possible, therefore, we need to attempt to engage in some form of 'triangulation', searching for another point of reference besides the text itself, whether this is a further document or archaeological remains or whatever, so that any conclusion drawn may be based not upon the unsubstantiated testimony of one witness.

Liturgical historians also need to adopt the hermeneutics of suspicion in other ways, as we shall see in later chapters. In particular, we need to be aware of being too ready to draw the following conclusions:

(a) That Authoritative-sounding Statements are Always Genuinely Authoritative

Many ancient Christian writers in their allusions to liturgical practices make very emphatic statements about what is or is not the case, and traditional liturgical scholarship has been inclined to accept such remarks as truly authoritative declarations of the established doctrine and practice of the Church at the time that they were written, especially as many of those making these apparently *ex cathedra* pronouncements did actually occupy the office of a bishop. Such statements therefore often need to be taken with a pinch of salt. When some early Christian author proudly proclaims, for example, that a certain psalm or canticle is sung 'throughout the world', it probably means at the most that he knows it to be used in the particular regions he has visited or heard about: it remains an open question whether a similar usage obtained in other parts of the world.[42] Similarly, when some ancient bishop solemnly affirms that a certain liturgical custom is 'unheard of' in any church, he is almost certainly excluding from his definition of 'church' those groups of Christians whom he judges to be heretical and among whom the practice might well still be flourishing as it once had done in many other places in earlier times, in spite of our bishop's confident (though ignorant) assertion to the contrary.[43] Hence, the development of ecclesiastical structures and liturgical practices seems to have been much slower than has traditionally been supposed. Though many things did emerge quite early in the life of the Church, they did not immediately achieve normative or universal status, however strongly some individuals might have thought that they should.

42 Caesarius of Arles, for example, makes this claim with regard to the use of Psalm 104 at the daily evening service (*Serm.* 136.1). He maintains that as a result it 'is so well known to everybody that the greatest part of the human race has memorized it'; whereas in reality its use at this service seems to have been restricted to parts of the West, and in the East Psalm 141 was instead the standard evening psalm.

43 For example, Demetrius, patriarch of Alexandria in the third century, made such a claim with regard to the practice of preaching by those who were not ordained ministers, though the custom was defended by the bishops of Caesarea and Jerusalem, and seems to have left other traces of its former existence: see Paul F. Bradshaw, *Liturgical Presidency in the Early Church* (GLS 36, 1983), pp. 18–20.

(b) That Liturgical Legislation is Evidence of Actual Practice

When attention is directed towards the decrees of ecclesiastical councils and synods in the search for information about the practice of worship in the early Church, there is a natural tendency to focus on the things that those decrees say shall or shall not be done. Thus, to cite a simple example, when the Council of Braga in 561 CE insists that 'one and the same order of psalmody is to be observed in the morning and evening services; and neither individual variations nor monastic uses are to be interpolated into the ecclesiastical rule', one might be tempted to conclude that liturgical practices in Spain must have been uniform thereafter. Such a conclusion, however, can be shown to be false by the fact that synods held in later years found it necessary to repeat over and over again this demand for a standardization in usage.[44] Just because an authoritative body makes a liturgical regulation does not mean that it was observed everywhere or ever put into practice anywhere at all. Conservatism in matters liturgical is notoriously intractable and, as we all know well, canonical legislation from even the highest level is frequently unable to dislodge a well-established and much-loved local custom.

This does not mean, however, that such pieces of legislation are entirely valueless in the search for clues to the liturgical customs of the early Church. Indeed, quite the opposite is the case: regulations provide excellent evidence for what was actually happening in local congregations, not by what is decreed should be done but by what is either directly prohibited or indirectly implied should cease to be done. That such regulations were made at all shows that the very opposite of what they were trying to promote must have been a widespread custom at that period. Synodical assemblies do not usually waste their time either condemning something that is not actually going on or insisting on the firm adherence to some rule that everyone is already observing. Thus, for example, the decree by the Council of Vaison in 529 CE that the response *Kyrie eleison* should be used does not prove that this foreign innovation was quickly accepted in that part of Gaul – and indeed we have virtually no trace of its subsequent adoption there – but it does show that, prior to this time, that response was not a common part of the worship of that region.

The same is true of the liturgical comments that are found in many of the writings and homilies of early Christian theologians and bishops. We generally cannot know whether the practices and customs that they advocated were ever adopted by their congregations, or just politely listened to and then ignored, as the pleas of preachers often are; but we can conclude that there must have been some real foundation to the contrary custom or

---

44 See further Paul F. Bradshaw, *Daily Prayer in the Early Church* (London 1981/New York 1982), p. 115.

practice which is either directly criticized or implicitly acknowledged in the advice being given. Such writers may sometimes be suspected of hyperbole in the things they say, but they do not usually tilt at non-existent windmills. So, for example, when John Chrysostom describes those who fail to stay for the reception of communion at the celebration of the Eucharist as resembling Judas Iscariot at the Last Supper,[45] we do not know if he had any success in reforming the behaviour of his congregation, but we can safely assume that what he is complaining about was an observable feature at that time.

(c) That Even When a Variety of Explanations Exist for the Origin of a Practice, One of Them Must be Genuine

One frequently encounters in early Christian writings not only a partial description of some liturgical practice but also an explanation as to how it originated. Sometimes it is very easy to detect when such an explanation seems to be no more than the product of a pious imagination. When one reads, for example, in Coptic tradition that it was Theophilus, patriarch of Alexandria in the fourth century, who introduced baptismal chrism into Christian usage in response to the instruction of an angel to bring balsam trees from Jericho, plant them, extract the balsam, and cook the spices,[46] one may well have serious doubts about the veracity of the claim.[47] But in other cases it is less clear whether the author has access to a reliable source of information or not. Sometimes several writers will allude to the same custom but offer widely differing stories as to its true meaning or origin. This is the case, to cite just two examples, with regard to the times of daily prayer commonly observed in the third century, and with regard to the custom, first evidenced in Syria in the late fourth century, of placing the book of the Gospels on the head of a bishop during his ordination.

It is tempting in such instances to opt for the explanation that one finds most congenial to one's point of view and to discount the rest. This is in fact what scholars have generally done with respect to the explanations for the two customs just mentioned,[48] but there seems no particular reason to suppose that any one of the ancient commentators had access to a more authoritative source of information than the others. Indeed, the very existence of multiple explanations and interpretations is itself a very good

---

45 John Chrysostom, *De baptismo Christi* 4.

46 See Louis Villecourt, 'Le livre du chrême', *Muséon* 41 (1928), pp. 58–9.

47 Yet even an historically inaccurate statement like this can yield useful evidence for the period in which it originated once its *Sitz im Leben* is properly appreciated: see Paul F. Bradshaw, 'Baptismal Practice in the Alexandrian Tradition, Eastern or Western?', in idem, ed., *Essays in Early Eastern Initiation* (A/GLS 8, 1988), pp. 5–17.

48 For further details see Paul F. Bradshaw, *Daily Prayer in the Early Church*, pp. 48–62, and idem, *Ordination Rites of the Ancient Churches of East and West* (New York 1990), pp. 39–44.

indication that no authoritative tradition with regard to the original purpose and meaning of the custom had survived, and hence writers and preachers felt free to use their imaginations. This is not to say that the true origin can never be unearthed by modern scholarship, with its access to sources and methods not known to the ancients, or that sometimes one of those early writers may not have hit upon the right solution. But it does suggest that in such situations it may often be necessary to look for the real answer in a quite different direction from that of the conventional accounts.

Conclusion

In the light of all the caution and uncertainty which I have expressed, some readers may feel that the whole attempt to reconstruct patterns of ancient Christian worship is doomed to failure, that it is not simply a matter of joining up the dots on a sheet of otherwise plain paper, but rather of finding the dots in the first place, buried as they are among countless others of different shades and hues, and of doing so with a blindfold over one's eyes. I can sympathize with some of that trepidation: the task is certainly not as easy as former generations often judged it. Yet, while we cannot hope to learn everything we would like to know about the Church's early worship, it is not impossible to say, even if only in a provisional way, a certain amount about how that worship began and developed in the first few centuries of the Christian tradition. When the dots are carefully joined, a faint picture can indeed emerge.

2

The Background of
Early Christian Worship

The Influence of Paganism

Apparently driven by a conviction as to the unique character of the Christian religion over against its pagan rivals, older studies of the early Church and its worship generally paid scant attention to the practices of contemporary pagan cults, except to draw attention to the differences which separated them from Christianity. Any influence that these other religions might have had on Christian liturgy was usually reckoned as belonging only to the period from the fourth century onwards, when they were seen as having had a corrupting effect upon the purity of the original practices. Jonathan Z. Smith has alleged that this point of view, particularly prominent among Protestant scholars, was shaped by their desire to equate Roman Catholic and pagan influences on 'pure' Christianity.[1]

It began to be challenged at the very end of the nineteenth century by the German *religionsgeschichtliche Schule*, 'history-of-religions school', a group of scholars who had a greater influence on biblical scholarship than on liturgical historians.[2] In their efforts to explain the Bible by relating it to other religions, they tried to trace the origins of the worship practices of Paul and the early Gentile Christians to the contemporary Greek mystery-religions.[3] Among them, to cite just a few examples, were Heinrich Julius Holtzmann (1832–1910), who set Paul's doctrine of baptism in Romans 6 against the ideas of the Greek mysteries,[4] Wilhelm Heitmüller (1869–1926), who argued that

---

1 *Drudgery Divine: On the Comparison of Early Christianities and the Religions of Late Antiquity* (Chicago 1990), pp. 21–46.
2 Though there were several among them who did try to explain later liturgical practices by references to other religions, most notably F. J. Dölger: see Theodor Klauser, *Franz Joseph Dölger 1879–1940* (Jahrbuch für Antike und Christentum Ergänzungsband 7; Münster 1980), esp. pp. 70–1.
3 See Gerd Lüdemann and Martin Schröder, *Die religionsgeschichtliche Schule in Göttingen. Eine Dokumentation* (Göttingen 1987).
4 *Lehrbuch der neustestamentlichen Theologie* (Freiburg/Leipzig 1897).

Paul's understanding of the Eucharist came from the Hellenistic world,[5] and Wilhelm Bousset (1865–1920), who put forward the thesis that it was the Gentile Christians who first worshipped Christ as *Kyrios*, seeing him as a new 'mystery-god'.[6] This school, which also had a strong influence on Rudolf Bultmann, gave rise to a deep division between scholars throughout a large part of the twentieth century, some insisting that the mystery-religions had little or no impact on New Testament Christianity, others believing that their effect was quite considerable.[7] In the long run, however, the weakness of the latter, both in focusing too narrowly upon mystery-religions and not on the wider religious and cultural milieu of which they were but a part, and also in too readily regarding apparent parallels, including those from texts later than the New Testament period, as constituting sources of Christian practice, has been generally acknowledged, even if in the case of Paul's baptismal theology it has only (finally?) been laid to rest quite recently by the work of A. J. M. Wedderburn.[8]

That is not to say, however, that Paul and other early Christians were completely uninfluenced by the pagan world around. Far from it. Although both Judaism and primitive Christianity were in certain important respects exclusivist and kept themselves apart from what other religious groups were doing, neither of them existed in a vacuum, insulated from the language, images, and practices of the religions and culture around them. Thus, albeit often quite unconsciously, they could not help but be affected by their contemporaries and have the words and actions of their worship shaped by the society in which they lived. In the last few decades, therefore, this broader interplay between Christian, Jewish and pagan practices has slowly begun to be acknowledged and explored. Beginning with an influential article by Gordon J. Bahr in 1970, which encouraged many subsequent scholars to look more closely at the Graeco–Roman background of both Jewish and Christian meals in their attempts to understand the early Eucharist,[9] there can be seen a

---

5 *Taufe und Abendmahl bei Paulus: Darstellung und religionsgeschichtliche Beleuchtung* (Göttingen 1903).
6 *Kyrios Christos: Geschichte des Christusglaubens von den Anfängen des Christentums bis Irenaeus* (Göttingen 1913); ET: *Kyrios Christos* (Nashville 1970).
7 See the list of representatives of both sides in Bruce M. Metzger, 'Considerations of Methodology in the Study of the Mystery Religions and Early Christianity', *Harvard Theological Review* 48 (1955), pp. 2–4, reprinted in revised form in idem, *Historical and Literary Studies: Pagan, Jewish and Christian* (Grand Rapids 1968), pp. 2–4.
8 *Baptism and Resurrection: Studies in Pauline Theology against its Graeco-Roman Background* (Tübingen 1987).
9 'The Seder of Passover and the Eucharistic Words', *NovT* 12 (1970), pp.181–202 = Henry A. Fischel, ed., *Essays in Greco–Roman and Related Talmudic Literature* (New York 1977), pp. 473–94. For a recent contribution, see Blake Leyerle, 'Meal Customs in the Greco–Roman World', in Paul F. Bradshaw and Lawrence A. Hoffman, eds, *Passover and Easter: Origin and History to Modern Times* (Notre Dame 1999), pp. 29–61.

growing trend to take more seriously the influence of the wider pagan environment on the earliest patterns of Christian worship.[10]

The Influence of Judaism

On the other hand, the recognition that Christianity inherited many of its liturgical practices from Judaism has been very long established, and can be traced back at least to the late seventeenth century. The Dutch Protestant theologian, Campegius Vitringa (1659–1722), appears to have been the first to suggest the connection,[11] and similar views appeared in the works of several eighteenth- and nineteenth-century scholars.[12] The early twentieth century saw an increasing number of such attempts to postulate a link between Jewish and Christian liturgical forms,[13] and after the publication in 1945 of Gregory Dix's magisterial work *The Shape of the Liturgy*,[14] it became axiomatic for those searching for the origins of every aspect of primitive Christian liturgical practice to look primarily for Jewish antecedents. However, because they generally continued to accept uncritically the conclusions reached by earlier generations of Jewish scholars and to be largely unaware of more recent developments in scholarship, it is hardly surprising that they tended to remain convinced that Jewish liturgical practices were fixed and uniform in the first century of the Common Era,[15] and this attitude has persisted in many cases down to the present day. Thus, while it is not surprising that the important study by Joseph Heinemann published in Hebrew in 1964 was almost totally unknown to Christian liturgical scholars until its appearance in English in 1977 (though an English abstract did accompany the original edition), even since then it has all too rarely been cited in studies of the origins of Christian worship; still less has the changing face of rabbinic scholarship under Jacob Neusner been taken into account, or the subsequent significant contributions to the debate about the roots of Jewish worship by

---

10 See, for example, the recent study of New Testament worship by Larry Hurtado, *At the Origins of Christian Worship* (Carlisle 1999), pp. 7–28.

11 *De synagoga vetere* (Francquerae 1696); ET by J. L. Bernard, *The Synagogue and the Church* (London 1842).

12 See, for example, Joseph Bingham, *Origines Ecclesiasticae: The Antiquities of the Christian Church* (London 1710), Bk. XIII, ch. V, sect. 4; William Smith, *Dictionary of the Bible* (London 1863), 'Synagogue, V.1'; Warren, *The Liturgy and Ritual of the Ante-Nicene Church*, pp. 201–7.

13 See, for example, W. O. E. Oesterley, *The Jewish Background of the Christian Liturgy* (Oxford 1925 = Gloucester, MA 1965); Frank Gavin, *The Jewish Antecedents of the Christian Sacraments* (London 1928 = New York 1969).

14 For this, see below, pp. 122–6.

15 Thus Dix himself wrote that 'the various formulae of blessing for the different kinds of food were fixed and well-known, and might not be altered' (*The Shape of the Liturgy*, p. 51).

Ezra Fleischer, Stefan Reif, Tzvee Zahavy and others been noted and appreciated.

Yet such studies challenge the very foundations upon which reconstructions of early Christian liturgy have been built. While at one time it seemed perfectly possible to state with a considerable degree of assurance what Jewish worship was like in the first century, now things are by no means so clear. What can only be described as a revolution in Jewish liturgical studies has taken place, a revolution which has almost completely changed our perception of how sources should be used to reconstruct the forms of worship of early Judaism. This has resulted in the need to be much more cautious about affirming what would have been the liturgical practices with which Jesus and his followers were familiar. As Reif himself has said, 'suddenly it becomes clear that the basic work in Jewish liturgy has, after all, not been definitively completed. *Au contraire*, even the most basic facts about the early liturgical relationship between Jews and Christians must be rethought.'[16]

The basic problem for the reconstruction of the early history of Jewish worship is that extant liturgical texts as such are of a late date. The earliest complete prayer book known to us is that compiled by Amram Gaon in the ninth century,[17] although there are in addition some liturgical fragments from the Cairo Genizah[18] which may antedate Amram by a century or so. Knowledge of the growth and development of Jewish liturgy prior to this time has to rely to a large extent on attempts to divine the pre-history of these later texts with the assistance of the comments on and discussion of liturgical matters found in the Mishnah, Tosefta, and Talmud; and recent scholarship has shown that the interpretation of this material presents not inconsiderable difficulties.[19] To complicate matters further, Amram's text is Babylonian in origin, whereas it is the less easily discernible Palestinian tradition which is of most immediate relevance to the search for the beginnings of Christian worship.

---

16 Stefan C. Reif, 'Jewish Liturgical Research: Past, Present and Future', *JJS* 34 (1983), pp. 161–70, here at p. 168; repeated in idem, *Judaism and Hebrew Prayer: New Perspectives on Jewish Liturgical History* (Cambridge 1993), p. 10.

17 *Seder R. Amram Gaon*, Part I ed. David Hedegård (Lund 1951), Part II ed. Tryggve Kronholm (Lund 1974).

18 For this, see below, p. 26.

19 The Mishnah is the first systematic collection of rabbinic judgements made at the end of the second century CE; the Tosefta is a later supplement to this; and the Talmud is an extensive compilation of rabbinic discussion spanning several centuries after the Mishnah's promulgation and organized as a running commentary on that work. There are two Talmuds, the Palestinian, which in its final form is traditionally dated *c.* 400 CE, and the Babylonian, which is said to have been completed *c.* 500–600, though in actuality it was not finally edited until some time thereafter, perhaps as late as the seventh century or even the eighth. For further details, see Roger Brooks, *The Spirit of the Ten Commandments* (San Francisco 1990), pp. 36–45; and his articles, 'Mishnah' and 'Gemara', in *The Anchor Bible Dictionary* (New York 1992).

Earlier Jewish Liturgical Scholarship[20]

The scientific study of the history of Jewish liturgy is usually regarded as having begun with Leopold Zunz (1794–1886), although its roots can be traced back even before his time. In his monumental work, *Die gottesdienstlichen Vorträge der Juden historisch entwickelt*,[21] Zunz became the first scholar to stress the gradual evolution of the liturgy in the course of history. His methods were those of classical philology, which he had learned at the University of Berlin from August Boeckh and Friedrich August Wolf. Zunz regarded differences in the wording of prayers in the various manuscripts to which he had access as being variations on, or additions to, a single archetype, an *Urtext*, which lay behind them all. Thus, he believed that words and phrases which were common to all the manuscripts must be of greater antiquity than those which differed from one to another, and hence by comparing the variant forms of the material and peeling off the layers of what appeared to be subsequent accretions, it was possible to recover the original, briefer core of the text.

Not only does his approach – and all those which are derived from it – presuppose that liturgical texts necessarily evolved from simplicity to greater complexity, but it also contains several other assumptions:

1   that throughout the process of historical evolution there was in existence, as the Talmudic literature itself implies, a centralized rabbinic authority which established and regulated a single, normative pattern of worship, which instituted all legitimate changes 'from above' in an orderly manner, and which effectively disseminated them throughout the Judaism of the period;

2   that textual variations were generally best understood sequentially (that is, as reflecting subsequent chronological stages along this single line of development, with the different changes following one after the other in the course of history in a cumulative fashion) rather than, for example, occurring simultaneously in parallel versions of similar material;

3   that variations which could not be explained within this linear progression must either be deliberate heretical deviations from the norm or unimportant modifications which were not part of the mainstream of liturgical life, or be examples of a later liturgical diversity which was brought about primarily by the geographical dispersion of the Jews, an assumption that once again the Talmudic literature encourages;

20 In what follows I am heavily indebted to the detailed survey and critique by Richard S. Sarason, 'On the Use of Method in the Modern Study of Jewish Liturgy', in W. S. Green, ed., *Approaches to Ancient Judaism: Theory and Practice* (BJS 1; Missoula, MT 1978), pp. 97–172 = Jacob Neusner, ed., *The Study of Ancient Judaism* I (New York 1981), pp. 107–79.

21 1832; 2nd edn, Frankfurt 1892 = Hildesheim 1966; Jerusalem 1946 = 1974 (in Hebrew).

4   that it was possible to postulate the date when each of the changes had
     taken place by looking for some appropriate historical context which
     would have caused that change to occur, or at least have been congruent
     with its development.

The methodological criteria established by Zunz were followed by the
scholars who came after him, and not even Solomon Schechter's discovery in
1896 in the Genizah of the Ben Ezra synagogue in Cairo of a vast quantity of
fragmentary liturgical texts of a distinctly Palestinian character which frequently differed in wording from the European manuscripts, was sufficient to
shake these foundations. Subsequent scholars may have made minor modifications to their conclusions, but the basic principles survived in the work of
such major figures as Ismar Elbogen (1874–1943) and Louis Finkelstein
(1895–1991). While Elbogen (whose comprehensive study, *Der jüdische
Gottesdienst in seiner geschichtlichen Entwicklung*,[22] continues to be used as a
basic source today) acknowledged that the precise wording of prayers had
not originally been fixed, but that there were several alternative versions in
existence for some time, he still used philological methods to analyse the
history of texts, viewing the original 'seed' of the liturgy as having been
gradually encapsulated in layers of 'rind'.[23]

Finkelstein, on the other hand, whose reconstructions of the supposed *Urtext*
of the *Tefillah* (the prescribed form of Jewish daily prayer) and of the *Birkat
ha-mazon* (the grace after meals)[24] still tend to be cited as authoritative by
Christian scholars, had no such reservations. On the contrary, he carried Zunz's
method to an extreme, articulating his operational rules as follows:

> In attempting to establish on the basis of these later forms the earliest
> text of the benedictions, we must bear in mind that for many centuries
> the prayers were not written down but transmitted orally. Under these
> circumstances new material could be added, but changes and omissions
> were difficult. It is comparatively easy to issue an edict changing the
> wording of written prayers, and in an age of printing it is a slight matter
> to prepare a new edition of a prayer book. But when people recited
> their prayers from memory, they were willing to learn new verses or
> phrases, but found it difficult to unlearn what they already knew.

22 Leipzig 1913; 2nd edn, Frankfurt 1924; 3rd edn 1931 = Hildesheim 1962; revised Hebrew
    edn, ed. J. Heinemann, *Ha-tefillah Be-Yisrael* (Tel-Aviv 1972); ET by Raymond P.
    Scheindlin, *Jewish Liturgy: A Comprehensive History* (Philadelphia 1993).
23 (3rd edn), pp. 41f., 254. See Sarason, 'On the Use of Method', p. 109 = 120.
24 'The Development of the Amidah', *JQR* 16 (1925/6), pp. 1–43, 127–70; 'The Birkat Ha-
    Mazon', *JQR* 19 (1929), pp. 211–62.

It follows that in dealing with various formulae of prayer we must remember that *in general* these rules hold. 1. The old text is retained as a nucleus of the later formula. 2. Where various versions differ, the part that is common to all of them is the more likely to contain the original form. 3. The briefest form is very often the most akin to the original.[25]

The Influence of Joseph Heinemann (1915–77)

Although form-critical methods had begun to be applied to biblical studies at the beginning of the twentieth century, they had virtually no impact upon the study of Jewish liturgy until much more recently. It is true that in the 1930s Arthur Spanier (1884–1944) began to question the appropriateness of the pure philological method and to suggest a generic classification of prayer-material according to characteristics of form and style, but this initiative came to an end when he perished in the Holocaust.[26]

It was not until the 1960s that this approach was taken up again. In his doctoral dissertation, published in Hebrew in 1964,[27] Joseph Heinemann posited the origin of individual Jewish liturgical texts on the basis of the particular stylistic features which they displayed, arguing that some forms appeared more congruent with the Temple, others with the nascent synagogue, the law court, the house of study, and so on. So, to take a simple example, he held that texts which addressed the congregation in the second-person plural ('you') were unlikely to have originated in the synagogue, where the prayer-leader was expected to use the first-person plural ('we, us') and include himself along with those on whose behalf he was praying. On the other hand, the second-person address was common in Temple services, where the priests were accustomed to bless the people.[28]

But Heinemann's work did much more than add a new analytical tool to the study of the history of Jewish worship: it challenged the fundamental principles of interpretation hitherto adopted, and set forth a completely different model of liturgical development. He did not deny the value of the philological method, when applied to genuine literary texts, but insisted that 'it cannot be transferred as a matter of course to the field of liturgy without first determining whether or not the methodological tools are appropriate to the subject matter which is to be analyzed by them'.[29] He argued that there never had

---

25 'The Birkat Ha-Mazon', p. 224 (emphasis in original).
26 See the analysis of his work in Sarason, 'On the Use of Method', pp. 140–5 = 155–60.
27 *Prayer in the Period of the Tanna'im and the Amora'im: Its Nature and its Patterns* (Jerusalem 1964; 2nd edn 1966); ET = *Prayer in the Talmud: Forms and Patterns* (Berlin 1977).
28 *Prayer in the Talmud*, pp. 104ff.
29 ibid., p. 6.

been a single *Urtext* of Jewish liturgical forms, but that a variety of oral versions had existed from the first, and only later were these subjected to standardization:

> The Jewish prayers were originally the creations of the common people. The characteristic idioms and forms of prayer, and indeed the statutory prayers of the synagogue themselves, were not in the first place products of the deliberation of the Rabbis in their academies, but were rather the spontaneous, on-the-spot improvisations of the people who gathered on various occasions to pray in the synagogue. Since the occasions and places of worship were numerous, it was only natural that they should give rise to an abundance of prayers, displaying a wide variety of forms, styles, and patterns. Thus, the first stage in the development of the liturgy was characterized by diversity and variety, and the task of the Rabbis was to systematize and to impose order on this multiplicity of forms, patterns, and structures. This task they undertook after the fact; only after the numerous prayers had come into being and were familiar to the masses did the Sages decide that the time had come to establish some measure of uniformity and standardization. Only then did they proceed carefully to inspect the existing forms and patterns, to disqualify some while accepting others, to decide which prayers were to be statutory on which occasions, and by which prayers a man 'fulfilled his obligation'.[30]

Heinemann thus called into question the underlying presuppositions of earlier scholarship. Since he denied that – at least in the earliest period of liturgical evolution – there had been a centralized rabbinic authority which regulated worship practices, textual differences were not necessarily always reflective of sequential stages of development, nor alternatively to be dismissed as deviations from some putative norm. On the contrary, they might often be indicative of simultaneous, parallel strands, some of which ultimately converged, while others in time disappeared from use. Hence, neither the simplest version nor that which has most features in common with others is necessarily the earliest. Similarly, parallel occurrences of the same phraseology in widely different contexts could well be the natural use of certain stock phrases rather than actual literary dependency.[31]

Heinemann argued that the process of standardization took place only gradually. By the second century CE 'only the number of the benedictions, their order of recitation, and their general content had been fixed, as well as

30 ibid., p. 37.
31 ibid., pp. 37–69.

the occasions of their recitation and the rules which governed them, but not their exact wording'.[32] At this time 'each worshipper was still basically allowed to formulate his own benedictions as long as he "mentioned in them" those items and idioms which, in the meantime, had become customary'. The next step came in the late Amoraic period (fifth century CE), 'when it was no longer deemed sufficient merely to set down the particular items which had to be mentioned in specific benedictions, but it was also felt necessary to fix exact wordings of the opening formula, the concluding eulogy, and ultimately certain important phrases in the body of the benediction itself'. However, even this did not prove that non-normative formulations did not go on being used.[33] The process, he believed, did not end until the Geonic period (600–1100 CE), and even when the exact wording of the prayers was finally determined, different versions became authoritative in Babylonia and in Palestine.[34]

More Recent Jewish Scholarship

Heinemann's methodology has since been adopted by other Jewish scholars, and most notably by Lawrence Hoffman, who has traced in greater detail the slow movement towards the standardization of the synagogue liturgy in later centuries.[35] However, not all have accepted Heinemann's conclusions unreservedly. E. Daniel Goldschmidt (1895–1973), for example, continued to defend the philological approach.[36] Even Heinemann's translator, Richard Sarason, while accepting the arguments for an original multiplicity of forms, has expressed caution about the detail of his theory of origins, since so little is known of the period in question:

> While Heinemann's general characterization of the synagogue as a popular folk institution over which the rabbis gradually came to exercise control seems valid, it is not at all clear that the prayer texts and formulae, as well as most of the structures, which the rabbis set down in the Mishnah, Tosefta, and the two Talmuds as 'normative' necessarily originated with the masses and not within rabbinic circles themselves.[37]

32 ibid., p. 26.
33 ibid., pp. 51–3.
34 ibid., p. 29.
35 *The Canonization of the Synagogue Service* (Notre Dame 1979). On this process, see also the study by Stefan C. Reif, 'The Early History of Jewish Liturgy', in Bradshaw and Hoffman, eds, *The Making of Jewish and Christian Worship*, pp. 109–36; revised version in Reif, *Judaism and Hebrew Prayer*, pp. 122–52.
36 See Sarason, 'On the Use of Method', pp. 124–7 = 137–40.
37 ibid., p. 146 = 161.

In other words, while Heinemann's theory of the origins of Jewish prayer may indeed be accurate, what survives in the later liturgy may derive from an elitist group rather than from these more populist prayer-patterns – which increases the difficulty of discovering just what the latter were. This suspicion is further encouraged by the existence of occasional incidental references in the rabbinic literature to ongoing ritual practices of the common folk which meet with disapproval. Such glimpses of alternative patterns of worship may well represent only the tip of the iceberg with regard to the customs of the masses.

Similarly, Tzvee Zahavy would maintain that more credence needs to be given to social and political influences in the shaping of Jewish prayers, and both Zahavy and Stefan Reif have argued that Heinemann went too far in his emphasis on the superiority of the form-critical over the philological method. They have advocated as the direction for the future a more comprehensive, integrated interdisciplinary approach, incorporating the use of such things as literary criticism, archaeology, art history, history of religions, and the history of law.[38] Hoffman, too, in his more recent work has criticized all schools of liturgical scholarship for being too narrowly focused on the textual dimension of worship to the exclusion of other perspectives.[39]

On the other hand, it can also be argued that in some respects Heinemann did not go far enough, in that he tended to accept the genuine historicity of statements in the Mishnah, Tosefta, and Talmud which were attributed to rabbinic figures of earlier centuries. In the period since he wrote, such an assumption has been seriously questioned by a new school of rabbinic studies which is particularly associated with Jacob Neusner. If Heinemann's contribution to Jewish liturgical study parallels the form-critical phase of biblical scholarship, then this new movement may be compared to the redaction-criticism which developed in scriptural studies in the second half of the twentieth century. Previously the compilers of biblical books, and especially those responsible for the final redaction of the canonical Gospels, had tended

38 Tzvee Zahavy, 'A New Approach to Early Jewish Prayer', in Baruch M. Bokser, ed., *History of Judaism: The Next Ten Years* (BJS 21; Chico, CA 1980), pp. 45–60; idem, 'The Politics of Piety: Social Conflict and the Emergence of Rabbinic Liturgy', in Bradshaw and Hoffman, eds, *The Making of Jewish and Christian Worship*, pp. 46–69; idem, 'Three Stages in the Development of Early Rabbinic Prayer', in Jacob Neusner *et al.*, *From Ancient Israel to Modern Judaism* I (BJS 159; Atlanta 1989), pp. 233–65, reproduced in expanded form in idem, *Studies in Jewish Prayer* (Lanham, MD 1990), pp. 1–44; Reif, 'Jewish Liturgical Research: Past, Present and Future', revised version in idem, *Judaism and Hebrew Prayer*, pp. 1–21. See also Richard S. Sarason, 'Recent Developments in the Study of Jewish Liturgy', in Neusner, ed., *The Study of Ancient Judaism* I, pp. 180–7.
39 *Beyond the Text: A Holistic Approach to Liturgy* (Bloomington, IN 1987); idem, 'Reconstructing Ritual as Identity and Culture', in Bradshaw and Hoffman, eds, *The Making of Jewish and Christian Worship*, pp. 28–45.

to be seen as little more than mere scribes, mechanically recording historical material more or less exactly in the form they received it. Redaction-criticism took the compilers' role rather more seriously and viewed them as playing a much more creative part in the process of composition, recognizing that they selected and shaped the written and/or oral traditions which they inherited according to their own particular theological outlook, literary purposes, and personal prejudices. They had thus impressed their individual viewpoint on the material, and in the process had sometimes obliterated our access to the earlier sources themselves.

In the same way, scholars had held until recently that the rabbinic literature contained a highly accurate record of the oral judgements of individual rabbis which had been carefully handed down, in some cases over many centuries. Hence it was believed that this material could be used as a reliable historical chronicle for the periods which it purported to represent. More than that, there was a tendency to treat texts which had been edited over a four-century span – from 200 to 600 CE – as a seamless whole, regardless of geographical or chronological provenance, and to see a harmonious picture of a developing 'normative Judaism', in which a single sage's opinion could be thought to represent the universal practice; and even the cataloguing of a multitude of differing claims as to the origin of some institution was not thought to cast any serious doubts on its antiquity.

The newer school of rabbinic scholarship, however, approaches the sources with an awareness that one cannot automatically assume a simple historical reading to be reliable. Rabbinic literature, like the biblical books, was created not simply to chronicle the past but to promote and justify the world-view of those responsible for its redaction. For that reason, they were inevitably selective in their approach, restricting themselves to those rabbinic opinions that came within their own view of acceptable limits and omitting whatever did not, and arranging and shaping the material that they did include so that it reflected their own intellectual and theological system.

In other words, the literature is seen as more revealing about the redactors and the age in which they lived than about the earlier periods of history from which it draws. Thus, a saying may be attributed to an ancient authority, but that does not necessarily mean that he must have said it or, if he did say it, that it had the same meaning in its original context as it is given by the redactor of the material or by a later commentator on it. A story may be told about a particular rabbi, but that does not necessarily mean that the events described actually took place in the historical period to which they are ascribed, or even at all. Transmitters and redactors of oral tradition regularly attribute anonymous stories and sayings to ancient authorities so as to increase their prestige, as well as supplementing and reinterpreting their content.[40]

Yet here, too, as in the case of philology versus form-criticism, one must beware of rushing to one extreme or another. As Stefan Reif has said,

> to accept uncritically the historicity of all talmudic reports, particularly as they relate to events in the pre-Christian period, and the attribution of all statements to particular personalities is as misguided as the approach that claims all previous studies antiquated and distinguished talmudists obsolete and refuses to credit the rabbis with any reliable information about the origin of their own religious traditions.[41]

On the other hand, we must not underestimate the radical transformation which Judaism underwent after the destruction of the Temple in 70 CE. The religion which emerged in the period afterwards was by no means identical with the religion which had been current in the decades preceding it. That catastrophic event spelled the demise of many varieties of thought and practice which had previously flourished within Judaism, as groups like the Sadducees and Essenes failed to adapt to the new situation and left the traditions of the Pharisaic party in a position of pre-eminence. And yet even those traditions did not simply continue unchanged: the loss of the Temple and of its sacrificial cult deprived Jews of the way of serving God which was prescribed in the Torah, and so for the faith to survive required a massive reinterpretation of much that they had previously believed. Indeed, the whole of post-70 CE Judaism may be viewed as a kind of cultic surrogate, in which the former sacrificial activities were metaphorically transferred to the daily life of the Jewish people – to the act of Torah study, to the obedient observance of the commandments, and to prayer in the synagogue.[42]

40 See Jacob Neusner, 'The Teaching of the Rabbis: Approaches Old and New', *JJS* 27 (1976), pp. 23–35; 'The Use of the Later Rabbinic Evidence for the Study of First-Century Pharisaism', in Green, ed., *Approaches to Ancient Judaism*, pp. 215–28; 'The Formation of Rabbinic Judaism: Methodological Issues and Substantive Theses', *Formative Judaism: Religious, Historical and Literary Studies* III (BJS 46; Chico, CA 1983), pp. 99–146.

41 'Some Liturgical Issues in the Talmudic Sources', *SL* 15 (1982/3), p. 190; repeated in idem, *Judaism and Hebrew Prayer*, p. 92. On the continuities within Judaism, see also Roger Brooks, 'Judaism in Crisis? Institutions and Systematic Theology in Rabbinism', in Jacob Neusner *et al.*, *From Ancient Israel to Modern Judaism* II (BJS 173; Atlanta 1989), pp. 3–18.

42 This idea is extensively developed in Richard S. Sarason, 'Religion and Worship: The Case of Judaism', in Jacob Neusner, ed., *Take Judaism, For Example: Studies toward the Comparison of Religions* (Chicago 1983), pp. 49–65. See also Arnold Goldberg, 'Service of the Heart: Liturgical Aspects of Synagogue Worship', in Asher Finkel and Lawrence Frizzell, eds, *Standing before God* (New York 1981), pp. 195–211; Ruth Langer, *To Worship God Properly: Tensions between Liturgical Custom and Halakhah in Judaism* (Cincinnati 1998); B. T. Viviano, *Study as Worship: Aboth and the New Testament* (Leiden 1978).

Consequently, many things which had earlier been a part of Temple liturgy alone gradually came to have a place within the daily life of ordinary Jews and within the worship of the synagogue. For example, the rules of ritual purity which had formerly pertained only to those engaged in the service of the cult were now reinterpreted as applying to everyone, and such ceremonies as the procession seven times around the altar at the festival of Sukkot were eventually transferred to the synagogue. While among the Pharisees some of these developments – and especially the application of the rules about ritual purity – certainly ante-dated the destruction of the Temple and thus prepared the way for further moves in that direction, it seems likely that others underwent transformation only after that event made it impossible to observe them in their original setting. This should lead to greater caution in assuming that many of the features of later Jewish worship would necessarily have been familiar to Jesus and his followers.

Reconstructing the Jewish Background to Christian Worship

In our efforts to assess the influence of Jewish practices upon Christian worship we ought to focus primarily upon the first century. It is true that contact between Jews and Christians did not end after 70 CE, and there is evidence for some continuing links down to at least the fourth century: some of the early Fathers were clearly influenced by Jewish sources, and John Chrysostom tells us that some ordinary Christians were attending both synagogue and church, though it is not clear how widespread, geographically or chronologically, this practice was.[43] On the other hand, after the close of the first century, liturgical influence from Judaism to a now predominantly Gentile Church is likely to have been relatively marginal, and any really significant effects must be sought in the earlier formative period.

Furthermore, in the task of reconstructing first-century Jewish worship, we should treat as primary sources chiefly material that is contemporary with, or older than, the period in question. The historicity of evidence from later sources that is not largely substantiated by these earlier witnesses must be regarded with a degree of suspicion. It is possible that such sources may contain genuine records of earlier times, but that cannot automatically be assumed. Even descriptions of Temple rituals may sometimes be projecting back what later Jews thought should have happened, rather than what

---

43 See James H. Charlesworth, 'A Prolegomenon to a New Study of the Jewish Background of the Hymns and Prayers in the New Testament', *JJS* 33 (1982), pp. 269–70; William Horbury, 'The Benediction of the Minim and Early Jewish–Christian Controversy', *JTS* 33 (1982), pp. 19–61; Robert Wilken, *John Chrysostom and the Jews* (Berkeley 1983).

actually was the case.[44] The probable veracity of statements like these must be carefully tested by considering such matters as the chronological proximity of the written testimony to the event or person mentioned in it and the possible motives which might lie behind the propagation of the narrative. In addition, we need to bear in mind the possibility that at least in some cases it may have been the Christian practice that influenced the later Jewish custom rather than the other way around.[45]

What is equally important for the background of Christian worship is that we should not single out any one Jewish tradition as normative and treat others as deviations, nor restrict our focus to asking which elements of later Jewish liturgy go back to the first century. While Pharisaism may have been the prevailing school of thought in the first century, it was not necessarily the chief influence on the early Christians. Hence, if we wish to see the whole picture without bias, our sources must encompass the total evidence for early Jewish worship – both those expressions that survived in the rabbinic corpus and those that found no place there but were just as much a part of earlier Jewish piety – and we should be as open to the possibility of a diversity as to a uniformity of practice, and not try to force the various pieces of evidence that we have into a false harmony with one another. Testimony that a custom was practised is not *ipso facto* proof that it was universally observed, to the exclusion of all alternatives.

A particular question is posed here by the various pieces of liturgical material scattered among the Qumran literature. There has been a common tendency to treat the findings from this source as representative only of marginal sectarian practice and so unable to shed any light on wider Jewish liturgical activity prior to the destruction of the Temple. Daniel Falk has recently argued, however, that a good deal of what has been discovered there does not bear any marks that would make it exclusive to that particular community, and so it should be treated as reflecting the broader prayer patterns of early Judaism.[46] But in any case, regardless of the resolution of that particular matter, the close parallels that have been observed between a number of other features of early Christianity and the Qumran texts should make us attentive to possible liturgical connections between the two as well.

Although not as much contemporary material pertaining to worship may

---

44 So, for example, the material in the Mishnah tractate *Middot* seems at times to be more closely related to biblical projections of the Temple than to what is now known through archaeological research to have been true of the actual Temple site. Similarly, the liturgical descriptions in the tractate *Tamid* do not yield a single consistent picture such as one might expect if its purpose had really been to record accurately the daily ritual.

45 For examples, see Israel J. Yuval, 'Easter and Passover as Early Jewish–Christian Dialogue', in Bradshaw and Hoffman, eds, *Passover and Easter: Origin and History to Modern Times*, pp. 98–124.

46 *Daily, Sabbath, and Festival Prayers in the Dead Sea Scrolls* (Leiden 1998).

have survived from this period as we might wish, there is in fact much more than is often assumed. James Charlesworth has catalogued what he describes as 'an abundance of unexamined data' relating to forms of Jewish hymns and prayers that pre-date 70 CE.[47] As he indicates, much work remains to be done on this material before it can yield useful results for our picture of first-century Jewish worship:

> We need a synthesis of this data. We need to explore the relationships of shared themes, perspectives, symbols, and metaphors. We need to explore the possibility of a development of the ancient forms of Semitic poetry, rhythm and rhyme. We need to clarify the social setting of the compositions, and to explore whether there is a significant relation between the prayers composed by the apocalypticists and the statutory prayers of the Synagogue, *Bet Midrash*, and other liturgically formalized Jewish settings. Especially, we need to probe the possible kinship among those that phenomenologically had a life within some liturgical setting. In terms of these concerns, the above outlined data is a promised land without maps.[48]

In the light of all this, what can be said about Jewish worship in the first century? For the purposes of this study, we shall omit consideration of the Temple. While it is beyond doubt that regular sacrifices were being offered there, there is very little literary evidence which provides reliable details of the cult at this period. In any case, although the sacrificial imagery of the Temple certainly did continue to figure in early Christian thought, and more strongly from the fourth century onwards in actual liturgical practice,[49] the source for this was the literary description of the Temple liturgy in the Hebrew Scriptures rather than the institution itself. Thus, we shall examine briefly four areas: possible elements of synagogue liturgy; the practice of daily prayer; forms of prayer themselves; and grace at meals. Reference to the

---

47 'A Prolegomenon', pp. 274–6. For an introduction to some of these sources, see Charlesworth, 'Jewish Hymns, Odes, and Prayers (ca. 167 BCE–135 CE)', in Robert A. Kraft and George W. E. Nickelsburg, eds, *Early Judaism and its Modern Interpreters* (Atlanta/Philadelphia 1986), pp. 411–36; David Flusser, 'Psalms, Hymns and Prayers', in Michael E. Stone, ed., *Jewish Writings of the Second Temple Period* (Assen, The Netherlands/Philadelphia 1984), pp. 551–77.
48 'A Prolegomenon', p. 277.
49 See Robert Daly, *The Origins of the Christian Doctrine of Sacrifice* (Philadelphia 1978); R. P. C. Hanson, *Eucharistic Offering in the Early Church* (GLS 19, 1979); Kenneth Stevenson, *Eucharist and Offering* (New York 1986), pp. 10–37; Rowan Williams, *Eucharistic Sacrifice: The Roots of a Metaphor* (GLS 31, 1982); Frances Young, *The Use of Sacrificial Ideas in Greek Christian Writers from the New Testament to John Chrysostom* (Cambridge, MA 1979).

Passover and its influence upon early Christian worship will be reserved to the next chapter.

Synagogue Liturgy in the First Century?

The Mishnah lists five actions which it says cannot be performed communally without the presence of a quorum of ten adult males: the recitation of the *Shema*, the recitation of the *Tefillah*, the priestly blessing, the reading from the Torah, and the reading from the Prophets.[50] Scholars have traditionally assumed that these constituted the main elements of the Sabbath synagogue service of the time, and took place in the order in which they are listed, especially as they correspond with the order of the later synagogue liturgy. But this assumption is open to doubt. Since they form merely the first part of a longer list of nine liturgical activities requiring ten males, in which the others clearly refer to different situations (weddings, funerals, and the grace after meals), it is by no means certain that all five must belong to a single occasion; and even if they do, it still remains an open question whether the Mishnah is here describing what was already the accepted practice of the period or attempting to prescribe some innovation. Hence, the further assumption that this form of service, even if not the rabbinic rule about the need for a minimum of ten men, was already in existence in the first century CE is even more questionable.

Indeed, on the basis of both archaeological and literary evidence, a growing number of scholars now doubt that any form of regular Sabbath liturgy as such was a feature of the synagogue before the third century.[51] Instead, it seems to have been an assembly for the primary purpose of studying a portion of the Torah on every Sabbath and festival (at which some praying might also have been done) that was a regular feature of the synagogue from the outset, and may even have constituted *the* fundamental reason for the emergence of that institution. Portions of the Torah also came

50 *Meg.* 4.3. For the *Shemah* and the *Tefillah*, see below, pp. 39–40. According to the Mishnah, the pronouncing of the Aaronic blessing, Numbers 6.24–6, over the people originated in the Temple ritual in connection with the daily sacrifices (*Tamid* 7.2). It is possible, therefore, that it was not transplanted to the synagogue until after 70 CE. Its position in the later synagogue service – after the *Shema* and *Tefillah* but before the scriptural reading(s) – is interesting, since one might have expected it to have been placed at the end of the whole liturgy. A possible explanation may be that the *Tefillah* and the blessing were viewed as a single liturgical unit, perhaps because the *Tefillah* came to be thought of as a substitute for the Temple sacrifices and hence the blessing followed it, as it had done in the cult.

51 See, for example, the detailed study by Heather A. McKay, *Sabbath and Synagogue: The Question of Sabbath Worship in Ancient Judaism* (Leiden 1994); and the briefer survey by Daniel K. Falk, 'Jewish Prayer Literature and the Jerusalem Church in Acts', in Richard Bauckham, ed., *The Book of Acts in its Palestinian Setting* (Carlisle/Grand Rapids 1995), pp. 267–301, esp. 277–85.

to be read at the Sabbath afternoon assembly and on Monday and Thursday mornings. This, however, is almost certainly a later development than the reading on Sabbath mornings, and the choice of Mondays and Thursdays for this purpose seems to be governed by the fact that these were market days in Palestine when people might be expected to gather in villages and towns in some numbers. The morning assembly on Sabbaths and festivals also included a second reading from the Prophets (which in the Jewish division of the Scriptures includes the historical books of Joshua, Judges, Samuel, and Kings). This too was probably a later development, though Luke 4.16–30 and Acts 13.15 indicate that it was established in the first century CE. The readings were followed by a translation into the vernacular and could be concluded with a discourse or homily.

The Babylonian Talmud prescribed that the entire Pentateuch should be read through in a year, on a consecutive basis, interrupted only by special lections on festal days. The Palestinian practice, on the other hand, was different, and the traditional scholarly theory has been that in this case there was a standard lectionary cycle lasting exactly three years, both for the Torah and for the Prophets.[52] Heinemann demonstrated, however, that any idea of a uniform cycle of readings in early times runs contrary to the evidence and 'belongs clearly to the realm of fiction'.[53] While, for example, the Mishnah prescribes 21 verses of the Torah as the minimum to be read each Sabbath morning (there are to be at least seven readers, who must each read no fewer than three verses: *Meg.* 4.4), it does not set any maximum, and consequently different synagogues could have reached different places in the Torah on any given occasion. Moreover, while some read passages consecutively on Sabbath mornings, Sabbath afternoons, Mondays, and Thursdays, others did not, but repeated the Sabbath morning reading on the other occasions in the week. Even less is known about how the Prophetic readings were originally arranged; whether, for instance, they were simply read consecutively or were chosen to complement the Pentateuchal lection or were determined by the season of the liturgical year.

52 This theory was first advanced by Adolph Büchler, 'The Reading of the Law and Prophets in a Triennial Cycle', *JQR* 5 (1893), pp. 420–68; 6 (1894), pp. 1–73.
53 'The Triennial Lectionary Cycle', JJS 19 (1968), pp. 41–8. See also Charles Perrot, *La lecture de la Bible dans la synagogue* (Hildesheim 1973); idem, 'The Reading of the Bible in the Ancient Synagogue', in M. J. Mulder, ed., *Mikra* (Assen, The Netherlands/Philadelphia 1988), pp. 137–59; Ezra Fleischer, 'Annual and Triennial Reading of the Bible in the Old Synagogue', *Tarbiz* 61 (1991), pp. 25–43 (in Hebrew; English summary, pp. ii–iii); idem, 'Inquiries Concerning the Triennial Reading of the Torah in Ancient Eretz-Israel', *Hebrew Union College Annual* 62 (1991), pp. 43–61 (in Hebrew).

The Question of Psalmody
Liturgical and musical historians have also tended to assert confidently that
psalmody was a standard part of the early synagogue liturgy, and some have
even gone so far as to suggest that there was once a triennial cycle for the
Psalter at the Sabbath afternoon service, corresponding to that for the Torah,
in which the psalms were read through in order.[54] As James McKinnon has
demonstrated, however, not only is there a lack of documentary evidence for
the inclusion of psalms in synagogue worship in the early centuries CE, but if
there was no Sabbath synagogue liturgy in the first century, then *a fortiori* it
cannot have included psalms![55]

Whatever the origin of the canonical psalms and their possible liturgical
use in the First Temple, evidence for the place of psalms in the Second Temple
and early synagogue is very limited. The Mishnah lists a psalm for each of the
seven days of the week (24, 48, 82, 94, 81, 93, 92) sung by the Levites at the
Temple sacrifices (*Tamid* 7.4), and at the important festivals the *Hallel*
(Psalms 113–18) accompanied the sacrifices. But, while the *Hallel* seems to
have been taken over into the domestic Passover meal at an early date, and
apparently also into the festal synagogue liturgy, the first mention of the
adoption of the daily psalms in the synagogue is not until the eighth century.[56]
Nor are there earlier references to the use of other psalms in the synagogue,
except for an enigmatic statement in the Mishnah concerning 'those who
complete a *hallel* every day' (*Meg.* 17b). The Babylonian Talmud identifies
this *hallel* as *pesukei de-zimrah*, 'verses of song' (*B. Shab.* 118b), a phrase
which was later used to denote Psalms 145–50, but there is no way of knowing
whether the Talmudic expression was originally understood in this sense or
not, still less whether the Mishnaic *hallel* referred to the same psalms.
Hoffman has suggested that both were probably intended simply as generic
terms for any group of psalms of praise.[57] In any case, it would appear that
what is envisaged is private recitation by pious individuals rather than a
formal part of synagogue liturgy, just as also seems to be true of the Baylonian
Talmud's reference to some who recite Psalm 145 three times a day
(*B. Ber.* 4b).

54 See the scholars cited in J. A. Lamb, *The Psalms in Christian Worship* (London 1962), pp.
    14–15.
55 'On the Question of Psalmody in the Ancient Synagogue', *Early Music History* 6 (1986),
    pp. 159–91, here at 170–80 = idem, *The Temple, the Church Fathers and Early Western
    Chant* (Aldershot 1998) VIII.
56 See ibid., pp. 180ff.; Zahavy, *Studies in Jewish Prayer*, pp. 103–9.
57 *The Canonization of the Synagogue Service*, pp. 127–8. See also Sarason, 'On the Use of
    Method', p. 130 = 145; and cf. a spirited defence of the notion that the *hallel* did
    comprise Psalms 145–50 in W. Jardine Grisbrooke, 'The Laudate Psalms: A Footnote',
    SL 20 (1990), pp. 175–9.

On the other hand, although there may be little evidence for the use of the canonical psalms in early Judaism, there are at least some indications that hymns and songs were being composed and used in some way.[58] These, however, may have belonged rather to more informal and domestic situations than to formal synagogue assemblies.

Daily Prayer

While there is no firm evidence for Sabbath synagogue liturgy in the first century, still less does there seem to be any foundation for the assertion by C. W. Dugmore (1910–90) that in first-century Judaism, at least in the larger towns, 'daily attendance at the public worship of the community would be the practice of every devout Jew'.[59] On the contrary, even the Mishnah gives the impression that the *Shema* and the *Tefillah* will normally be said each day by individuals on their own, and their corporate recitation in the synagogue belongs only to those days of the week when people might gather together to read the Scriptures – the Sabbath, Mondays, and Thursdays.[60] Moreover, while the community life of the Essenes apparently did lead to daily prayer in common,[61] Matthew 6.5 regards public prayer by some Pharisees at street corners *and in synagogues* as a particular act of ostentation rather than as a regular religious custom.

In its fully developed form the *Shema* consists of three Pentateuchal passages (Deuteronomy 6.4–9; 11.13–21; Numbers 15.37–41) and takes its name from the opening Hebrew word of the first passage ('Hear'). The Mishnah presupposes that it is recited twice each day, in the morning and in the evening, accompanied by *berakot*: in the morning, two before it and one after, in the evening, two before it and two after (*Ber.* 1.1–4). It also claims that the *Shema* had been recited by the priests in the Jerusalem Temple, where it had been preceded by the recitation of a single *berakah* and the Decalogue, and followed by three *berakot* (*Tamid* 5.1).[62] It appears, therefore, that the general obligation to recite the *Shema* developed out of an earlier

58 See, for example, the collection of Qumran *Hodayoth*; Philo, *In Flaccum* 121–4 and *De vita contemplativa* 29, 80, 83, 84.
59 *The Influence of the Synagogue upon the Divine Office* (London 1944; 2nd edn, ACC 45, London 1964), p. 43.
60 See McKinnon, 'On the Question of Psalmody in the Ancient Synagogue', pp. 176–8; Roger T. Beckwith, *Daily and Weekly Worship – From Jewish to Christian* (A/GLS 1, 1987), pp. 11–12; Zahavy, *Studies in Jewish Prayer*, pp. 45–52.
61 See Josephus, *Jewish War* 2.128–9; 1QS6.3. The Therapeutae described by Philo, however, lived in recluse and only assembled for worship on the Sabbath (*De vita contemplativa* 30).
62 See R. Hammer, 'What Did they Bless? A Study of Mishnah Tamid 5.1', *JQR* 81 (1991), pp. 305–24. For the meaning of *berakah*, *berakot*, see below, p. 43.

Temple ritual. Zahavy, however, has disputed this and proposed instead that it originated as a popular scribal rite, the alleged link with the Temple being an attempt by the scribal group to give added authority to the practice.[63] If this is so, it seems a little surprising that this group did not make their description of the Temple ritual correspond more exactly in its details (and especially the number of *berakot*) with the form which later became normative.

Whatever its origins, there are a number of signs that the twice-daily recitation of the *Shema* was already more widely practised prior to the destruction of the Temple. There are apparent allusions to it in the *Letter of Aristeas* (which was probably composed in the middle of the second century BCE), in Philo, in Josephus, and in the Dead Sea Scrolls.[64] The Decalogue and the beginning of the *Shema* occur in the Nash papyrus (*c.* 150 BCE),[65] and the scriptural verses of the *Shema* appear in the earliest phylacteries found at Qumran. While the Mishnah does not refer to the use of the Decalogue with the *Shema* outside the Temple, both the Nash papyrus and the evidence of the Cairo Genizah suggest that at least in some places the two were at one time combined, but that this practice eventually fell into disuse.

The *Tefillah*, 'prayer' (later also known as the *Amidah*, 'standing', from the posture to be adopted for it), was also called the *Shemoneh Esreh* (the 'Eighteen [*berakot*]'), from the fact that its contents came to be fixed at 18 (later 19) separate sections, each of which eventually had a short *berakah* appended to its conclusion in order to conform to the later rabbinic requirement that all prayers must have the *berakah* form. According to the Mishnah, the *Tefillah* was to be said three times each day, in the morning, the afternoon, and the evening (*Ber.* 4.1), but scholars today dispute whether the custom of threefold daily prayer existed in the first century or was a later development. Rabbinic literature records a variety of explanations as to the origin of the practice, among them that the prayers were instituted by the patriarchs (*B. Ber.* 26b), by Moses (*J. Ber.* 7.11c), or by 120 elders, including several prophets (*B. Meg.* 17d). Heinemann, having listed these and other rabbinic claims, confidently concluded that

63 'The Politics of Piety', pp. 53–6; 'Three Stages in the Development of Early Rabbinic Prayer', pp. 238–9; *Studies in Jewish Prayer*, pp. 87–94.

64 *Letter of Aristeas* 158–60; Philo, *De spec. leg.* 4.141; Josephus, *Ant.* 4.8.13; 1QS10.10. ET of the *Letter of Aristeas* in James H. Charlesworth, ed., *The Old Testament Pseudepigrapha* II (Garden City, NY 1985/London 1986), pp. 7–34. Falk, *Daily, Sabbath, and Festival Prayers in the Dead Sea Scrolls*, pp. 21–57, believes that the collection of daily prayers found in 4Q503 were probably *berakot* to accompany the recitation of the *Shema*.

65 See W. F. Albright, 'A Biblical Fragment of the Maccabean Age: The Nash Papyrus', *JBL* 56 (1937), pp. 145–76.

since almost every one of these dicta attributes the institution of fixed prayer to a different generation, public body, or personage, nothing can be deduced from their joint testimony with any degree of surety, save for the great antiquity of that institution itself ... The evolution of the fixed prayers began hundreds of years before the destruction of the Second Temple.[66]

His conclusion, however, does not necessarily follow. The testimony reveals only that rabbis of the fourth and fifth centuries CE are said to have *thought* that the practice was an ancient one, not that it really was. An important dimension of post-70 CE Judaism was the obvious need to stress its continuity with the past, and to give authority to the practices it then prescribed by affirming their antiquity. It is, moreover, a natural tendency of all religions to regard whatever is current as having always been observed. Thus Ezra Fleischer has argued that when the Babylonian Talmud (*B. Meg.* 18b) claims that prayer three times a day was organized and regulated by Simeon of Paqoli at Yavneh (*c.* 90 CE), that was when it first emerged as a fixed, obligatory practice in substitution for the former daily sacrifices of the Temple.[67] Although he seems to be basically correct with regard to the attempt to impose the general obligation to pray three times a day at that time, we need to distinguish that from the practice of threefold daily prayer as such, which may well have existed within some religious groups long before that time, an aspect which Fleischer wants to underplay.[68] After all, even if some of the evidence adduced for the existence of an earlier custom of threefold daily prayer may be challenged,[69] the practice is unlikely to have been simply invented out of thin air at the end of the first century. Moreover, the connection of *thrice*-daily prayer with the times of the *twice*-daily sacrifices looks more like a secondary adaptation than its primary motivation, since there is no equally significant correspondence in the Temple cult for the evening hour of prayer, and the Mishnah's own suggestion that it was linked to the closing of the Temple gates (*Taan.* 4.1) has the appearance of a later rationalization.

66 *Prayer in the Talmud*, p. 13.
67 'On the Beginnings of Obligatory Jewish Prayer', *Tarbiz* 59 (1990), pp. 397–441 (in Hebrew; English summary, pp. iii–v).
68 See the critical comments by Stefan Reif, 'On the Earliest Development of Jewish Prayer', *Tarbiz* 60 (1991), pp. 677–81 (in Hebrew; English summary, p. viii), and Fleischer's response, 'Rejoinder to Dr Reif's Remarks', ibid., pp. 683–8 (in Hebrew; English summary, pp. viii–ix).
69 See the critique by Falk, 'Jewish Prayer Literature and the Jerusalem Church in Acts', pp. 295–6, of Bradshaw, *Daily Prayer in the Early Church*, pp. 2–11. He misses the point, however, with regard to threefold daily prayer in Daniel 6.10: this certainly was a sign of Daniel's exceptional piety, but the mention of prayer *thrice* a day (rather than, say, four, five, or six times) might be thought to point to the existence of such a practice in some contemporary pious groups, as Falk himself seems to admit on p. 292.

On the other hand, this does not mean that the content of the first-century daily prayer was already the *Shemoneh Esreh*. Nor did that text spring fully formed out of the convocation at Yavneh at the end of the century, as Fleischer also argues,[70] still less did it achieve immediate universal compliance, as he supposes. As Ruth Langer has remarked in a recent critique of his work, he assumes that 'Rabban Gamliel could decree that everyone must pray a new complex set of prayer three times a day, and people simply rearranged their lives to accommodate this'.[71] On the contrary, it is much more likely that all that was fixed then was the number of *berakot*, together with the general theme of each and the order in which they were to be said, not their precise wording, and that prior to this date a number of different forms of prayer were in use, of varying lengths and with a diversity of themes, according to local custom.[72] Even afterwards, some of these other customs no doubt still persisted, and the permission granted to substitute a different order of only seven *berakot* on Sabbaths and festivals appears to be a concession to a rival tradition that could not be entirely eradicated.

Zahavy has argued that the *Shemoneh Esreh* originated as the main liturgical practice of the deposed priestly aristocracy after the destruction of the Temple, and hence both *Shema* and *Tefillah* represent the prototypical liturgies of competing social factions. Only later, during the second century, he believes, was a compromise reached and the two were amalgamated to form the core of rabbinic liturgy.[73] His identification of the priestly aristocracy as the *originating* group, rather than as those who adopted a pre-existent practice, is questionable, but the notion that the two customs – reciting the *Shema* with its accompanying prayers twice each day and praying three times a day – first emerged as the distinctive practices of quite different religious groups and began to be harmonized only later, in the second or third century, does seem to be well founded, especially as even within later Judaism the rules pertaining both to the time limits for the fulfilment of the duty and to the persons who were obligated to perform it were quite different in each case.

---

70 See further his article, 'The *Shemone Esre* – Its Character, Internal Order, Contents and Goals', *Tarbiz* 62 (1993), pp. 179–223 (in Hebrew; English summary, pp. vi–vii).

71 'Revisiting Early Rabbinic Liturgy: The Recent Contributions of Ezra Fleischer', *Prooftexts* 19 (1999), pp. 179–94, here at p. 190.

72 See Jacob Petuchowski, 'The Liturgy of the Synagogue: History, Structure, and Contents', in W. S. Green, ed., *Approaches to Ancient Judaism* IV (BJS 27; Chico, CA 1983), pp. 6ff.

73 'The Politics of Piety', pp. 58–63; 'Three Stages in the Development of Early Rabbinic Prayer', pp. 242–52; *Studies in Jewish Prayer*, pp. 94–101.

First-century Jewish Prayer-patterns

While it is true – as Christian scholars have constantly asserted – that the *berakah* was a first-century Jewish prayer-form, it was not the only form that prayer could then take in the Jewish tradition, nor was there only one standard form of *berakah* in current use.[74] The *berakah* (plural *berakot*) derives its name from the Hebrew verb *barak*, 'to bless', and several variant types of liturgical formulae utilizing its passive participle *baruk* (or in Greek, *eulogetos*) in reference to God can be detected in the Hebrew Bible and in intertestamental literature. As well as very short doxological formulae, such as 'Blessed is the Lord for ever' (Psalm 89.52), there are also longer acclamations containing either a relative clause or a participial phrase. The use of a relative clause to express the particular actions of God which were the reason for the blessing (as in Exodus 18.10: 'Blessed is the Lord, who has delivered you out of the hands of the Egyptians and out of the hand of Pharaoh') appears to be older than the use of the participial phrase, which tends to speak in more general terms of the qualities of God, as in Tobit 13.1: 'Blessed is God, the one living for ever, and [blessed is] his kingdom.'

In either case, however, this simple *anamnesis* of God might be expanded into a more complex structure by the addition of other elements. A more detailed narrative description of God's works (as, for example, in 1 Kings 8.15–21 or in Tobit 13.2) is very common, as are supplication and intercession – the remembrance of God's past goodness constituting the ground on which he might be asked to continue his gracious activity among his people (as in 1 Kings 8.56–61) – but confession of sin or protestations of unworthiness and faithfulness are also found. The petitionary element often ends with a statement that its purpose is not just the benefit of the suppliants but the advancement of God's glory (as in 1 Kings 8.60: 'that all the peoples of the earth may know that the Lord is God'), and both the narrative description and such petition may lead back to praise in a concluding doxology. Although in the Hebrew Bible these *berakot* are nearly all cast in the third person, there developed in the intertestamental period an increasing preference for the second person instead, as, for example, in 1 Maccabees 4.30ff.: 'Blessed are you, O Saviour of Israel, who ...'

On the other hand, the praise of God might be expressed in ways other than the *berakah*. An alternative construction (sometimes called the *hodayah*) instead used the Hebrew verb *hodeh*, or sometimes some other verb, but in an active and not a passive form, with God addressed directly in the second person. Although *hodeh* is usually translated into English as 'give thanks', its primary meaning is not the expression of gratitude but rather confession or acknowledgement that something is the case, the same verb also

---

74 See further, Bradshaw, *Daily Prayer in the Early Church*, pp. 11–16.

being used for the confession of sin. It was at first rendered into Greek by compound forms of the verb *homologeo*, although later *eucharisteo* became established as an alternative. Like *barak*, it could be used in brief doxologies, as in Psalm 30.12, 'O Lord my God, I will give thanks to you for ever', or with a subordinate clause to articulate the reason for the praise, usually introduced with the conjunction *ki*, 'that' (in Greek *hoti*), as in Isaiah 12.1: 'I will give thanks to you, O Lord my God, that though you were angry with me, your anger turned away and you comforted me'; and the formula could be expanded with further narrative description or by the addition of supplication before returning to a doxological conclusion. This liturgical form is common among the material from Qumran.

Similarly, Jewish prayers of praise in this period might dispense entirely with any introductory formula, and begin directly to recount the mighty works of God, either speaking of God in the third person or addressing God directly in the second person, and could then pass on to supplication and to a concluding doxology, as in the Prayer of Manasses. More complex liturgical forms might combine elements of different types. So, for example, Daniel 2.20–3 begins with a *berakah* and continues (v. 23) with the *hodayah* form; 2 Maccabees 1.11–17 is in *hodayah* form but with a *berakah* conclusion; and 1 Esdras 4.59–60 has all three elements: 'From you comes victory, from you comes wisdom, and yours is the glory, and I am your servant. Blessed are you, who has given me wisdom; for to you I give thanks, O Lord of our fathers.' Furthermore, the difference between the constructions could be blurred to some extent by the fact that the *hodayah* might occasionally use a relative clause, like the *berakah*, and the *berakah* a subordinate clause like the *hodayah*.

Grace at Meals

According to the Mishnah, nothing was to be eaten without God having first been blessed for it, and the short *berakot* to be used for each kind of food are quoted (*Ber.* 6.1–3). Zahavy has suggested, however, that this fully-fledged system of food-blessings, recited before eating, was not formalized until at least the middle of the second century, and was built upon an older tradition of saying blessings over wine and grace at the end of a meal,[75] although his methodology can be questioned. While the Mishnah does not give the text of the grace at the end of a meal, its general outline must by then have been well established, for it is referred to as comprising three *berakot* (*Ber.* 6.8). It is

---

75 'Three Stages in the Development of Early Rabbinic Prayer', pp. 240–1, 252–3; 259–63 = *Studies in Jewish Prayer*, pp. 14–16, 24, 31–4. See also Baruch M. Bokser, '*Ma'al* and Blessings over Food: Rabbinic Transformation of Cultic Terminology and Alternative Modes of Piety', *JBL* 100 (1981), pp. 557–74.

usually assumed that at least the substance of the later *Birkat ha-mazon* was already in regular use, as this too has a tripartite structure: a *berakah* for the gift of food; a *hodayah* for the gift of the land, the covenant, and the law; and a supplication for mercy on the people, the city of Jerusalem, and the Temple.[76] Some confirmation of the antiquity of this form is provided by the *Book of Jubilees*, usually dated somewhere in the middle of the second century BCE. There a grace which is put into the mouth of Abraham displays a very similar tripartite structure: a blessing of God for creation and the gift of food; thanksgiving for the long life granted to Abraham; and a supplication for God's mercy and peace.[77]

We should beware, however, of too readily drawing the conclusion that this grace after meals had a standardized form in the first century. Since we have already observed a considerable degree of variation and fluidity in other prayer-patterns from this time, it would be natural to expect some similar diversity in domestic food rituals prior to the attempts to set limits to orthodoxy after the destruction of the Temple. There is obviously an element of continuity between the general structure and themes of the grace known to the author of *Jubilees* and the later *Birkat ha-mazon*, but it is likely that the precise contents varied considerably between different groups of people in the intervening centuries. A fragmentary text of what may be a somewhat different meal-prayer has survived from the synagogue at Dura-Europos,[78] and another from the Qumran literature,[79] and so it is possible that some traditions within early Judaism had forms of grace which diverged more widely still from this pattern.

Unfortunately, no more detailed information about meal-prayers in this period has been preserved. While, for example, both Josephus and the rest of the Qumran literature witness to the fact that the Essenes prayed before and after eating, they do not give any clear indication of the content of the prayers.[80] On the other hand, the *Letter of Aristeas* refers to prayer before eating as a regular Jewish custom, and the only words which it cites are petitionary rather than an act of blessing or thanksgiving.[81] It should also be noted that Philo consistently uses *eucharisteo* rather than *eulogeo* to refer to prayer at meals, which may possibly be an indication that there were forms of grace in Hellenistic Judaism which began with that verb.[82]

76 ET in R. C. D. Jasper and G. J. Cuming, eds, *Prayers of the Eucharist: Early and Reformed* (3rd edn, New York 1987), pp. 7–12.
77 *Jubilees* 22.6–9; ET in Charlesworth, *Old Testament Pseudepigrapha* II, p. 97.
78 See Jacob Neusner, *A History of the Jews in Babylonia* I (Leiden 1965 = BJS 62; Chico, CA 1984), p. 161, n. 3.
79 Moshe Weinfeld, 'Grace after meals in Qumran', *JBL* 111 (1992), pp. 427–40.
80 Josephus, *Jewish War* 2.8.5; 1QS6.3–8; 1QSa2.17f.
81 *Letter of Aristeas* 185.
82 See Jean Laporte, *La doctrine eucharistique chez Philon d'Alexandrie* (Paris 1972), pp. 82–4; ET = *Eucharistia in Philo* (New York 1983), pp. 53–5.

Furthermore, the Mishnah directed that when three or more people ate together, one of them was to say the grace on behalf of all, and it prescribed before the prayer a formula of invitation and a communal response, which varied according to the number of people present (*Ber.* 7.1–3). Thus, for example, the form for use with one hundred people was:

> Let us bless the Lord our God.
> Blessed be the Lord our God.

Heinemann argued that this bidding must be of great antiquity and that its wording would have become fixed at an early date.[83] However, that some variation in wording could apparently still be countenanced when the Mishnah was compiled seems a strong indication that its text had not been definitively established at an earlier time. This in turn suggests the possibility that there may once have existed even more diverse forms both of the bidding and of the grace itself which lay beyond the limits that the rabbinic tradition was prepared to recognize.

83 'Birkath ha-Zimmun and Havurah Meals', *JJS* 13 (1962), pp. 23–9.

3

Worship in the New Testament

The number of studies in the last 50 years relating to various aspects of worship in the New Testament has been so great that a comprehensive and detailed account is quite impossible within the limits of this chapter. We shall content ourselves, therefore, with indicating a number of major trends or tendencies that can be observed within this literature, and noting some methodological criticisms which may be raised in connection with them. Some of these trends belong chiefly to older generations of scholarship, while others persist down to the present. Some are more pronounced in the work of biblical scholars; some are more evident in the work of liturgical historians; while others are common to both groups.

The Tendency Towards 'Panliturgism'

While some scholars have been inclined to deny that the New Testament supplies much evidence at all for what the early Christians were doing in their regular worship, others have sometimes displayed what has been called a certain 'panliturgism' – a tendency to see signs of liturgy everywhere,[1] which, as C. F. D. Moule observed, brings with it 'the temptation to detect the reverberations of liturgy in the New Testament even where no liturgical note was originally struck'.[2] This tendency can be clearly illustrated in the multifarious attempts to discern a liturgical context behind the New Testament writings themselves. Many scholars have claimed to see here reflections of certain Jewish liturgical practices which more recent research into the origins of Jewish worship would consider post-date the composition of the New Testament books.

---

1 W. C. van Unnik, '*Dominus vobiscum*: The Background of a Liturgical Formula', in A. J. B. Higgins, ed., *New Testament Essays: Studies in Memory of T. W. Manson* (Manchester 1959), p. 272 = *Sparsa Collecta* 3 (NovT Supplement 31; Leiden 1983), p. 363.
2 *Worship in the New Testament* (London/Richmond, VA 1961 = GLS 12/13, 1983), p. 7.

For example, it has often been stated that the Gospels were intended for public reading within regular Christian worship, and hence their composition would have been shaped to some extent by the Jewish lectionary which they would then have accompanied and on which they would have constituted a commentary. Thus, attempts have been made to discern the lectionary material lying behind them. R. G. Finch in 1939 seems to have been the first to do this, maintaining that Jesus' teaching was not only given in the synagogue but affected by what was read there.[3] Subsequently G. D. Kilpatrick suggested that Matthew was intended for public reading at worship, but did not attempt to propound a detailed lectionary arrangement.[4] Philip Carrington developed the idea in relation to Mark, seeing it as laid out in accordance with an annual cycle of Sabbaths and feasts.[5] Michael Goulder went further, and regarded all three Gospels as lectionary books – Mark for half a year, Matthew for a full year following the festal cycle, and Luke for a full year following the Sabbath cycle[6] – while Aileen Guilding tried to show that the fourth Gospel was intended as a commentary on the Jewish triennial lectionary and was attempting to preserve the traditions about Jesus in a form suitable for liturgical use in the churches.[7]

Most of these theories do not have the slightest evidence to support them. Not only has recent Jewish scholarship revealed that there was no fixed Sabbath lectionary in existence in the first century,[8] but we have no reason to

---

3 *The Synagogue Lectionary and the New Testament* (London 1939).

4 *The Origins of the Gospel according to St Matthew* (Oxford 1946), ch. V.

5 *The Primitive Christian Calendar: A Study in the Making of the Markan Gospel* (Cambridge 1952). He was severely criticized by W. D. Davies, 'Reflections on Archbishop Carrington's "Primitive Christian Calendar"', in W. D. Davies and D. Daube, *The Background of the New Testament and its Eschatology* (Cambridge 1954), pp. 124–52, reprinted in W. D. Davies, *Christian Origins and Judaism* (London/Philadelphia 1962), pp. 67–95. Carrington, however, defended his position in a long appendix to his *According to Mark* (Cambridge 1960), pp. 346–71.

6 *Midrash and Lection in Matthew* (London 1974); *The Evangelists' Calendar* (London 1978). Goulder subsequently admitted that 'in the present state of knowledge the Sabbath readings in the synagogue are speculative', and so the hypothesis of a correspondence between the Gospels and a Sabbath lectionary 'needs to be shelved, though it does not need to be abandoned'; but he still insisted that correspondence with the main feasts of the year is much stronger: *Luke: A New Paradigm* (Journal for the Study of the New Testament Supplement Series 20; Sheffield 1989) I, pp. 147–77.

7 *The Fourth Gospel and Jewish Worship* (Oxford 1960), pp. 54–7. But cf. the criticisms in Leon Morris, *The New Testament and the Jewish Lectionaries* (London 1964); idem, 'The Gospels and the Jewish Lectionaries', in R. T. France and David Wenham, eds., *Gospel Perspectives* 3 (Sheffield 1983), pp. 129–56. While not going as far as Guilding, Oscar Cullmann, *Early Christian Worship* (London/Philadelphia 1953), pp. 37–59, considered that one of the chief concerns of the Fourth Gospel was to set forth the connection between the contemporary Christian worship and the historical life of Jesus.

8 See above, p. 37.

suppose that Gentile churches would necessarily have wanted to preserve a Jewish system of Scripture reading in their worship, nor is there any sign that Christians assigned particular passages of Scripture to specific occasions. On the contrary, Justin Martyr, writing in the middle of the second century, stated that the readings lasted 'for as long as time allows'.[9]

Efforts to find a liturgical background in Judaism have not been restricted to the Gospels alone. T. W. Manson thought that the early part of Romans took its form from the liturgy of the Day of Atonement, and that the Corinthian letters contained reminiscences of the feasts of Passover, New Year, and Tabernacles.[10] Carrington believed that some of the themes of the Corinthian correspondence were derived from a synagogue lectionary used during the period from Passover to Pentecost, and that Hebrews may have been intended for reading at a Jewish–Christian celebration of the Day of Atonement.[11] Ernst Lohmeyer also saw a reflection of the Day of Atonement in Colossians 1.13–20,[12] while James Charlesworth has suggested that the influence of that feast lies behind Philippians 2.6–11.[13] Here, too, the connection is tenuous. While it is possible at least in some cases that the author's experience of Jewish festivals and the concepts associated with them have coloured the expression of the theological ideas of some of the New Testament material, it is a quite unjustified leap from there to posit the text's original *Sitz im Leben* within that worship.

Closely related to these claims is the question of the extent to which Christianity separated itself from Judaism from the outset, and therefore the degree to which Jewish liturgy would have continued to exercise a formative influence on Christian worship, especially in the predominantly Gentile churches founded by Paul. Scholars have adopted different positions on this issue. Some have stressed the element of continuity with Judaism in almost every aspect of Christian liturgy; others have minimized the connection between Church and synagogue, often seemingly more on the basis of a dogmatic conviction that the Christian faith necessarily involved a radical transformation or even rejection of the former religion than on the basis of a dispassionate examination of the evidence. Gerhard Delling, for example, asserted that 'the Worship which belongs to the

---

9 Justin Martyr, *I Apol.* 67.3. See below, pp. 98–9, 123–4.
10 '*Hilasterion*', *JTS* 46 (1945), pp. 1–10.
11 *The Primitive Christian Calendar*, pp. 42–4. See also T. W. Manson, *The Epistle to the Hebrews* (London 1951), p. 131.
12 *Die Briefe an die Philipper, an die Kolosser und an Philemon* (Göttingen 1930), pp. 41–7. See also Stanislas Lyonnet, 'L'hymne christologique de l'Épître aux Colossiens et la fête juive du Nouvel An', *Recherches de science religieuse* 48 (1960), pp. 92–100.
13 'A Prolegomenon', p. 279, n. 46.

kingdom which has come in Jesus is fundamentally and completely detached from that of Israel'.[14]

Other attempts have been made to discover a specifically Christian liturgical context behind New Testament material. Carrington concluded that the similar moral exhortations in Colossians, Ephesians, 1 Peter, and James implied that the writers were drawing upon a common pattern of teaching designed for pre-baptismal catechesis.[15] E. G. Selwyn added material from Romans and 1 Thessalonians and believed that he had discovered a baptismal catechism with five different sections which circulated *c.* 50–55 CE.[16] While many scholars have subscribed to the view that 1 Peter contains a baptismal homily of some sort,[17] Herbert Preisker and F. L. Cross went further and argued that the epistle incorporates a complete baptismal liturgy.[18] J. C. Kirby extended this idea to Ephesians and claimed to find there an act of worship which 'may have had a close connection with baptism, though not necessarily with the administration of the sacrament itself', but was more likely 'a Christianized form of the renewal of the covenant'.[19] John Coutts argued that similar forms of prayer, which were baptismal in context, could be seen in 1 Peter and Ephesians;[20] A. T. Hanson discerned elements of a baptismal liturgy in Titus 2–3;[21] Ernst Käsemann saw Colossians 1.12–20 as a primitive Christian baptismal liturgy;[22] and Massey Shepherd put forward the notion that the outline of the Book of Revelation was probably suggested by the order of the paschal liturgy.[23]

Other scholars have rightly questioned many of these claims. James Dunn,

14 *Worship in the New Testament* (London 1962), p. 6. See also Ferdinand Hahn, *The Worship of the Early Church* (Philadelphia 1973), pp. 32ff., 50–2, who believed that the early Christians were originally free from Jewish ritual practices, but gradually returned to such customs as fasting and Sabbath observance.

15 *The Primitive Christian Catechism* (Cambridge 1940).

16 *The First Epistle of St Peter* (London 1947). Cf. the careful evaluation of a possible liturgical background for 1 Thessalonians by Raymond F. Collins, 'I Thes. and the Liturgy of the Early Church', *Biblical Theology Bulletin* 10 (1980), pp. 51–64.

17 See, for example, F. W. Beare, *The First Epistle of Peter* (2nd edn, London 1958), pp. 196–202 (3rd edn, Oxford 1970), pp. 220–6.

18 H. Preisker, revision of H. Windisch, *Die katholischen Briefe* (3rd edn, Tübingen 1951), pp. 49–82, 156–62; F. L. Cross, *1 Peter – A Paschal Liturgy* (London 1954). See also M.-E. Boismard, 'Une liturgie baptismale dans la Prima Petri', *Revue biblique* 63 (1956), pp. 182–208; 64 (1957), pp. 161–83; idem, *Quatre hymnes baptismales dans la Première Épître de Pierre* (Paris 1961); A. R. C. Leaney, 'I Peter and the Passover: An Interpretation', *NTS* 10 (1963/4), pp. 238–51.

19 *Ephesians: Baptism and Pentecost* (London 1968), pp. 150, 170.

20 'Ephesians 1.3–14 and 1 Peter 1.3–12', *NTS* 3 (1956/7), pp. 115–27.

21 *Studies in the Pastoral Epistles* (London 1968), ch. 7.

22 *Essays on New Testament Themes* (London/Naperville, IL 1964 = Philadelphia 1982), pp. 149–68.

23 *The Paschal Liturgy and the Apocalypse* (London/Richmond, VA 1960).

for example, doubts whether it is valid to argue from similarities in teaching to established catechetical forms, and his 'unease grows when these catechetical forms become explicitly *baptismal* catechisms', since not only is testimony for a formal catechumenate lacking in the first century, but the New Testament itself implies that one did not exist; and the evidence for elaborate baptismal liturgies at this period is 'even more flimsy'.[24]

The Tendency to Read Back Later Liturgical Practices

Many conclusions about worship in the New Testament – including some of those listed above – are arrived at only by assuming that liturgical customs found in later centuries must have been in continuous existence from the first century. But that is precisely to beg the question: if there is no unambiguous witness in the New Testament documents themselves to a particular liturgical practice but it can only be detected by interpreting obscure allusions there in the light of evidence from several centuries later (and often from a quite different geographical region), are we justified in making such a connection? While it is certainly possible that in some cases a line of historical continuity *may* run from New Testament times to the liturgical practices of later ages, there are enough instances where recent scholarship is able to demonstrate the improbability of such a trajectory (and to propose instead a much more likely genesis for a particular liturgical custom in the circumstances of a later period) as to make all similar speculation highly risky.

Abundant illustrations could be offered of the pitfalls of such an approach, but Massey Shepherd's theory about the link between the Book of Revelation and the paschal liturgy will serve as a good example. Although he admitted the danger of reading the liturgical developments of a later period back into early sources, and agreed that 'it would be very difficult, if not impossible, to construct from the Apocalypse an order of Paschal celebration, if we did not have the outline of such an order in the *Apostolic Tradition* of Hippolytus', yet he was so convinced of the reliability of the claim of this third-century document to embody genuine first-century traditions that he believed that, 'apart from certain details of ceremonial, there is nothing in the general *ordo* of the Paschal rite described by Hippolytus that could not have been in use in the first century'.[25] He therefore proceeded to see behind the structure of the Book of Revelation a full-blown baptismal liturgy,

24 *Unity and Diversity in the New Testament* (London/Philadelphia 1977), pp. 143–7 (2nd edn 1990), pp. 141–8. See also C. F. D. Moule, 'The Nature and Purpose of 1 Peter', *NTS* 3 (1956/7), pp. 1–11; T. C. G. Thornton, '1 Peter a Paschal Liturgy', *JTS* 12 (1961), pp. 14–26.

25 *The Paschal Liturgy and the Apocalypse*, pp. 78–9. For the *Apostolic Tradition*, see below, pp. 80–3.

comprising: scrutinies, vigil with readings, the initiation itself, prayers, readings from the Law, Prophets, and Gospel, psalmody, and Eucharist. Many of these elements, however, are not in fact found in the *Apostolic Tradition*, but are also being read back from even later sources; and more recent scholarship (as we shall see later in Chapter 7) casts serious doubt on the notion that such a standardized paschal initiation liturgy existed anywhere before at least the fourth century.

A further illustration of the dangerous temptation posed by this tendency is provided by Michael Goulder's claim that the precise chronology of the death of Jesus given in the Gospels is an indication that the first Christians turned the Passover into a memorial of their Lord's Passion lasting 24 hours. He justifies this conclusion by reference to the evidence of the fourth-century Jerusalem pilgrim, Egeria, and what he calls 'hints' in second- and third-century sources.[26] While there may perhaps be a liturgical dimension to the Passion chronology, possibly in relation to the hours of daily prayer observed throughout the year by some early Christians,[27] there is no evidence to support a connection with a Christian Passover. Not only does the Jerusalem commemoration of the Passion of Jesus seem to be a fourth-century creation derived from the Gospel chronology and the earlier 'hints' turn out to be allusions merely to an all-night paschal vigil and not to a more extended observance, but what positive testimony there is to the earliest Christian Pascha suggests that it was celebrated at cock-crow and not prolonged throughout the following day.[28]

The Tendency Towards Harmonization

Not least because of the paucity of evidence in the New Testament for first-century Christian worship, there has been a tendency among some scholars to amalgamate the various scraps of information that do exist in order to form a single composite picture. Thus, for example, references to liturgical activities from the Acts of the Apostles or from the Pauline letters may be combined with apparent allusions to worship from the Johannine literature or from one of the synoptic Gospels to constitute a supposed description of how the first Christians worshipped. Behind this approach lies the assumption of a basic unity of liturgical practice within the apostolic period.[29]

Contemporary currents in New Testament scholarship, however, present a strong challenge to this presupposition, since they stress the essentially

---

26 *Luke: A New Paradigm* I, pp. 151–2. For Egeria, see below, pp. 115–16.
27 See Bradshaw, *Daily Prayer in the Early Church*, pp. 60–2.
28 See below, pp. 179–82.
29 Cullmann, *Early Christian Worship*, pp. 7–36, is one of those guilty of this fault.

pluriform nature of primitive Christianity,[30] and so render improbable the traditional idea that a single, uniform archetype ultimately underlies the later diversity in Christian worship practices. Each of the New Testament books, therefore, needs to be examined for what it may have to reveal about the worship of the particular Christian community from which it emerges, as well as for remnants of even earlier liturgical traditions which it may have preserved, before any attempt is made to look for common features shared by these different churches.[31]

There is a further danger inherent in the process of harmonization, and that is of treating as standard liturgical customs those practices which are described or advocated by the authors whose works happen to have come down to us. Since these represent only a limited number of the many diverse forms which early Christianity appears to have taken, we simply do not know whether all Christian communities worshipped in this way or not. It is even difficult to be sure, when a series of liturgical references is given in a New Testament source, whether they reflect an actual sequence within a rite or are mentioned in that order for some quite different reason.[32]

Liturgy in the Acts of the Apostles

One of the major problems with regard to the New Testament is that nearly all the explicit references to and descriptions of Christian worship occur in one book – the Acts of the Apostles. Because of the shortage of other evidence, there has been a not unnatural tendency for scholars to generalize about forms of worship in the New Testament period on the basis of this source alone. In the light of the recognition of the extent of the diversity of thought and practice within first-century Christianity, however, such a tendency is called into serious question. This work may possibly be able to tell us about what went on in one tradition within the early Church, but we have no grounds for assuming that it was necessarily typical of all the rest.

But which tradition of worship, if any, does it reflect? When, for example, the author describes the procedure adopted to appoint a replacement for Judas (Acts 1.23–6) and the initiation of Cornelius and his household (Acts 10.44–8), just what is it that is being described? Are these accounts reasonably

---

30 See, for example, Raymond E. Brown, *The Churches the Apostles Left Behind* (New York 1984), pp. 19–30; Dunn, *Unity and Diversity in the New Testament*, passim; Käsemann, *Essays on New Testament Themes*, pp. 95–107.

31 Despite some weaknesses, Hahn's *Worship of the Early Church* (to which reference has already been made) is a notable attempt to trace patterns of worship in the New Testament in this way.

32 See, for example, G. J. Cuming, 'Service-endings in the Epistles', *NTS* 22 (1975/6), pp. 110–13: and cf. J. M. Gibbs, 'Canon Cuming's "Service-endings in the Epistles": A Rejoinder', *NTS* 24 (1977/8), pp. 545–7.

reliable historical records of what actually went on in the earliest Palestinian Christian communities, carefully preserved and communicated to the author? Or do they, on the contrary, derive from the author's own experience of Christian liturgy, so that, while they may not tell us anything about the first generation of Christians, they do instead offer valuable evidence about what ordination and baptismal practices were like in a predominantly Gentile church in the second half of the first century?[33] Or are they neither of these, but rather the products of the author's own imagination, intended perhaps by their form to make specific theological points – for instance, the casting of lots in the appointment of Matthias symbolizing that the choice was not human but divine,[34] and the gift of the Spirit preceding the act of immersion in the case of the household of Cornelius symbolizing a Gentile equivalent of the Pentecost experience[35] – and consequently say nothing about what ordinary Christians actually did at any time in the first century?

Similar questions can be posed about other descriptions of acts of worship elsewhere in the Book of Acts. When, for example, the Jerusalem church gather at night to pray for the imprisoned Paul (Acts 12.5, 12), and Paul and Silas pray and sing hymns to God at midnight while in prison (Acts 16.25), are these reflections of a regular custom of night-prayer known to the author, or an unusual activity occasioned by the special circumstances?[36] Again, does the occurrence of the 'breaking of the bread' at Troas after midnight on the first day of the week, preceded by a lengthy sermon (Acts 20.7–11), reflect the regular time and manner of the eucharistic celebration with which the author was familiar, or is it an exceptional form and occasion brought about by Paul's impending departure?[37] In any case, which evening is meant: Saturday

---

33 Ernst Haenchen, *The Acts of the Apostles* (Oxford/Philadelphia 1971), p. 354, suggests that because Peter himself does not perform the actual baptism of Cornelius and his household, 'Luke is no doubt reproducing here the position obtaining in his own day'.

34 See William A. Beardslee, 'The Casting of Lots at Qumran and in the Book of Acts', *NovT* 4 (1960), pp. 245–52.

35 See, for example, Geoffrey Lampe, *The Seal of the Spirit* (London 1951; 2nd edn 1967), p. 75. Gerd Lüdemann, *Early Christianity according to the Traditions in Acts* (Minneapolis 1989), p. 129, claims that 'the bestowal of the Spirit comes before the baptism only for reasons of narrative technique'.

36 Hans Conzelmann, *A Commentary on the Acts of the Apostles* (Philadelphia 1987), p. 132, suggests that in Acts 16.25 the midnight hour is simply part of the 'numinous mood' and the singing of hymns of praise is a common motif of the 'prison release'.

37 Haenchen (*The Acts of the Apostles*, p. 586) suggests the former: a Eucharist, without a meal, preceded by a sermon. Conzelmann, however (*A Commentary on the Acts of the Apostles*, p. 169), would see verses 7 and 11 as a liturgical embellishment to an older form of the story, and maintains that 'no conclusions about the course and the components of the liturgy can be drawn from the redactional additions, since they do not intend to provide ritual exactitude'. For a recent interpretation of the phrase, 'breaking of the bread', see Justin Taylor, 'La fraction du pain en Luc-Actes', in J. Verheyden, ed., *The Unity of Luke-Acts* (Leuven 1999), pp. 281–95.

(which in Jewish reckoning would be the beginning of the first day of the week) or Sunday?[38] The account of the resurrection appearance on the Emmaus road (Luke 24.13–32) has caused similar speculation: is the sequence of events – the explanation of Moses and the prophets followed by the meal – indicative of the regular order of the Eucharist known to the compiler or not?

Such questions have perhaps been raised most acutely in connection with the various references to baptism which occur in Acts. In 8.14–17, for example, the apostles at Jerusalem send Peter and John to the Samaritans who have been baptized by Philip. They pray that the Samaritans may receive the gift of the Holy Spirit 'for it had not yet fallen on any of them . . . Then they laid their hands on them and they received the Holy Spirit.' Some would see this merely as a more detailed description of what would have happened at all baptisms. Ernst Haenchen, for example, affirms that 'in Luke's community baptism and the laying on of hands must still have been associated';[39] Hans Conzelmann concludes that 'the laying on of hands must have been customary at baptism, even if Tertullian is the first to state it explicitly';[40] and Wolfgang Dietrich thinks that in the early Jerusalem community there was a rule that the bestowal of the Spirit was reserved to the apostles.[41] Others argue that what is described is an exceptional practice occasioned by the particular situation: the story provides a means whereby the mission of the Hellenists in Samaria can be seen to be endorsed by the Jerusalem apostles, and tells us nothing about normal initiatory practice in the author's community.[42]

A similar difference of opinion exists over the parallel instance in Acts 19.1–7, where the baptism is followed by the imposition of Paul's hands and the reception of the Holy Spirit. Was the post-baptismal imposition of hands conveying the gift of the Spirit a standard initiation procedure in the author's experience, or alternatively is the account constructed in an unusual way to make the point that only after baptism in the name of Jesus can the Holy Spirit be received?[43]

Although various scholars have expressed a strong preference for one position or another in both these and other instances in the Book of Acts, the

---

38 See the discussion in Willy Rordorf, *Der Sonntag* (Zurich 1962) = *Sunday* (London/Philadelphia 1968), pp. 196–202; Samuele Bacchiocchi, *From Sabbath to Sunday* (Rome 1977), pp. 101–11.
39 *The Acts of the Apostles*, p. 304. See also ibid., p. 308.
40 *A Commentary on the Acts of the Apostles*, p. 65.
41 *Das Petrusbild der lukanischen Schriften* (Stuttgart 1972), pp. 249f.
42 See Lampe, *The Seal of the Spirit*, pp. 66–75; Lüdemann, *Early Christianity according to the Traditions in Acts*, pp. 96–7.
43 See Lampe, *The Seal of the Spirit*, pp. 75ff.; Lüdemann, *Early Christianity according to the Traditions in Acts*, pp. 210–11.

inevitable uncertainty which is raised by the alternative explanations means that it is difficult to use the evidence of this source with any degree of confidence to reconstruct first-century Christian liturgy.

Literary Metaphor or Liturgical Practice?

The other New Testament books, and especially the Epistles, tend to offer possible allusions to what Christians were doing liturgically more often than explicit descriptions of practices. But once again there is a serious difficulty about how these should be interpreted. For instance, when 1 Corinthians 5.8 says that 'Christ our Passover is sacrificed for us; therefore let us keep the feast', is this to be understood as a purely ethical exhortation or as encouragement to participate in a Christianized Passover liturgy?[44] And when Galatians 3.27 speaks of the baptized as having 'put on Christ', and Colossians 3.9–10 and Ephesians 4.22–4 speak of putting off the old nature and putting on the new, are these images occasioned by an already existing baptismal custom of stripping off one's clothing before being immersed and of being clothed with a white garment after emerging from the water, such as we find in fourth-century evidence?[45] Or are they simply vivid metaphors coined by the writer, which only much later encouraged or gave rise to the liturgical usage? The latter might seem the more probable explanation, but to these examples may be added the accounts in Mark's Gospel of the young man at the arrest of Jesus who left the linen cloth he was wearing and ran away naked (14.51–2) and of the young man sitting on the right side of the empty tomb, dressed in a white robe (16.5). Robin Scroggs and Kent Goff have put forward the suggestion that this pair of stories is intended as a baptismal image,[46] and this is certainly an attractive interpretation of passages which have often puzzled commentators.

The same questions have been asked of other baptismal images in the New Testament. For example, Christians are spoken of as having been sealed with the Holy Spirit (see 2 Corinthians 1.22; Ephesians 1.13; 4.30), and Revelation 7.3f. describes the sealing of the servants of God as being 'upon their foreheads'. Is this merely a metaphor, or an allusion to a liturgical ceremony of making the sign of the cross on the foreheads of the newly baptized, such as we find in later practice? Do references to anointing (see 1 John 2.20, 27) reflect an actual use of oil or are they meant metaphorically?

Obviously, in all such cases there is a real danger of the unwarranted

---

44　See Gerlach, *The Ante-Nicene Pascha*, pp. 35–6.
45　Cf. also the similar eschatological images of 2 Corinthians 5.1–5.
46　Robin Scroggs and Kent I. Goff, 'Baptism in Mark: Dying and Rising with Christ', *JBL* 92 (1973), pp. 531–48.

reading back of later practices into New Testament times that we have spoken of earlier. Yet, at least in some instances, we cannot entirely rule out the possibility that the development may not always have been from metaphor to later literal fulfilment, but rather from early practice to literary image. The difficulty consists in knowing which direction the development took in any given case.

The Book of Revelation presents a particular problem in this area. Some have regarded much of its imagery of heavenly worship as a clear reflection of liturgical practices familiar to the author. So, for example, Oscar Cullmann could say: 'the whole Book of Revelation from the greeting of grace and peace in chapter 1.4 to the closing prayer: Come Lord Jesus, in chapter 22.20, and the benediction in the last verse, is full of allusions to the liturgical usages of the early community'.[47] Other scholars, on the other hand, question the too-ready assumption of the existence of parallels between heavenly and earthly worship in many of the details described.[48] After all, it is generally taken for granted that the early Christians did not use incense in their worship, in spite of the references to it in Revelation 5.8 and 8.3f. How then can we be sure that other elements do correspond to regular Christian liturgical customs?

Possible Early Christian Hymns and Prayers

One aspect of research into early Christian worship which has received considerable attention is the detection of actual liturgical texts, and especially hymns, within the New Testament books themselves.[49] Among the more obvious examples of hymnic material are the Lukan canticles (1.46–55, 68–79; 2.29–32);[50] John 1.1–16;[51] Philippians 2.6–11;[52] Colossians 1.15–20;[53] and the

47 *Early Christian Worship*, p. 7.
48 See, for example, Delling, *Worship in the New Testament*, pp. 44–8; Hahn, *Worship of the Early Church*, pp. 80–1.
49 Important studies of hymnic material include: Reinhard Deichgräber, *Gotteshymnus und Christushymnus in der frühen Christenheit* (Göttingen 1967); J. M. Robinson, 'Die Hodajot-Formel in Gebet und Hymnus des Frühchristentums', in W. Eltester, ed., *Apophoreta. Festschrift für Ernst Haenchen* (Berlin 1964), pp. 194–235; J. T. Sanders, *The New Testament Christological Hymns* (Cambridge 1971); J. Schattenmann, *Studien zum neutestamentlichen Prosahymnus* (Munich 1965); G. Schille, *Frühchristliche Hymnen* (Berlin 1965); K. Wengst, *Christologische Formeln und Lieder des Urchristentums* (Gütersloh 1972).
50 For full discussion and bibliography, see Raymond E. Brown, *The Birth of the Messiah* (Garden City, NY 1977), pp. 346–66.
51 See Rudolf Schnackenburg, *The Gospel according to St John* I (London 1968/New York 1980), pp. 229–30.
52 See especially the study by R. P. Martin, *Carmen Christi* (Cambridge 1967; 2nd edn, Grand Rapids 1983).
53 See the bibliography in W. G. Kümmel, *Introduction to the New Testament* (London 1966/Nashville 1975), p. 343.

various acclamations and songs in the Book of Revelation.[54] Some scholars
would add to this list such passages as Hebrews 1.3; 1 Timothy 3.16; 1 Peter
3.18–22, and others still more, but these suggestions immediately reveal how
extremely difficult it is to establish objective criteria to distinguish actual
hymns from mere poetic passages,[55] or to know whether the composition
simply originated with the author or some other anonymous person, or was in
real liturgical use in a Christian community. It is often equally difficult to
determine when the New Testament authors are citing typical prayer-forms
with which they are familiar and when they are not,[56] or even to separate
hymns from prayers, since both may employ a similar construction.

Some scholars have attempted not only to identify passages as hymnic
material but also to classify them as being either

1   Jewish compositions with little or no Christian editing;
2   Christian redactions of Jewish originals;
3   pre-Christian Hellenistic compositions; or
4   purely Christian compositions, though perhaps influenced by Jewish or
    other traditions.

Some would further subdivide the material as being of either Palestinian or
Hellenistic Jewish–Christian origin, or even envisage different types of Hellenistic Jewish–Christianity.[57] While, however, there might be some measure of
agreement as to the categories, there is a conspicuous lack of consensus about
where the various hymns ought to be located. So, for example, while Käsemann
regards Colossians 1.15–20 as in origin a Gnostic hymn,[58] Reinhard Deichgräber[59] and Eduard Lohse[60] trace it back to Hellenistic Judaism, and others
would attribute its composition entirely to the author of the Epistle.[61]

---

54   For these, see E. Cothenet, 'Earthly Liturgy and Heavenly Liturgy according to the
     Book of Revelation', in *Roles in the Liturgical Assembly* (New York 1981), pp. 115–35;
     K.-P. Jörns, *Das hymnische Evangelium* (Gütersloh 1971); Pierre Prigent, *Apocalypse et
     liturgie* (Neuchâtel 1964). See also Ugo Vanni, 'Liturgical Dialogue as a Literary Form
     in the Book of Revelation', *NTS* 37 (1991), pp. 348–72.
55   See the comments by Charlesworth, 'A Prolegomenon', p. 280.
56   See, for example, P. T. O'Brien, *Introductory Thanksgivings in the Letters of Paul*
     (Leiden 1977); and G. P. Wiles, *Paul's Intercessory Prayers* (Cambridge 1974), who tends
     to see rather more such passages than are actually there.
57   See, for example, Dunn, *Unity and Diversity in the New Testament*, pp. 132–41.
58   *Essays on New Testament Themes*, pp. 154–9.
59   *Gotteshymnus und Christushymnus in der frühen Christenheit*, p. 154.
60   *Colossians and Philemon* (Philadelphia 1971), p. 45.
61   See, for example, A. Hamman, *La Prière, I: Le Nouveau Testament* (Tournai 1959), pp.
     255–6. Some have even judged it to be an example of a eucharistic prayer rather than a
     hymn: see Klaus Gamber, 'Anklänge an das Eucharistiegebet bei Paulus und das jüdische
     Kiddusch', *Ostkirchliche Studien* 9 (1960), pp. 254–64; E. J. Kilmartin, 'Sacrificium Laudis:
     Content and Function of Early Eucharistic Prayers', *Theological Studies* 35 (1974), p. 273.

Nevertheless, in spite of all this uncertainty, those passages which have been identified by general consensus as hymns and prayers can legitimately be seen as reflecting the sort of liturgical material which early Christians would have used. Even if these particular examples are not taken directly from common worship but are the product of the authors' creativity, they would inevitably have been influenced to a considerable extent by the liturgical forms with which they were familiar. This conclusion is confirmed by a comparative analysis of the passages in question, which reveals a large number of common stylistic and linguistic features persisting across differences of author, theology, and background, and so suggests that this commonality derives from the similarities within their various liturgical traditions. For example, early Christian forms of prayer reveal an apparently growing preference for *eucharisteo* over *eulogeo*. Although it is frequently said that these verbs are simply synonyms, our study of Jewish prayer-patterns has indicated that this is not the case, but that each word was used in a quite different liturgical construction. Thus, the preference points to the dominance of the *hodayah/eucharistia* form over the *berakah/eulogia* in primitive Christianity.[62]

In addition to the general methodological questions outlined so far in this chapter, there are some further, specific problems with regard to the interpretation of the baptismal and eucharistic references in the New Testament, and to these we now turn.

The Origins of Christian Baptism[63]

The custom of baptizing new converts to Christianity appears to have been derived from John the Baptist, but the source of his practice is uncertain. Some scholars have argued that it was based on the ablutions of the Essene community at Qumran, but these were repeated washings related to the need for ritual purity and do not seem to have included an initiatory baptism. Others have suggested that John was influenced by the practice of baptizing new converts to Judaism, but there is some doubt whether this was being done in his time or whether it was only adopted at a later date. A third possibility is

---

62 See above, pp. 43–4, and also Bradshaw, *Daily Prayer in the Early Church*, pp. 30–7.
63 Recent studies include: Adela Yarbro Collins, 'The Origin of Christian Baptism', *SL* 19 (1989), pp. 28–46 = Maxwell E. Johnson, ed., *Living Water, Sealing Spirit: Readings on Christian Initiation* (Collegeville 1995), pp. 35–57; Gordon W. Lathrop, 'Baptism in the New Testament and its Cultural Settings', in S. Anita Stauffer, ed., *Worship and Culture in Dialogue* (Geneva 1994), pp. 17–38; Lars Hartman, *'Into the Name of the Lord Jesus': Baptism in the Early Church* (Edinburgh 1997) with substantial bibliography; and some of the essays in S. E. Porter and A. R. Cross, eds, *Baptism, the New Testament and the Church*, Journal for the Study of the New Testament Supplement Series 171 (Sheffield 1999).

that it arose out of the Israelite traditions of ritual purification (see, for example, Leviticus 15.5–13) and/or of prophetic symbolism, which had spoken of God's people being cleansed with pure water in preparation for the advent of the messianic age (see, for example, Ezekiel 36.25–8).

Whether the Christian adoption of baptism began with Jesus himself or only in the Church after his resurrection cannot easily be resolved. All three synoptic Gospels record Jesus' own baptism by John but say nothing of him baptizing his followers. The Gospel of John, on the other hand, does not mention Jesus being baptized but does speak of him baptizing others (John 3.22, 26; 4.1; but cf. 4.2). Matthew 28.16–20 contains the command to baptize all nations, but there are difficulties in accepting this as an authentic saying of the risen Lord, not least because Christian baptisms seem at first to have been 'in the name of Jesus' rather than of the Trinity, as in the Matthean text.[64]

Whatever its origins, however, it appears that from early times it became the usual – though perhaps not yet universal – custom to initiate new converts into the Church through a process which included baptism, performed in a river, a pool, or a domestic bath-house. What else besides the immersion might have been involved is not made explicit in the New Testament. We have already noted the difficulties in deciding whether allusions to anointing and clothing are to actual baptismal practices and whether the references to a post-baptismal imposition of hands in Acts are to a regular part of the initiation rite (cf. also Hebrews 6.2). There may possibly have been a preliminary period of instruction, especially when converts came from a Gentile background, and it is likely that the ritual included a confession of faith in Jesus in one form or another.[65] It is uncertain whether infants and young children were baptized as well as adults.[66]

64 See Benjamin J. Hubbard, *The Matthean Redaction of a Primitive Apostolic Commissioning: An Exegesis of Matthew 28:16–20* (Missoula, MT 1974). The trinitarian formula may even be a much later addition to the Matthean text: see H. B. Green, 'Matthew 28:19, Eusebius, and the lex orandi', in Rowan Williams, ed., *The Making of Orthodoxy* (Cambridge/New York 1989), pp. 124–41. The criticism made by Cyprian, *Ep.* 74.5; 75.18, appears to indicate that the church at Rome in the third century was still willing to accept the sufficiency of baptisms in the name of Jesus alone, even if its own practice was now trinitarian.

65 The baptismal confession of faith, 'I believe that Jesus Christ is the Son of God', in Acts 9.37 looks like an early addition to the text based on actual liturgical practice, but how typical a form this was cannot be known.

66 The classic discussion of this question is between Joachim Jeremias, *Infant Baptism in the First Four Centuries* (London/Philadelphia 1960), and Kurt Aland, *Did the Early Church Baptize Infants?* (London/Philadelphia 1963). See also Jeremias' response to Aland, *The Origins of Infant Baptism* (London/Naperville, IL 1963); Everett Ferguson, 'Inscriptions and the Origin of Infant Baptism', *JTS* 30 (1979), pp. 37–46; and the series of essays by David F. Wright, 'The Origins of Infant Baptism – Child Believers' Baptism?', *SJT* 40 (1987), pp. 1–23; 'How Controversial Was the Development of Infant Baptism in the Early Church?', in J. E. Bradley and R. A. Muller, eds, *Church, Word, and Spirit: Essays in Honor of Geoffrey W. Bromiley* (Grand Rapids 1987), pp. 45–63; 'At What Ages were People Baptized in the Early Centuries?', *SP* 30 (1997), pp. 389–94.

On the other hand, what is clear from the New Testament is that the process of becoming a Christian was interpreted and expressed in a variety of different ways. So, for example, in some traditions the emphasis was clearly placed on the forgiveness of sins and the gift of the Holy Spirit (see Acts 2.38); in others the metaphor of birth to new life was used (John 3.5f.; Titus 3.5–7); in others baptism was understood as enlightenment (Hebrews 6.4; 10.32; 1 Peter 2.9); and in Paul's theology the primary image was union with Christ through participation in his death and resurrection (Romans 6.2ff.). This variation in baptismal theology encourages the supposition that the ritual itself may also have varied from place to place. Indeed, the account of Jesus washing the disciples' feet in John 13.1–20, coupled with the inclusion of a similar foot-washing within the baptismal rites of some later Christian traditions, suggests the possibility that it, rather than whole-body baptism, may have functioned as *the* initiation ritual within some early Christian communities, and hence its appearance as an ancillary rite in later times was a deliberate compromise with the mainstream practice.[67] In other communities, anointing with oil rather than water may once have been the central ritual, and again its combination with the water bath in early Syrian baptismal practice (with unction here preceding immersion, in spite of its deviation from the Gospel archetype of the baptism of Jesus, where water precedes the descent the Spirit) being yet another liturgical compromise.[68]

Last Supper and Lord's Supper

One of the major difficulties faced by scholars with regard to the origins of the Eucharist is the question of how far the accounts of the Last Supper (Matthew 26.17–30; Mark 14.12–26; Luke 22.7–38; 1 Corinthians 11.23–6) may be treated as reliable descriptions of an actual historical event and how far they have been affected by the later liturgical practices of the first genera-tion of Christians. A number of scholars from Rudolf Bultmann onwards have argued that, while Jesus may indeed have held a final meal with his disciples, the narratives as we have them are creations of the early Church and so can tell us nothing about the actual historical roots of the Eucharist

---

67 See further Martin F. Connell, '*Nisi pedes*, except for the feet: Footwashing in the community of St John's Gospel', *Worship* 70 (1996), pp. 20–30; and the observations of Maxwell E. Johnson, *The Rites of Christian Initiation: Their Evolution and Interpreta-tion* (Collegeville 1999), pp. 20–2.
68 For later instances of it as a baptismal ceremony, see below, pp. 146–9. And for the sug-gestion that the mixed chalice at the Eucharist may also have been a similar compromise between two traditions, see p. 69, n. 108.

but can only witness to its later development.[69] Other scholars, however, would accept that the accounts have certainly been influenced by the liturgical practices of the first Christians, but maintain that still discernible within them is a firm historical core.[70]

Since there are significant differences between the various narratives, scholars have been divided over which of them, if any, has best preserved the historical details. Joachim Jeremias, for example, opted for the Markan version of the interpretative words of Jesus over the bread and the wine as coming closest to the original,[71] Heinz Schürmann expressed a strong preference for the Lukan narrative, with its eschatological emphasis,[72] and Eduard Schweizer considered the Pauline account the most primitive in form, in spite of its more obvious liturgical character.[73] More recently, Xavier Léon-Dufour has taken up a mediating position and argued that older and newer elements are combined in all the traditions.[74]

To speak of the narratives as possibly being 'influenced by the liturgical practices of the first Christians' requires some clarification. This does not necessarily mean that they were regularly recited as part of the eucharistic liturgy itself from early times, whether within the eucharistic prayer or as an independent formula, as many scholars have concluded. There is no firm evidence at all for the liturgical use of an institution narrative until the fourth century, and then it has the marks of an innovation rather than a well-established custom.[75] Prior to that time, its use seems to have been catechetical rather than liturgical, and its stylized form is just as likely a result of this function as of employment as a liturgical formula. Thus, the most that we can say is that, because the narratives were passed on within Christian communities which

---

69 See, for example, R. Bultmann, *Theology of the New Testament* (London/New York 1952) I, pp. 144–51; Eduard Schweizer, *The Lord's Supper according to the New Testament* (Philadelphia 1967); W. Marxsen, *The Lord's Supper as a Christological Problem* (Philadelphia 1970); John Dominic Crossan, *The Historical Jesus: The Life of a Mediterranean Jewish Peasant* (San Francisco 1991), pp. 360–7.

70 For recent contributions to this debate, see John Meier, 'The eucharist at the Last Supper: Did it happen?', *Theology Digest* 42 (1995), pp. 335–51; John Koenig, *The Feast of the World's Redemption: Eucharistic Origins and Christian Mission* (Harrisburg, PA 2000).

71 *Die Abendmahlsworte Jesu* (Göttingen 1935, 3rd edn 1960) = *The Eucharistic Words of Jesus* (London/New York 1966). Many other scholars have followed him, including Rudolf Pesch, *Das Abendmahl und Jesu Todesverständnis* (Freiburg 1978).

72 *Eine quellenkritischen Untersuchung des lukanischen Abendmahlsberichtes Lk 22, 7–38*, published in three parts (Münster 1953, 1955, 1957). A similar position was adopted by H. Merklein, 'Erwägungen zur Überlieferungsgeschichte der neutestamentlichen Abendmahlstraditionen', *Biblische Zeitschrift* 21 (1977), pp. 88–101, 235–44.

73 *The Lord's Supper according to the New Testament*. See also Paul Neuenzeit, *Das Herrenmahl. Studien zur paulinischen Eucharistieauffassung* (Munich 1960).

74 *Sharing the Eucharistic Bread* (New York 1987); see especially pp. 82–5, 96–8, 158–9.

75 See below, p. 219.

celebrated the Eucharist, their liturgical experience may have had some effect on the way in which they told the story of the Last Supper.

Passover and Last Supper

Whether or not the Last Supper was a Passover meal has also been a topic of great debate. Some scholars accept as genuine the claim made in the synoptic Gospels that it was indeed a Passover meal, and regard the different chronology of the Fourth Gospel (which situates the Supper on the day before the Passover) as an adjustment made by the Evangelist for a theological purpose – so that the death of Jesus would coincide with the very time that the Passover lambs were being sacrificed in the Temple. Others note a number of details in the synoptic versions which do not seem to fit with the Passover explanation, and so prefer to accept John's chronology as historical.[76] Some have even tried to solve the apparent contradiction by ingenious attempts at harmonization. Annie Jaubert, for example, suggested that Jesus ate the Passover meal on Tuesday evening, following the solar calendar current among the Essenes, and died on Friday, the day of the Passover according to the official calendar.[77] I. Howard Marshall resurrected the explanation originally put forward by Paul Billerbeck, that the different methods of calendrical reckoning adopted by the Pharisees and the Sadducees led to the former keeping the Passover on Thursday (the practice followed by Jesus and recorded in the synoptic Gospels) and the Sadducees observing it on Friday (as the Fourth Gospel reports).[78]

Those who reject the notion that the Last Supper was a Passover meal have not been slow to offer alternative hypotheses for the occasion. From the end of the nineteenth century onwards a number of scholars espoused the theory that it was a '*kiddush* meal'. Jeremias, however, conclusively argued that there never was such a thing: a *kiddush* was simply a special blessing pronounced at the beginning of each Sabbath or festival, and 'the idea of a passover *kiddush* which takes place twenty-four hours before the beginning of the feast is *pure fantasy*; not one shred of evidence can be adduced for it'.[79] Others, including Gregory Dix,[80] followed Hans Lietzmann in describing it as a *haburah* meal –

---

76 The various arguments are set out by Jeremias, *The Eucharistic Words of Jesus*, pp. 15–88, who supports the idea that the supper was a Passover meal; cf. Léon-Dufour, *Sharing the Eucharistic Bread*, pp. 306–8, who reaches the opposite conclusion; and Étienne Nodet and Justin Taylor, *The Origins of Christianity* (Collegeville 1998), pp. 89–123, who rehearse the arguments fully, and propose a connection to Pentecost instead!

77 *La date de la Cêne* (Paris 1957) = *The Date of the Last Supper* (New York 1965).

78 *Last Supper and Lord's Supper* (Exeter 1980/Grand Rapids 1981), pp. 71–5.

79 *The Eucharistic Words of Jesus*, pp. 26–9 (emphasis in original).

80 *The Shape of the Liturgy*, pp. 50ff.

a Jewish meal, 'invested with religious solemnity, which might be held by a company of friends'.[81] Once again Jeremias pointed out the total lack of evidence for such an institution: the meals of the *haburot mishwah*, which did exist, were exclusively in connection with obligations such as circumcisions, weddings, and funerals; and, moreover, every Jewish meal had 'religious solemnity', whether it was taken alone or in company.[82] This, of course, does not deny the possibility that Jesus ate a meal with his friends which was not the Passover, but only that this would not have been a part of the tradition of the *haburot mishwah*.

Another possible connection which has been explored by some scholars is with the communal meals of the Essene movement at Qumran. Although only a few would see the Supper itself as having been directly influenced from this source, others suggest that early Christian eucharistic practice, and hence the accounts of the Supper, may have been affected by experience of such meals. But the similarities are only in elements common to all Jewish festal meals and not in elements unique to the Essenes.[83] Likewise, attempts to see a link with the Jewish tale of Joseph and Asenath fail to be convincing, not least because of uncertainties with regard to the date and provenance of that text.[84]

A more recent proposal for an alternative to the Passover meal as the source of Christian eucharistic practice has been the *zebah todah* ('sacrifice of praise/thanksgiving'), a cultic thank-offering by an individual or a group for divine deliverance, which in addition to the sacrifice itself involved a joyful hymnic proclamation (*todah*) of what God had done, and a communion meal including, among other things, the consumption of leavened bread (Leviticus 7.12–15).[85] Only Hartmut Gese has gone so far as to suggest that the Last Supper itself was intended by Jesus as a *todah*-meal, eaten in anticipation of his own imminent sacrificial death.[86] Other scholars have proposed either that

---

81 *Messe und Herrenmahl* (Bonn 1926) = *Mass and Lord's Supper* (Leiden 1953–1978), pp. 170–1, 185.
82 *The Eucharistic Words of Jesus*, pp. 29–31.
83 ibid., pp. 31–6.
84 See Christoph Burchard, 'The Importance of Joseph and Asenath for the Study of the New Testament: A General Survey and a Fresh Look at the Lord's Supper', *NTS* 33 (1987), pp. 102–34.
85 See further, Henri Cazelles, 'L'Anaphore et l'Ancien Testament', in *Eucharisties d'Orient et d'Occident* I (Paris 1970), pp. 11–21.
86 'Die Herkunft des Abendmahles', *Zur biblischen Theologie* (Munich 1977), pp. 107–27 = 'The Origin of the Lord's Supper', *Essays on Biblical Theology* (Minneapolis 1981), pp. 117–40. But his position has received support from Joseph Ratzinger, 'Form and Content in the Eucharistic Celebration', in idem, *The Feast of Faith: Approaches to a Theology of the Liturgy* (San Francisco 1986), postscript 2; Dennis Lindsay, '*Todah* and the Eucharist: The Celebration of the Lord's Supper as a "Thank Offering" in the Early Church', *Restoration Quarterly* 39 (1997), pp. 83–100.

the Christian Eucharist came into being as a *todah*-meal in thanksgiving for the deliverance wrought by Jesus, or merely that early eucharistic prayers were influenced in their form by the *todah*.[87] To a great extent these theories have been occasioned by the need to explain why it is that later eucharistic prayers did not retain the *berakah* form commonly thought to have been standard in first-century Jewish meal-prayers, but apparently show a preference for the *hodayah/eucharistia* form supposedly characteristic of the *todah*. If, however, as we have suggested in the preceding chapter,[88] Jewish meal-prayers were not standardized in the first century and the *hodayah* could be used in contexts other than the *zebah todah*,[89] then these hypotheses are rendered unnecessary. In any case, they do not account very satisfactorily for the Last Supper itself, nor for the strongly eschatological emphasis in the tradition.[90]

From the point of view of liturgical scholars, the question of whether the Last Supper was a Passover meal does not seem particularly crucial. Even if it *were* a Passover meal, no exclusively paschal practices appear to have been retained in the primitive Church's eucharistic celebrations, least of all restricting it to an annual occasion; and even if it *were not* a Passover meal, it still took place within a Passover atmosphere and context. In any case, we are far from certain about the precise details of the Passover meal in the first century, and it is probable that it was considerably different from the form that it took after the destruction of the Temple. To cite just one example, it seems likely that it did not become a true family meal until the Passover ceased to be a Jerusalem pilgrimage festival after 70 CE.[91]

Breaking of Bread and Eucharist

In his monumental work, *Messe und Herrenmahl*, Lietzmann developed a theory originally advanced by Friedrich Spitta at the end of the nineteenth century[92] that there were from the first two quite different types of eucharistic liturgy in the Church. One was the joyful fellowship meal of the early Jewish–Christian communities, the 'breaking of bread' as in Acts 2.42; the other arose within the Pauline churches and was dominated by the theme of

---

87 See Léon-Dufour, *Sharing the Eucharistic Bread*, pp. 41–5, and the works cited in n. 46 there. Cf. also below, pp. 131–3.
88 See above, pp. 43–6.
89 As Léon-Dufour himself admitted: *Sharing the Eucharistic Bread*, p. 42.
90 See further Paul F. Bradshaw, '*Zebah Todah* and the Origins of the Eucharist', EO 8 (1991), pp. 245–60.
91 See Baruch M. Bokser, *The Origins of the Seder* (Berkeley/Los Angeles 1984); Joseph Tabory, 'Towards a History of the Paschal Meal', in Bradshaw and Hoffman, eds, *Passover and Easter: Origin and History to Modern Times*, pp. 62–80.
92 *Zur Geschichte und Litteratur des Urchristentums* (Göttingen 1893) I, pp. 207–337.

the memorial of the death of Christ. According to Lietzmann, the former type was a continuation of the meals shared by the disciples with Jesus during his earthly ministry and was not related to the Last Supper; it had no narrative of institution, did not involve the use of wine, and had a strong eschatological dimension, being the anticipation of the messianic banquet. The second type arose from Paul's belief that Jesus intended the Last Supper to be repeated as a liturgical rite ('Do this in remembrance of me' – found only in 1 Corinthians 11.24, 25 and Luke 22.19); it was characterized by Hellenistic sacrificial concepts and eventually supplanted the former type everywhere.

Several other scholars adopted variations of this thesis. Ernst Lohmeyer differentiated between a Galilean tradition of bread-breaking stemming from the meals of Jesus with the disciples, and a Jerusalem tradition descended from the Last Supper which evolved into the Pauline memorial rite.[93] Cullmann defended Lietzmann's original hypothesis, but with the qualification that the common origin of both types was to be sought in the historical Last Supper, 'even if only indirectly in the case of the first type'.[94] The direct origin he attributed to the post-resurrection meal appearances of Jesus. While earlier scholars from Spitta onwards[95] had seen a possible connection between the Eucharist and these Christophanies, they had usually viewed the eucharistic experiences of the early Christians as having been responsible for the emergence of the stories, or at least as having influenced their form. Hence Cullmann appears to have been the first to explore the opposite idea, that the resurrection events themselves gave rise to the eucharistic practice. This approach has since been followed by some other scholars, including Willy Rordorf,[96] but it has also met with criticism.[97]

The majority of scholars, however, rejected Lietzmann's theory of a dual origin of the Eucharist as being based on extremely tenuous evidence and as making the improbable assumption of a radical dichotomy between the thinking and practice of the primitive Jerusalem church and the Pauline communities. Nevertheless, there was a widespread acknowledgement of the existence of what R. H. Fuller called a 'double strand' in the Supper tradition – the eschatological focus and the interpretative words over the bread and

93 'Vom urchristlichen Abendmahl', *Theologische Rundschau* 9 (1937), pp. 168–227, 273–312; 10 (1938), pp. 81–99; 'Das Abendmahl in der Urgemeinde', *JBL* 56 (1937), pp. 217–52.
94 'La signification de la Sainte-Cêne dans le christianisme primitif', *Revue d'histoire et de philosophie religieuses* 16 (1936), pp. 1–22 = 'The Meaning of the Lord's Supper in Primitive Christianity', in O. Cullmann and J. Leenhardt, *Essays on the Lord's Supper* (London/Richmond, VA 1958), pp. 5–23; see also his *Early Christian Worship*, p. 17, n. 1.
95 *Zur Geschichte und Litteratur des Urchristentums* I, pp. 292f.
96 *Sunday*, pp. 215–37. See below, p. 178.
97 See Gese, 'The Origin of the Lord's Supper', p. 128; Léon-Dufour, *Sharing the Eucharistic Bread*, pp. 39–40.

cup.[98] While there might still have been disagreement as to whether or not the interpretative words went back to the historical Last Supper, there seemed to be a general consensus that in the earliest period of the Church's existence it was the eschatological theme which dominated eucharistic practice, but that it became combined with the remembrance of the death of Christ in the early Palestinian tradition.

So, for example, while A. J. B. Higgins supported the essentials of Cullmann's position, he disputed the notion that the pre-Pauline type would not have involved the use of wine. As for the remembrance of Christ's death,

> although to be sure it is not actually mentioned any more than the partaking of wine, it must long have been present in the *Palestinian* as well as in the Hellenistic communities. It is very probable, especially in view of the dependence of both so-called types of Eucharist on the Last Supper, that what Paul did was to lay a renewed emphasis on the remembrance of the death of Christ which was already present, but which at Corinth was in danger of being forgotten . . .[99]

Eduard Schweizer similarly observed that the eschatological sayings in the Last Supper narratives were always attached to the wine and not the bread, and concluded that it was

> impossible to establish the existence of two wholly distinct and independent types of the Lord's Supper in the early church . . . If these two factors – the eschatological joy connected with the presence of the Lord at the table and his imminent return, and the proclamation of Jesus' death connected with the granting of the salvation wrought in this death – did not belong together from the very beginning, they must certainly have merged very early in the Palestinian church.[100]

Léon-Dufour, on the other hand, spoke of a double tradition not in terms of the difference of its content but on the basis of its literary form. He believed that there was what he described as a 'cultic' tradition about the Last Supper and a non-cultic or 'testamentary' tradition, which belonged to the genre of the 'farewell discourse'.[101]

98 'The Double Origin of the Eucharist', *Biblical Research* 8 (1963), pp. 60–72.
99 *The Lord's Supper in the New Testament* (London 1952), pp. 56–63 (emphasis in original).
100 *The Lord's Supper according to the New Testament*, p. 25.
101 *Sharing the Eucharistic Bread*, pp. 90ff.

Recent Trends in the Search for Eucharistic Origins

Although some scholars continue to pursue variations of the dual origin approach,[102] two other principal trends can be seen in more recent New Testament scholarship. One is to look at the Last Supper within the context of the significance of human meals in general and of the cultural background of Graeco–Roman practice in particular, and especially the pattern of the *symposion*, where drinking wine followed the meal.[103] The other is to locate the roots of the Eucharist more broadly within the context of other meals in Jesus' life and not merely the Last Supper, and largely following the trajectory established by redaction-criticism, to take seriously various layers of meaning that can be discerned within the New Testament, and the different ways that the individual New Testament writers describe those meals. Whereas earlier generations of scholars were concerned to try to find the common core behind the variety, scholars today tend to be more interested in what the variety says about the particular theologies of the Eucharist which were espoused by the individual writers and their communities, even if they cannot always agree on the specific layers of meaning that exist in the New Testament texts or on the special emphasis being given to the material by a writer.[104]

Perhaps the most significant contributions, however, have come from Andrew McGowan, who has not only suggested that there may be more evidence for early eucharistic meals where the cup ritual *preceded* the bread ritual than previously assumed, but has also sought to rescue instances of celebrations with bread and water (instead of wine) from the marginalized status of the abnormal and deviant to which other scholars have tended to relegate them.

With regard to the former, in addition to Luke 22.15–19 (the well-known 'shorter' text of the Last Supper attested by a number of manuscripts, where

102 See, for example, Gerard Rouwhorst, 'Le célébration de l'Eucharistie dans l'Église primitive', *QL* 74 (1993), pp. 89–112, who puts forward the strange idea that there was an annual type, celebrated at Passover/Easter, which explicitly commemorated the death of Christ and included an institution narrative; and a weekly type, a Christianized Sabbath meal celebrated on Sundays and not directly influenced by the Last Supper tradition.

103 See above, p. 22, n. 9.

104 See for example Léon-Dufour, *Sharing the Eucharistic Bread*, pp. 181–277; Jerome Kodell, *The Eucharist in the New Testament* (Wilmington, DE 1988), pp. 71–132; Bernd Kollman, *Ursprung und Gestalten der Frühchristlichen Mahlfeier* (Göttingen 1990); Dennis E. Smith and Hal E. Taussig, *Many Tables: The Eucharist in the New Testament and Liturgy Today* (London/Philadephia 1990), pp. 21–69; Bruce Chilton, *A Feast of Meanings: Eucharistic Theologies from Jesus through the Johannine Circle*, NovT Supplement 72 (Leiden 1994); Eugene LaVerdiere, *The Eucharist in the New Testament and in the Early Church* (Collegeville 1996).

the cup precedes the breaking of the bread and no second cup follows after supper), 1 Corinthians 10.16 (where Paul mentions the 'cup of blessing' before 'the bread which we break'),[105] and above all *Didache* 9–10 (where the same pattern is found),[106] McGowan drew attention to another apparent instance of the same so-called 'inverted' sequence in a fragment of Papias preserved in the writings of Irenaeus, and observed that the same order appears to underlie the account of the community supper in the *Apostolic Tradition* of Hippolytus.[107] Most of these can of course be dismissed – and indeed they have often been dismissed – either as aberrations from so-called mainstream Christianity or as characteristic only of the *agape* and not of the Eucharist itself. But that is to allow one's pre-determined conclusions to dictate what evidence may be admitted into the argument.

With regard to 'wineless' Eucharists, McGowan noted that not only are there a number of sources in which it is clear that water rather than wine was used, and some where bread alone is mentioned, or bread with other food-stuffs, but in addition a number of early Christian writers – including the authors of some New Testament books – speak of the use of a cup without making reference to its content at all. There has been a natural tendency to interpret this silence in favour of the presence of wine, but this may not be true in every case, especially since there are numerous indications that the use of wine was controversial in early Christianity. For example, Irenaeus, Clement, and other significant early witnesses to the use of wine, all polemi-cize against the use of water in the cup, which would have been unnecessary were it merely the practice of a few deviant groups.[108] From his examination

---

105 Although some scholars would dismiss this as simply an inversion for rhetorical reasons, others argue that it reflects an actual ritual sequence known to Paul, very likely that of the Corinthian church which he is addressing: see Enrico Mazza, *The Origins of the Eucharistic Prayer* (Collegeville 1995), pp. 66–97.

106 See below, pp. 119–21.

107 ' "First regarding the Cup . . . ": Papias and the Diversity of early Eucharistic Practice', *JTS* 46 (1995), pp. 551–5.

108 The importance attached by Cyprian to the mingling of both wine and water in the cup, while at the same time inveighing against the use of water alone, is suggestive of a deliberate compromise between variant practices rather than merely the continuation of a standard custom in the ancient world, which is the usual explanation advanced by scholars for the practice of the mixed chalice. Indeed, long ago Adolf von Harnack ('Brod und Wasser: Die eucharistischen Elemente bei Justin', in *Über das gnostische Buch Pistis-Sophia; Brod und Wasser: die eucharistischen Elemente bei Justin. Zwei Untersuchungen* [TU 7, 1891], pp. 115–44) made the suggestion, which deserves more serious attention than it has ever received, that the references to wine had been inter-polated into the accounts of the Christian Eucharist in Justin Martyr's *First Apology*, and that the original text had referred to water alone. It is certainly true that the phrase 'water and wine mixed with water' is an odd one for Justin to have used, and it would be truly ironic if the text constantly cited by scholars as the earliest description that we have of the 'conventional' Christian Eucharist turns out to have originally been describing one with water alone instead of wine. For Justin Martyr, see below, p. 98.

of the wide range of diverse evidence that exists, McGowan reached the conclusion that quite a number of early Christian groups seem to have used
water rather than wine not only for the cup of the eucharistic meal, but also
for meals in general, and that this seems to be closely linked to another
dietary restriction of a more general kind – the avoidance of meat. He
proposed therefore that the rejection of both meat and wine by certain
groups of Christians pointed to a form of asceticism which was based not so
much on concern for the purity of the individual body as on marking out their
particular group from others around them by the avoidance of all food and
drink that was associated with pagan sacrifice.[109]

This conclusion in turn supports the idea that, in the light of the general
pluriformity of primitive Christianity, early eucharistic meals may have varied
not only in theological emphases between the different traditions but also in
the very form of the meal itself,[110] variations that we cannot easily dispose of
by consigning those that do not fit our ideal to the supposed category of an
agape rather than a Eucharist, since the evidence will not allow us to divide
Christian practice neatly this way: for some communities, *agape* was the name
given to their eucharistic meal.[111] Moreover, while in some places the
eucharistic action proper may have become detached from the meal at an
early stage, in others the two may have remained united for much longer than
is often supposed.[112]

Did the Eucharist Ever Conform to the Shape of the Last Supper?

At this point it seems worth asking the question as to whether the Eucharist
ever conformed to the pattern presented in the New Testament narratives of
the Last Supper, in which the bread and cup rituals were separated by the
meal. It must be remembered that we possess no evidence at all for such a
practice: it is simply inferred from the narratives. But that is to assume that
the narratives once functioned as the detailed 'script' or 'ordo' for the

---

109 *Ascetic Eucharists: Food and Drink in Early Christian Ritual Meals* (Oxford 1998).
110 Cyrille Vogel, 'Le Repas sacre au poisson chez les chrétiens', *RevSR* 40 (1966), pp.
   1–16, and Richard H. Hiers and Charles A. Kennedy, 'The Bread and Fish Eucharist in
   the Gospels and Early Christian Art', in *Perspectives in Religious Studies* 3 (1976), pp.
   20–47, suggested the possible existence of an early Christian fish-meal; but McGowan,
   Ascetic Eucharists, pp. 127–40, doubts this.
111 See Andrew B. McGowan, 'Naming the Feast: *Agape* and the Diversity of Early
   Christian Meals', *SP* 30 (1997), pp. 314–18.
112 It is often assumed that 1 Corinthians 11.17ff. represents a halfway stage, in which the
   meal immediately preceded the celebration of the Eucharist proper, but this discounts
   the possibility that at Corinth the Eucharist, whatever its *meaning*, may have been very
   little different in *appearance* from a normal communal meal.

community's celebration and not simply as aetiological stories,[113] and that may be a mistake.

Why should the early Christians have felt bound to follow in exact detail in their weekly community meals together the description of what Jesus did at what was allegedly the special annual event of the Passover meal? Even if they thought that Jesus had said, 'Do this in remembrance of me', they did not necessarily interpret this to mean, 'Do this, *in exactly the same order*, in remembrance of me.' It is more likely that they understood the command to mean that whenever they ate a ritual meal together, whatever form it took, they were to eat and drink in remembrance of him. And although recent studies have looked to the *symposion* as the model on which both Jewish and Christian formal meal practice would have been based, that was not the only pattern that Christian meals might have followed in the first century. At Qumran the community meal is described as involving blessings over the bread and new wine together at the very beginning (1 QS6; 1QSa), and later rabbinic legislation states that saying a blessing over wine before a meal exempts one from the obligation to say a blessing over wine after the meal (Mishnah, *Ber.* 6.5A).[114]

It would therefore not necessarily have appeared unusual if first-century Jewish–Christian communal meals had involved blessings being said over wine and bread at the same time, at the very beginning of the meal. And while we have no evidence for Christian meals where the cup blessing came at the end, we do have at least some evidence of a Christian practice where the cup blessing seems to have come at the beginning, along with the blessing over the bread, as we have already seen. And that pattern is very close to the one that we find in Justin Martyr in the second century (and also the later tradition), where bread and cup are brought together to the one presiding, who then gives thanks over them, although the meal has now apparently disappeared.[115] It is true that this displays a bread–cup sequence rather than a cup–bread one, but that there might have been a difference in their order in different communities should not surprise us, especially as similar variations in the order of blessings and disputes between different schools as to which one was correct characterize a great deal of the later rabbinic literature. What both sequences have in common is that the two blessings/thanksgivings take place in close proximity to one another at the beginning of a meal, and this

---

113 On the role of the institution narrative in early Christianity, see Andrew B. McGowan, 'Is there a Liturgical Text in this Gospel?: The Institution Narratives and Their Early Interpretative Communities', *JBL* 118 (1999), pp. 73–87.

114 See further, Andrew B. McGowan, 'The Inordinate Cup: Issues of Order in Early Eucharistic Drinking', *SP* 35 (2001), pp. 283–91.

115 On this, see further below, pp. 99–100, and also Paul F. Bradshaw, 'Did the Early Eucharist ever have a Sevenfold Shape?', *Heythrop Journal* 43 (2002).

would have continued unchanged even when the meal was no longer included.

Conclusion

This chapter has offered many more questions than answers, and that indeed was its purpose. Too often in the past, over-confident assertions have been made about the nature of Christian worship in the first century on the basis of false assumptions and methods, or of dogmatic rather than historical criteria. There is relatively little about which we can be sure with regard to this subject, and so the New Testament generally cannot provide the firm foundation from which to project later liturgical developments that it has frequently been thought to give. We must therefore be content to remain agnostic about many of the roots of Christian worship practices which we observe clearly for the first time in the following centuries.

4

Ancient Church Orders:
A Continuing Enigma

Ancient church orders constitute one of the more fascinating *genres* of early Christian literature, purporting to offer authoritative 'apostolic' prescriptions on matters of moral conduct, liturgical practice, and ecclesiastical organization and discipline. What these pseudo-apostolic texts have to say about the apostolic age itself may be of little interest, but they are potentially valuable sources of evidence for the thought and practices of the periods in which they were composed. Although they were apparently originally written in Greek, in some cases all that has survived are translations into other languages.

Their Discovery

Prior to 1800 only one such document was generally known, the *Apostolic Constitutions*, first published in 1563. Although its authenticity did not go entirely unchallenged, it was accepted by many as a genuinely apostolic work in the centuries which followed its discovery. During the nineteenth century, however, discoveries of other church orders came thick and fast. In 1843 J. W. Bickell published the Greek text of a short treatise which he called 'the Apostolic Church Order'.[1] In 1848 Henry Tattam produced an edition of what turned out to be a translation into the Bohairic dialect of Coptic, made as recently as 1804, of a composite work comprising three elements: Bickell's *Apostolic Church Order*; another previously unknown document, which for want of a better title was later designated by Hans Achelis as 'the Egyptian Church Order'; and a different recension of the final book 8 of the *Apostolic Constitutions*.[2] This collection is usually called the Clementine Heptateuch or Alexandrine Sinodos.

In 1854 Paul de Lagarde edited a Syriac version of a document generally referred to as the *Didascalia Apostolorum*;[3] and in 1856 he published a Syriac

---

1 *Geschichte des Kirchenrechts* I (Giessen 1843), pp. 107–32.
2 *The Apostolical Constitutions or the Canons of the Apostles in Coptic with an English Translation* (London 1848).
3 *Didascalia Apostolorum syriace* (Leipzig 1854 = Osnabrück 1967).

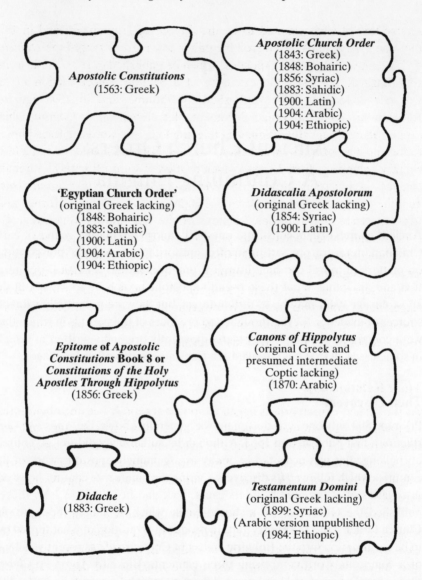

Figure 4.1: The publication of the pieces of the puzzle

translation of the *Apostolic Church Order* and the Greek text of a work known as the *Epitome* of *Apostolic Constitutions* 8, or alternatively by the title which appears in some manuscripts, 'The Constitutions of the Holy Apostles through Hippolytus'.[4] In 1870 Daniel von Haneberg produced the

4 *Reliquiae iuris ecclesiastici antiquissimae* (Leipzig 1856 = Osnabrück 1967), pp. 1–23.

Arabic text of what claimed to be the *Canons of Hippolytus*;[5] and in 1875 Philotheos Bryennios discovered the only known Greek text of the *Didache*, or 'Teaching of the Twelve Apostles', which he published in 1883.[6] In the same year Lagarde disclosed the existence of a Sahidic dialect version of the Bohairic collection earlier published by Tattam,[7] and in 1899 Ignatius Rahmani produced a Syriac document, the *Testamentum Domini*, which capped all other apostolic claims by feigning to be the words of Jesus himself to the apostles after his resurrection.[8] In 1900 Edmund Hauler edited a fifth-century palimpsest from Verona which contained – unfortunately with many lacunae – Latin translations of the *Didascalia*, the *Apostolic Church Order*, and the 'Egyptian Church Order'.[9] Finally, in 1904 George Horner contributed Arabic and Ethiopic versions of the Alexandrine Sinodos to the Bohairic and Sahidic texts earlier published by Tattam and Lagarde.[10]

Although no new church orders have been added to the list of discoveries since the beginning of the twentieth century, some new manuscripts of various recensions have been found, including in some cases a few small fragments of otherwise missing Greek originals. These have affected the task of establishing the text, and consequently better editions have since been produced for most of the individual documents.

Their Relationship

As the various church orders began to appear, it rapidly became obvious that they were more than merely parallel examples of a particular type of literature. Parts of the different documents exhibited such a marked similarity to one another that it clearly pointed to a direct literary relationship. But what was that relationship? How did these various pieces of the jigsaw puzzle fit together?

There was no shortage of theories, and almost every possible combination was suggested. Thus in 1891 Achelis proposed that the genealogy ran from the *Canons of Hippolytus* through the so-called 'Egyptian Church Order', and also another work subsequently lost, to the *Epitome* and then to *Apostolic Constitutions* 8;[11] while in the same year F. X. Funk suggested almost exactly

5 *Canones S. Hippolyti arabice* (Munich 1870).
6 *DIDACHE TON DODEKA APOSTOLON* (Constantinople 1883).
7 *Aegyptiaca* (Göttingen 1883 = 1972), pp. 209–91.
8 *Testamentum Domini nostri Jesu Christi* (Mainz 1899 = Hildesheim 1968).
9 *Didascaliae apostolorum fragmenta Veronensia latina. Accedunt canonum qui dicuntur apostolorum et aegyptiorum reliquiae* (Leipzig 1900).
10 *The Statutes of the Apostles or Canones Ecclesiastici* (London 1904); later edition of the Arabic by Jean and Augustin Périer, *Les 127 Canons des Apôtres* (PO 8/4; Paris 1912 = Turnhout, Belgium 1971).
11 *Die Canones Hippolyti* (TU 6/4; Berlin 1891).

the opposite order: *Apostolic Constitutions* 8 → *Epitome* → 'Egyptian Church Order' → *Canons of Hippolytus*.[12] When Rahmani published the *Testamentum Domini* in 1899, he claimed that it was a second-century work from which *Apostolic Constitutions* 8 and the 'Egyptian Church Order' were both derived, with the *Canons of Hippolytus* in turn being dependent upon the latter. In 1901 John Wordsworth propounded the theory that there was a lost church order from which all the known ones had emanated.[13]

What is ironical to later eyes is that at this stage nobody proposed a combination which would have put the 'Egyptian Church Order' first in this line. Instead, it was unanimously judged to be descended from one or other of the documents to which it had close similarity. It was not until 1906 that Eduard von der Goltz suggested that this anonymous text might in reality be a work by Hippolytus of Rome, the *Apostolic Tradition*, previously believed to have been lost.[14] This theory was taken up and elaborated, first by Eduard Schwartz in 1910, and then quite independently and much more fully by R. H. Connolly in 1916.[15] Although some scholars still entertain doubts about its attribution to Hippolytus or its Roman origin (about which more will be said later), it is now universally accepted that this document is the original source of the other church orders from which it was formerly presumed to be derived.

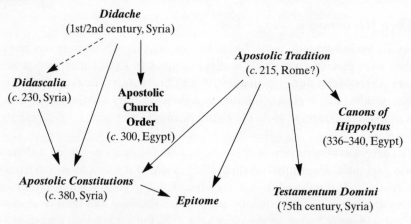

Figure 4.2: The relationship between the individual church orders

12 *Die apostolischen Konstitutionen, eine litterar-historische Untersuchung* (Rottenburg 1891 = Frankfurt 1970).
13 *The Ministry of Grace* (London 1901), pp. 18–21. A similar view was taken by A. J. Maclean, *The Ancient Church Orders* (Cambridge 1910), pp. 141–73.
14 'Unbekannte Fragmente altchristlicher Gemeindeordnungen', *Sitzungsberichte der Preussischen Akademie der Wissenschaften* (1906), pp. 141–57.
15 Eduard Schwartz, *Über die pseudoapostolischen Kirchenordnungen* (Strasbourg 1910); R. H. Connolly, *The So-called Egyptian Church Order and Derived Documents* (Cambridge 1916 = Nendeln, Liechtenstein 1967).

Thus, as can be seen from Figure 4.2, a family tree can now be established for the whole collection of church orders with a high degree of certitude. Because they claim to be apostolic, they reveal neither the names of their true authors nor the place and date of their real origin, and hence such questions usually have to be answered largely on the basis of the internal evidence of the documents themselves.

The Individual Documents

1. The Didache

The first part of this church order (chapters 1–6) is usually known as the 'Two Ways' because it presents moral teaching in the form of the way of life and the way of death. Then follow brief instructions about baptism (7),[16] the practices of twice-weekly fasting (on Wednesdays and Fridays) and thrice-daily prayer (8),[17] forms of prayer for use at either an *agape* or a Eucharist (9–10),[18] the treatment of 'apostles and prophets' (11–13), the celebration of the Eucharist 'on the Lord's Day of the Lord' (14),[19] and the appointment of bishops and deacons (15).[20] It concludes with an admonition to eschatological vigilance (16).

At first the only witness to the original was the Greek text discovered by Bryennios, but subsequently other Greek fragments were discovered at Oxyrhynchus, and also parts of translations into Ethiopic and Coptic (although whether the latter is translated directly from the Greek or from Syriac is uncertain). A complete translation into Georgian has also been found, but scholars are divided over its antiquity: while the manuscript itself dates only from the nineteenth century, some think the translation may have been made in the fifth century. Also of assistance in determining the reading of the original is the use of the *Didache* in the *Apostolic Church Order* and in *Apostolic Constitutions* 7.[21] The most accessible edition of the text is by Willy Rordorf and André Tuilier,[22] and an English translation of the *Didache* with a

---

16 See below, pp. 153–4.

17 For these, see below, pp. 179 and 175.

18 For this heavily debated issue, see below, pp. 119 ff.

19 C. W. Dugmore, 'The Lord's Day and Easter', in *Neotestamentica et Patristica* (Festschrift for Oscar Cullmann, Supplements to NovT 6; Leiden 1962), pp. 272–81, thought that this was a reference to Easter, but Rordorf (*Sunday*, pp. 209–10) rightly denied this and affirmed that it was speaking of Sunday.

20 See below, pp. 197–8.

21 Some scholars have thought that the latter may give evidence of a better text than the Bryennios ms. at some points. For example, they would accept as part of the original the prayer over *myron* ('ointment') found both in the Coptic version and in *Apostolic Constitutions* 7: see below, pp. 153–4.

22 *La doctrine des douze apôtres* (SC 248, 1978; 2nd edn, SC 248bis, 1998).

comprehensive commentary and bibliography of secondary literature by Kurt Niederwimmer appeared in 1998.[23]

Although the *Didache* is generally accepted as having originated in Syria, estimates of its date have varied widely. Some place it in the second century, others assign it to the first century, and some argue that it ante-dates many of the New Testament writings. Perhaps the most extreme claim in this direction was that made by Joan Hazelden Walker, who asserted that the *Didache* reflects a less sophisticated eucharistic theology than that of the canonical Gospels, and so must have been composed before they were written.[24] But her conclusion is flawed, since it cannot be assumed that Christianity developed at the same speed in every place, and hence a more primitive theology does not necessarily mean an earlier date.[25]

Obviously, the literary dependence of the *Didache* on other early Christian writings could be a significant point in establishing its date, but once again there has not been any scholarly consensus as to which, if any, of the New Testament books may have been known to the author. Some scholars have argued that the author of the *Didache* knew the Fourth Gospel, chiefly on the basis of the belief that the word *klasma* ('broken bread') in *Didache* 9.4 was dependent on John 6.3 and 11.52. This theory was strongly challenged by Arthur Vööbus, who argued that the other versions of the document clearly revealed that the original reading was *artos* ('bread') and not *klasma*, and that in any case the sequence of ideas in the *Didache* was very different from those in John's Gospel.[26]

2. *Didascalia Apostolorum*

This church order is obviously modelled on the *Didache*, and begins with admonitions concerning the Christian life (1–3). It continues with a lengthy section on the qualifications, conduct, and duties of a bishop (4–11). Here, and

---

23 *The Didache: A Commentary* (Minneapolis 1998). See also the volumes of essays, *The Didache in Context*, ed. Clayton N. Jefford (Leiden 1995) and *The Didache in Modern Research*, ed. Jonathan A. Draper (Leiden 1996), and the works cited therein, together with the recent essay by Draper, 'Ritual Process and Ritual Symbol in Didache 7–10', *VC* 54 (2000), pp. 121–58.

24 'A pre-Marcan Dating for the Didache: Further Thoughts of a Liturgist', *Studia Biblica 1978* III (Sheffield 1980), pp. 403–11.

25 The same criticisms can be levelled against Mazza, *The Origins of the Eucharistic Prayer*, pp. 92, 96, who postulates an extremely early date for the prayer material in *Didache* 9–10.

26 *Liturgical Traditions in the Didache* (Stockholm 1968), pp. 35–9, 137–57; idem, 'Regarding the Background of the Liturgical Traditions in the Didache: The Question of the Literary Relation between Didache ix, 4 and the Fourth Gospel', *VC* 23 (1969), pp. 81–7. Jean Magne, 'Klasma, sperma, poimnion. Le voeu pour la rassemblement de Didachè ix, 4', in *Mélanges d'histoire des religions offerts à Henri-Charles Puech* (Paris 1974), pp. 197–208, went further and proposed that *Didache* 9.4 originally spoke of sheep, and only later was this changed, first to corn, and then to bread.

at other points, the possibility of the remission of serious post-baptismal sins after a period of penance is presupposed, including adultery and apostasy: this contrasts with the more rigorist approach which tended to be taken in the West at this period. The physical disposition of bishop, presbyters, deacons, lay men, lay women, and children in the church building is dealt with next (12), and the people are exhorted to be constant in their attendance at church, and to avoid heretical assemblies and pagan festivities (13). Then follow injunctions concerning widows (14–15), male and female deacons (16), and the adoption of orphans (17). Bishops and deacons are forbidden to accept alms from those leading evil lives or following unacceptable occupations (18), and all Christians are exhorted to care for those who are imprisoned for the faith, and to be ready to face persecution and death themselves, comforted by the hope of the resurrection (19–20). Every Wednesday and Friday in the year, and the six days prior to Easter, are to be observed as days of fasting (21), and the treatise then moves on to refer to the upbringing of children (22), and to denounce heresy and schism (23). Chapters 24 and 25 purport to describe the composition of the work by the Apostles as a defence against heresy, and the final lengthy chapter (26) argues strongly for the freedom of Christians from the ritual legislation of the Old Testament.

With the exception of a small fragment of chapter 15 and a reworked form of the document in *Apostolic Constitutions* 1–6, the original Greek has been lost, and our main knowledge of the text therefore has to rest on two early translations, one into Latin and the other into Syriac. The Latin is known only from the Verona palimpsest, which preserves about two-fifths of the work. The Syriac, which thus constitutes the sole witness to the complete text, is preserved wholly or partially in a number of manuscripts, the oldest of which dates from the eighth century. The fourth century has been proposed as a possible date for this translation, but certain features of it might suggest a somewhat later period.[27] A possible Coptic fragment of the text has recently been found,[28] but Arabic and Ethiopic versions are dependent on *Apostolic Constitutions* 1–6.

The *Didascalia* was almost certainly composed in North Syria during the first half of the third century, probably *c.* 230. From the prominence that it

---

27 Edition and ET by Arthur Vööbus, *The Didascalia Apostolorum in Syriac* (Corpus Scriptorum Christianorum Orientalium 401, 402, 407, 408; Scriptores Syri 175, 176, 179, 180; Louvain 1979); English extracts in Sebastian Brock and Michael Vasey, *The Liturgical Portions of the Didascalia* (GLS 29, 1982); bibliographies of secondary literature in B. Altaner, *Patrologie* (9th edn, Freiburg 1978), pp. 85, 558; Paul F. Bradshaw, 'Kirchenordnungen I: Altkirchliche', *Theologische Realenzyklopädie* 18 (Berlin 1989), p. 666.

28 Alberto Camplani, 'A Coptic Fragment from the *Didascalia Apostolorum* (M579 F.1)', *Augustinianum* 36 (1996), pp. 47–51.

gives to the episcopate, it has been concluded that its author may himself
have been a bishop, and because he exhibits some medical knowledge, some
have supposed that he may also have been a physician. Claims sometimes
made that he was a convert from Judaism seem to have little justification, as
interest in the relationship between Christianity and the Old Testament Law,
which figures in this church order, was something which concerned other
Christians too.

3. Apostolic Church Order

This small treatise was given this name when it was first published in 1843 by
J. W. Bickell, though it has also received other appellations, among them 'The
Ecclesiastical Constitution of the Apostles'. The title which appears in the
Greek text is 'The instructions through Clement and ecclesiastical canons of
the holy Apostles'. After a short introduction (1–4), the first half (5–14) is an
adaptation of *Didache* 1–4, and the second half (15–30) issues brief regulations for the appointment of bishops, presbyters, readers, deacons, and
widows, and directives concerning the duties of deacons, lay men, and lay
women. Only one manuscript, of the twelfth century, contains the entire text
of the Greek original, though an excerpt from the first part is extant in four
other codices, and there are Latin, Syriac, Sahidic, Bohairic, Arabic, and
Ethiopic translations. It appears to have been written in Egypt, although
some scholars would assign it to Syria, and in its final form it dates very
probably from the end of the third century.[29]

4. Apostolic Tradition

After a very brief prologue this church order begins with directions for the
ordinations of a bishop, presbyter, and deacon, and provides an ordination
prayer for each one. In the case of the episcopal ordination it also sets out a
specimen form of eucharistic prayer for the new bishop to use, although permitting him to substitute his own words if he wishes. It then proceeds to the
appointment of widows, readers, virgins, subdeacons, and those with the gift of
healing. Lengthy instructions follow concerning the process of Christian initiation, beginning with the procedure for admission to the catechumenate and
a list of occupations forbidden to prospective Christians, and continuing with
the baptismal rite itself, which is intended for both adults and children and
leads into the first communion of the neophytes. The final part of the work

---

29 There is no recent edition, and the only recent studies are by Alexandre Faivre, 'Le texte
grec de la Constitution ecclésiastique des apôtres 16–20 et ses sources', *RevSR* 55
(1981), pp. 31–42; and Arthur Vööbus, 'Die Entdeckung der ältesten Urkunde für die
syrische Übersetzung der Apostolischen Kirchenordnung', *Oriens Christianus* 63
(1979), pp. 37–40. For older editions and studies, see Bradshaw, 'Kirchenordnungen', pp.
666–7.

deals with other liturgical matters, among them the conduct of a community supper, the observance of a two-day fast before Easter, the times of daily prayer and instruction in the word, and the use of the sign of the cross.

Since a Greek text of the work has not survived, except in the form of a few isolated fragments, attempts have been made to reconstruct the original – principally by Gregory Dix and Bernard Botte[30] – from the various extant translations (which differ considerably from one another) and from the adaptations made of it in the other church orders. It is commonly assumed that these reconstructions present us – at least substantially – with what the author originally wrote. This assumption, however, is very much open to question, and some scholars have argued that parts of the original work may have been retouched by later hands in order to bring it into line with current doctrine and practice.[31] Hence, even the task of establishing the original is by no means straightforward and there remains considerable uncertainty over the true reading of many parts of the text.

There are further doubts concerning its place of origin and authorship. The majority of scholars have supported the view that it originates from Rome and is the genuine work of Hippolytus, written *c.* 215, but this is far from sure. No existing manuscript bears a title for the work, and it was really the attribution to Hippolytus of two of the derived church orders (the *Epitome* of *Apostolic Constitutions* 8 and the *Canons of Hippolytus*) that encouraged the identification of this document with that author, as well as the prologue and epilogue of the work apparently using the expression 'apostolic tradition'. This evidence can be challenged.

The tendency to associate documents with apostolic figures or with those believed to have close connections to such persons so as to enhance their authority is very common in the ancient Christian world, and there are certainly other works that are known to have been falsely attributed to Hippolytus.[32] Moreover, Christoph Markschies has recently argued not only that the ascription of the *Canons of Hippolytus* to Hippolytus and the reference to him in the subheading of the *Epitome* were not made until the late fourth or

---

30 Gregory Dix, *The Treatise on the Apostolic Tradition of St Hippolytus* (London 1937; 2nd edn 1968 with preface and corrections by Henry Chadwick = London/Ridgefield, CT 1992); Bernard Botte, *La Tradition apostolique de saint Hippolyte* (Münster 1963; 4th edn 1972). See also the edition by G. J. Cuming, *Hippolytus. A Text for Students* (GLS 8, 1976).

31 See A. F. Walls, 'The Latin Version of Hippolytus' Apostolic Tradition', *SP* 3 (1961), pp. 155–62. With regard to the eucharistic prayer, see below, pp. 140–1; with regard to the post-baptismal ceremonies, see below, pp. 161–4; with regard to the hours of daily prayer, see below, p. 176; and with regard to the ordination rites, see below, pp. 206–9.

32 See Pierre Nautin, ed., *Homélies pascales* (SC 27; Paris 1950), pp. 34–6; J. M. Hanssens, *La liturgie d'Hippolyte* (OCA 155; Rome 1959, 2nd edn 1965), pp. 84–5; Allen Brent, *Hippolytus and the Roman Church in the Third Century* (Leiden 1995), pp. 192–3.

early fifth century (and thus much too late to credit them with any historical reliability), but that the apparent references to 'apostolic tradition' in the prologue and conclusion of the document have been misinterpreted by other scholars and consequently cannot allude to the title of the work.[33]

In any case, even the very existence of a work entitled *Apostolic Tradition* by Hippolytus of Rome is not above suspicion. The title is found among an anonymous list of works on the right-hand side of the base of a statue discovered in Rome in 1551, but this list does not correlate exactly with the works of Hippolytus that are catalogued both by Eusebius and by Jerome. Very surprisingly, it omits those that are most strongly attested as genuinely his,[34] and this has led some scholars to propose the existence of two authors or even a school of authors as responsible for the works on the list.[35] In a final bizarre twist to the tale, recent research has revealed that the statue itself was in origin not a representation of Hippolytus at all but of a female figure, which was restored in the sixteenth century as a male bishop because of the list of works inscribed on its base, using parts taken from other statues.[36]

Furthermore, a series of articles by Marcel Metzger has opened up a new line of approach to the document.[37] He developed an idea earlier advanced both by Jean Magne and by Alexandre Faivre, that not only is it not the *Apostolic Tradition* of Hippolytus, it is not the work of any single author at all but rather a piece of 'living literature'.[38] Metzger argued that its lack of unity

33 'Wer schrieb die sogenannte *Traditio Apostolica*? Neue Beobachtungen und Hypothesen zu einer kaum lösbaren Frage aus der altkirchen Literaturgeschichte', in W. Kinzig, Ch. Markschies, and M. Vinzent, *Tauffragen und Bekenntnis* (Arbeiten zur Kirchengeschichte 74; Berlin/New York 1999), pp. 8–43.

34 Hanssens, *La liturgie d'Hippolyte*, pp. 229–30, 247–9, 254–82; Brent, *Hippolytus and the Roman Church in the Third Century*, pp. 115–203.

35 Pierre Nautin, *Hippolyte et Josipe* (Paris 1947) and 'Notes sur le catalogue des oeuvres d'Hippolyte', *Recherches de science religieuse* 34 (1947), pp. 99–107; Vincenzo Loi, 'L'identità letteraria di Ippolito di Roma', in *Ricerche su Ippolito* (Studia Ephemeridis Augustinianum 13; Rome 1977), pp. 67–88; M. Simonetti, 'A modo di conclusione: Una ipotesi di lavoro', ibid., pp. 151–6; Brent, *Hippolytus and the Roman Church in the Third Century*, pp. 204–366; Paul Bouhot, 'L'auteur romain des *Philosophumena* et l'écrivain Hippolyte', *EO* 13 (1996), pp. 137–64.

36 See Margherita Guarducci, 'La statua di "Sant'Ippolito"', in *Ricerche su Ippolito*, pp. 17–30; idem, 'La "Statua di Sant'Ippolito" e la sua provenienza', in *Nuove ricerche su Ippolito* (Studia Ephemeridis Augustinianum 30; Rome 1989), pp. 61–74; Hanssens, *La liturgie d'Hippolyte*, pp. 217–31; Brent, *Hippolytus and the Roman Church in the Third Century*, pp. 3–114; and Markus Vinzent, '"Philobiblie" im frühen Christentum', *Das Altertum* 45 (1999), pp. 116–17, who has made the intriguing proposal that the figure was originally of an Amazon woman named Hippolyta.

37 Marcel Metzger, 'Nouvelles perspectives pour la prétendue *Tradition apostolique*', *EO* 5 (1988), pp. 241–59; 'Enquêtes autour de la prétendue *Tradition apostolique*', *EO* 9 (1992), pp. 7–36; 'A propos des règlements écclesiastiques et de la prétendue *Tradition apostolique*', *RevSR* 66 (1992), pp. 249–61.

38 Jean Magne, *Tradition apostolique sur les charismes et Diataxeis des saints Apôtres* (Paris 1975), pp. 76–7; Alexandre Faivre, 'La documentation canonico-liturgique de l'Eglise ancienne', *RevSR* 54 (1980), p. 286.

or logical progression, its frequent incoherences, doublets, and contradictions, all point away from the existence of a single editorial hand. Instead, it has all the characteristics of a composite work, a collection of community rules from quite disparate traditions. His arguments have been accepted by a number of scholars, and Maxwell Johnson, L. Edward Phillips, and I have taken his work a stage further in a major commentary on the church order.[39] We judge it to be an aggregation of material from different sources, quite probably arising from different geographical regions and almost certainly from different historical periods, from perhaps as early as the middle of the second century to as late as the middle of the fourth, since none of the textual witnesses to it can be dated with any certainty before the last quarter of that century. We therefore think that it is most improbable that it represents the actual practice of any single Christian community, and that it is best understood by attempting to discern the various individual elements and layers of which it is made up. Moreover, the composite character which the document displays extends also the individual ritual units within the text, such as ordination, baptism, and even the Eucharist itself, which appear to be artificial literary creations, made up of elements drawn from different local traditions rather than comprising a single authentic rite that was ever celebrated in that particular form anywhere in the world.

This church order therefore deserves to be treated with greater circumspection than has generally been the case, and one ought not automatically to assume that it provides reliable information about the life and liturgical activity of the church in Rome in the early third century.

5. Canons of Hippolytus

Although attention had been drawn as early as the seventeenth century to this Arabic collection of 38 canons with a concluding sermon, Haneberg's 1870 edition was the first published text, and it was from this that Achelis made his 1891 translation into Latin, containing many doubtful conjectures. As indicated above, Achelis accepted the attribution to Hippolytus as genuine and arrived at the conclusion that this was the original from which all the other church orders containing similar material were derived. As a consequence, interest was aroused in the document among liturgical scholars, but after the researches of Schwartz and Connolly had demonstrated that it was in reality merely a derivative of the *Apostolic Tradition*, it came to be considered as the latest of the group of related church orders, dating from the fifth or sixth century, and interest in it declined.

---

39   Paul F. Bradshaw, Maxwell E. Johnson, and L. Edward Phillips, *Apostolic Tradition: A Commentary* (Minneapolis 2002).

However, in 1956 Bernard Botte suggested that it had been composed in Egypt around the middle of the fourth century,[40] and in 1966 René-Georges Coquin, in the first and only proper critical edition of the text, followed up and amplified Botte's arguments, proposing on the basis of internal evidence a date between 336 and 340 for the work.[41] This would make it not the latest but the earliest known derivative of the *Apostolic Tradition*. On the other hand, Christoph Markschies has recently contested this conclusion and argued that, while the lost Greek original may date from that period, both the text in the form in which we now have it and the attribution to Hippolytus are no older than the late fourth or early fifth century.[42]

Nevertheless, it warrants more attention than it has hitherto received, both because it constitutes an important source for our knowledge of fourth-century Egyptian church life, about which we have relatively little other evidence, and because it may actually have something to contribute to the reconstruction of the original text of the *Apostolic Tradition*. Although the author seems to have freely paraphrased, supplemented, and adapted that source in the light of his own ecclesiastical situation and liturgical tradition, yet at least a few of these apparent drastic recastings may not be that at all, but rather points at which he alone has retained primitive readings which have been revised by the other later witnesses to the text.

Although it is now extant only in Arabic, there is general agreement that this text is derived from a lost Coptic version, which was in turn a translation of an original Greek text. Coquin considered that it had been written by a priest rather than a bishop – though his arguments are not totally convincing[43] – and that its place of composition was Alexandria: this latter view has since been challenged by Heinzgerd Brakmann, who has argued instead that it originates from elsewhere in northern Egypt.[44]

6. Apostolic Constitutions

This is a composite work, comprising the *Didascalia* (forming Books 1–6 of the work), the *Didache* (Book 7), and the *Apostolic Tradition* together with some other material (Book 8) – all of the sources having been extensively reworked in the process. It is generally agreed that it was written in Syria, and probably in Antioch, between 375 and 380. It is unlikely to be much earlier

---

40 'L'origine des Canons d'Hippolyte', in *Mélanges en l'honneur de Mgr Michel Andrieu* (Strasbourg 1956), pp. 53–63.
41 *Les Canons d'Hippolyte* (PO 31/2, 1966); ET based on this edition in Paul F. Bradshaw, *The Canons of Hippolytus* (A/GLS 2, 1987).
42 'Wer schrieb die sogenannte *Traditio Apostolica*?', pp. 8–11, 63–9.
43 See Bradshaw, *The Canons of Hippolytus*, p. 8.
44 'Alexandreia und die Kanones des Hippolyt', *Jahrbuch für Antike und Christentum* 22 (1979), pp. 139–49.

than that, because it includes a reference to the feast of Christmas, which was only just beginning to make an appearance in Eastern churches, and it is unlikely to be much later, because its doctrine of the Holy Spirit is incompatible with the definition agreed at the Council of Constantinople in 381. The identity and theological position of the compiler, on the other hand, have been long debated. Indeed, the orthodoxy of the document became suspect at an early date, and it was thought by the Trullan Synod (691–2) that heretics must have falsified the original apostolic work. Photius, the patriarch of Constantinople (d. 891), criticized the whole compilation for its Arianism, although subsequently opinion was divided over this question.

Among modern scholars, Funk in his 1905 edition of the text (which has generally been treated as definitive) tended to play down the heterodoxy of the work by preferring orthodox variant readings wherever possible and by claiming that any suspect formulae came from the compiler's source and thus ante-dated the Arian controversy.[45] C. H. Turner criticized Funk's textual methods and argued strongly for an Arian compiler,[46] and Bernard Capelle later demonstrated that the text of the *Gloria in Excelsis* found in the *Apostolic Constitutions* was not the original form of the hymn, as had been thought, but that the compiler had changed a hymn addressed to Christ into one addressed to the Father.[47] Because of similarities of language with the longer recension of the letters of Ignatius of Antioch, scholars have usually concluded that the compiler of the *Apostolic Constitutions*, whatever his theological stance, was also the interpolator of these letters.

The most recent contributions to the authorship debate are by Georg Wagner (who drew linguistic parallels with the writings of Eunomius),[48] by Dieter Hagedorn (who attributed the composition to an obscure bishop named Julian),[49] and by Marcel Metzger, who built upon Hagedorn's suggestion and concluded that, although Julian's commentary on Job is much more explicitly Arian than the more moderate subordinationism of the *Apostolic Constitutions*, this difference could be explained by the fact that the latter was

45 *Didascalia et Constitutiones Apostolorum* (Paderborn 1905 = Turin 1979); ET based on this edition by James Donaldson, *Constitutions of the Holy Apostles* (Edinburgh 1886/New York 1926), pp. 387–505.

46 'A Primitive Edition of the Apostolic Constitutions and Canons', *JTS* 15 (1913), pp. 53–65; 'Notes on the Apostolic Constitutions', *JTS* 16 (1914), pp. 54–61, 523–38; 21 (1920), pp. 160–8.

47 'Le texte du "gloria in exclesis"', *Revue d'histoire ecclésiastique* 44 (1949), pp. 439–57.

48 'Zur Herfunkt der apostolischen Konstitutionen', in *Mélanges liturgiques offerts au R. P. Dom Bernard Botte OSB* (Louvain 1972), pp. 525–37.

49 *Der Hiobkommentar des Arianers Julian* (Berlin/New York 1973), pp. XXXVII–LVII. See also T. A. Kopecek, 'Neo-Arian Religion: The Evidence of the Apostolic Constitutions', in R. C. Gregg, ed., *Arianism: Historical and Theological Reassessments* (Philadelphia 1985), pp. 153–80.

a liturgical work and so drew upon traditional material. Metzger did not think, however, that its compiler could be considered a strict Arian.[50] He also published a new edition of the text, making use of a wider range of manuscripts and free from the orthodox bias of Funk's edition.[51]

What is known as the *Epitome* or 'Constitutions of the Holy Apostles through Hippolytus' seems to be a series of extracts from *Apostolic Constitutions* 8 (1–2, 4–5, 16–28, 30–4, 42–6),[52] but at two points – the prayer for the ordination of a bishop and the instructions for appointing a reader – its text seems to be closer to the original Greek of the *Apostolic Tradition* rather than the expanded form in the *Apostolic Constitutions.* In addition, one manuscript alone also has, for some reason or another, a similar version of *Apostolic Tradition* 23. Thus, whether in origin this was a first draft of *Apostolic Constitutions* 8 or – as seems more likely – a later condensation of it, its editor appears also to have had access to a text of the *Apostolic Tradition* itself, although Christoph Markschies has recently contended that this was not the original Greek text of that church order as such but a version of it that had already undergone some modification.[53]

7. Testamentum Domini

This church order is a much enlarged version of the *Apostolic Tradition*, set within the context of instructions given by Jesus himself to his disciples before his ascension, and beginning with an apocalytic discourse. The author displays a somewhat perverse fidelity to his source: although he has retained much of its wording, he has interpolated so many words and phrases of his own that it frequently has an entirely different appearance and sense from the original. Thus all the various prayers are retained, but in a much expanded form, and others are added.

The original Greek text is lost, and reliance has usually been placed on the Syriac version published by Rahmani,[54] but here there are two problems. First, his edition was based on only one family of manuscripts, while a

50 'La théologie des Constitutions apostoliques par Clement', *RevSR* 57 (1983), pp. 29–49, 112–22, 169–94, 273–94.
51 *Les Constitutions apostoliques* (SC 320, 329, 336, 1985–7); partial ET based on this edition in W. Jardine Grisbrooke, *The Liturgical Portions of the Apostolic Constitutions: A Text for Students* (A/GLS 13-14, 1990); bibliography of secondary literature in Altaner, *Patrologie*, p. 256.
52 Text in Funk, *Didascalia et Constitutiones Apostolorum* II, pp. 72–96. For further details, see Botte, *Tradition apostolique*, pp. XXV–XXVI; Hanssens, *La Liturgie d'Hippolyte* I, pp. 78–9.
53 'Wer schrieb die sogenannte *Traditio Apostolica*?', pp. 15–19.
54 ET by James Cooper and A. J. Maclean, *The Testament of Our Lord Translated into English from the Syriac* (Edinburgh 1902); partial ET and bibliography of secondary literature in Grant Sperry-White, *The Testamentum Domini: A Text for Students* (A/GLS 19, 1991).

different manuscript tradition seems to underlie the text of the *Testamentum Domini* found in the West Syrian Synodicon,[55] which may offer indications of better readings at some points. Second, even if the earliest text of the Syriac can be established, it is not certain that it always accurately reproduced the original Greek, especially as there are also extant Arabic and Ethiopic versions of the document with significantly different readings. These are both probably dependent upon a lost Coptic translation. Until relatively recently any comparison with these versions was extremely problematic, as neither had ever been published, but in 1984 Robert Beylot produced a critical edition of the Ethiopic,[56] which goes some way to meet the difficulty, though the quality of his work has been questioned.[57] Since both these versions are later than the Syriac, many differences can be dismissed as the emendations – intentional and unintentional – of translators and copyists, but at least at some points they may retain older readings. The doxologies in the Ethiopic, for example, have a much simpler – and hence seemingly more primitive – form than those in the Syriac.[58]

Most scholars believe that the work originates from Syria, though Asia Minor and Egypt have also been suggested, and it has usually been regarded as the last of the church orders to have been written, dating most probably from the fifth century. Grant Sperry-White, however, has more recently proposed its origin as being in the second half of the fourth century.[59]

The Collections

That it has been possible to put these particular pieces together in what appears to be their correct order should not fool us into thinking that the whole church-order puzzle has been solved. It would be rather like thinking that once the literary relationship between Matthew, Mark, and Luke had been established, no further critical work on the synoptic Gospels was necessary. Other questions still remain with regard to the church-order literature, and it is to these that we now turn.

---

55 Arthur Vööbus, ed., *The Synodicon in the West Syrian Tradition* (Corpus Scriptorum Christianorum Orientalium 367, 368; Scriptores Syri 161, 162; Louvain 1975). This is based on MS. 8/11 of the Syrian Orthodox Patriarchate of Damascus, 1204 CE.
56 *Le Testamentum Domini éthiopien* (Louvain 1984).
57 See the review by Roger Cowley, *Journal of Semitic Studies* 31 (1986), pp. 292–5.
58 Compare the Syriac 'to you be praise and to your only-begotten Son our Lord Jesus Christ and to the Holy Spirit honourable and worshipped and life-giving and consubstantial with you, now and before all worlds and to the generation of generations and to the ages of ages' (Rahmani, p. 99) with the Ethiopic 'Glory to the Father, to the Son, and to the Holy Spirit, now and always and to the ages of ages' (Beylot, p. 206).
59 *The Testamentum Domini*, p. 6.

Apostolic Constitutions (Greek)

| *Didascalia* | *Didache* | *Apostolic Tradition* |

Verona Palimpsest LV (53) (Latin)

| *Didascalia* | *Apostolic Church Order* | *Apostolic Tradition* |

Alexandrine Sinodos (Sahidic, Bohairic, Arabic, Ethiopic)

| *Apostolic Church Order* | *Apostolic Tradition* | *Apostolic Constitutions* 8 |

Clementine Octateuch (Syriac)

| *Testamentum Domini* (in two books) | *Apostolic Church Order* | *Apostolic Constitutions* 8 |

Clementine Octateuch (Arabic)

| *Testamentum Domini* | *Apostolic Church Order* | *Apostolic Tradition* | *Apostolic Constitutions* 8 |

Table 4.1: The collections of church orders

Until relatively recently no attention was paid to the fact that the majority of the church orders were known to us not as individual documents at all but only as part of larger collections of such material. Even now only two scholars in the last 30 years, Bernard Botte and J. M. Hanssens, have tried to explore the nature of that interrelationship. As can be seen from Table 4.1, there are four such collections:

1 the *Apostolic Constitutions*;
2 a Latin translation of three Greek works thought to have been made about the same time as the *Apostolic Constitutions*, but known to us only through one manuscript, a fifth-century palimpsest;[60]
3 the collection known as the Alexandrine Sinodos, or the Clementine Heptateuch, found in several different language versions – in the two dialects

---

60 Most recent edition by Erik Tidner, *Didascaliae apostolorum Canonum ecclesiasticorum Traditionis apostolicae versiones Latinae* (TU 75, 1963).

of Coptic (Sahidic and Bohairic), in Arabic, and in Ethiopic – of which the Sahidic is the oldest and the others all in one way or another ultimately depend on it;

4   what is known as the Clementine Octateuch, which is found in different forms in two different languages, Syriac and Arabic, neither of which has yet ever been published in full. It consists of the *Testamentum Domini*, followed by the material included in the Alexandrine Sinodos, except that the Syriac version differs from the Arabic in omitting the text of the *Apostolic Tradition* of Hippolytus, and consequently dividing the *Testamentum Domini* into two books in order to retain the eightfold form.

What is particularly interesting about these collections is that the various church orders tend to appear in them in the same sequence. Thus we have the *Didascalia*, the *Didache*, and the *Apostolic Tradition* in the *Apostolic Constitutions*; and the *Didascalia*, the *Apostolic Church Order* (which, we saw earlier, itself incorporates part of the *Didache*), and the *Apostolic Tradition* in the Latin palimpsest. The Alexandrine Sinodos retains the latter two works in the same order as in the Latin translation, but appends to them another version of *Apostolic Constitutions* 8. The same is true of the Octateuch, though here the *Testamentum Domini* is prefixed. It appears impossible to dismiss all these similarities as merely coincidental, and it seems that there is a literary relationship between the collections, as well as between the individual church orders.

One simple answer – that there is direct dependency – must be ruled out. The Latin translation is certainly not derived from the *Apostolic Constitutions*, nor is the latter a re-translation back into Greek from the Latin: its Greek is too close to that of the sources – where we can check it – for such an idea to be conceivable; and in any case, one has the *Didache* and the other the *Apostolic Church Order* as its middle document. It is equally difficult to imagine that the Sahidic version of the Sinodos obtained its material from anywhere except a Greek source, and the same is true of the Syriac version of the Octateuch: indeed the colophon attached to the *Testamentum Domini* in this collection explicitly affirms that it at least was translated from Greek into Syriac by James of Edessa in the seventh century.

Thus, we need to seek some other solution to their similarities. Botte proposed the existence of an early Greek 'tripartite collection', subsequently lost, which consisted of the *Didascalia*, the *Apostolic Church Order*, and the *Apostolic Tradition* – in that order.[61] This would mean that the Latin collection was a translation of that work, while the author of the *Apostolic Constitutions* would have been influenced by it with regard to his order, but

---

61 'Les plus anciennes collections canoniques', *L'Orient syrien* 5 (1960), pp. 331–49.

for some reason preferred to replace the *Apostolic Church Order* with the *Didache*, since the two were similar to one another.

Botte's theory, however, still leaves a number of difficulties. It suffices to explain the relationship between two of the collections, but is not really adequate when it comes to the other two. If the author of the Sinodos had a triple collection in front of him, why should he discard the first of its three works but retain the other two? Botte suggested that it may have been because the *Didascalia* did not lend itself as easily as the others to the division into separate canons which we find in this collection. But, in any case, why should both the Sinodos and the Octateuch have chosen to add to this supposed triple collection a version of *Apostolic Constitutions* 8? That cannot surely be put down to coincidence, especially as there is nothing to suggest that this particular extract ever circulated on its own. Moreover, at the very least we seem obliged to posit the existence of an earlier, Greek form of the Octateuch, from which both our present versions, the Syriac and the Arabic, are ultimately descended. The Arabic cannot be descended directly from the Syriac, because the Syriac lacks the *Apostolic Tradition* (presumably omitted because it was so similar to the material in the *Testamentum Domini*), and the Syriac was obviously aware of a previous eightfold form of its material, since it divided the *Testamentum Domini* into two in order to retain that structure after the omission of the *Apostolic Tradition*.

It looks, therefore, as though we are forced to take seriously something like the more complicated theory put forward by Hanssens.[62] He held that originally only the *Apostolic Church Order* and the *Apostolic Tradition* circulated together in the fourth century. From this combination developed two further collections: one comprising the *Didascalia*, the *Apostolic Church Order*, and the *Apostolic Tradition*, from which the *Apostolic Constitutions* and the Latin translation were derived; the other made up of the *Apostolic Church Order*, the *Apostolic Tradition*, and a version of *Apostolic Constitutions* 8. This latter document would thus have constituted the original Greek collection of which the Alexandrine Sinodos was a translation; and our conjectured Greek Octateuch would then have been an expanded form of this, prefixed by the *Testamentum Domini*, since the supposed words of Jesus himself would naturally be placed before, and not after, what were then taken to be injunctions of the apostles.

Although the outlines of the process of transmission and aggregation of the various documents may thus be discerned, many questions of detail still remain unanswered. To give just one example, how are we to account for the existence of an Ethiopic version of the *Testamentum Domini*? Was it derived from our conjectured Sahidic Octateuch, and if so, why were the rest of its contents not translated as well? Was it perhaps because they already existed in the Ethiopic version of the Sinodos, or does the Ethiopic *Testamentum* emerge by some other route?

'Living Literature'

Even if we can begin to see *how* the various church orders were transmitted and combined, our puzzle is still far from complete. We may have been able to account for the process at a physical level, but that does not explain *why* it ever happened at all. Why should anyone take the time and trouble repeatedly to copy out these texts, translate and revise them, and combine them with others? What lies behind this gigantic spider's web? Strange though it may seem, this is not a question which those who have made use of the documents as historical source-material have often stopped to ask. They have simply plundered what they wanted to fit the picture of the early Church that they were attempting to paint, without asking themselves why it ever came to be there in the first place, and what this might have to say about its value as historical evidence.

As suggested in an earlier chapter, documents dealing with liturgical matters are particularly prone to editorial corrections so as to give authoritative status to current worship practices.[63] This development can be seen not only between the individual church orders in the series, as each one revised its predecessor, but also in the process of the copying of manuscripts, the translation from one language to another, and even the aggregation into collected works. At each step along the way, the aim was not simply to reproduce exactly the last example of the material, but to amend and update it. Thus, these texts are not always copies or translations in the sense in which we usually mean those words, but are instead really versions of the original, and frequently differ markedly from one another. Prayer-texts may be modified, for example, or even entirely omitted, if they do not resemble the prayers with which the copyists or translators were familiar; and additional prayer-material from their own tradition may be inserted among that from the source-document.

The church orders, therefore, should not be treated in the same way as other ancient works. When we encounter variant readings between different manuscript traditions, we are not always looking at accidental dislocation and copyists' errors: we are frequently seeing deliberate emendations designed to alter the sense of the text. This of course makes the task of restoring the original more difficult than it is in other types of literature. But we must also keep in mind that, in looking at this material, the original is not the only

---

63 See above, pp. 4–5.

important historical source: we should be equally interested in the changes which were made by the first, second, and even third translators, as indicating something about the world in which each lived, about what had changed and what had remained the same in the ongoing life of the Church, about the matters which were of vital importance to each translator's generation and those issues which had now ceased to be of concern.

Perhaps the best way of thinking of this material is as 'living literature',[64] constantly growing, changing, and evolving as it moves from generation to generation, or from one ecclesiastical tradition to another, with each stage, and not just the first, offering valuable source-material for historical study. Indeed, we may even be mistaken in what we regard as the beginning of the process, as the original documents in the series. If we may vary the metaphor a little, and look upon the literature as a great river which is made up of a number of smaller tributaries, what we consider the sources of the streams may perhaps not be where the water first begins at all, but only where it bursts forth into our view from beneath the ground – another stage in its long journey, and not the point at which it is formed.

Sources

There are certainly signs which suggest that at least some of the documents are made up of a number of different strata of material. They may have been drawing upon older sources which are otherwise unknown to us, or may themselves have gone through a number of different editions, as it were, being amplified and revised in response to changing situations, before attaining the form which we mistakenly treat as 'the original text'.

For example, it is acknowledged that the *Apostolic Constitutions* probably made use of other sources besides the works known to us, especially in Book 7, where prayer-texts of a strongly Jewish character are found.[65] It has also long been recognized that not only is the first half of the *Apostolic Church Order* dependent upon the first part of the *Didache* (or some earlier form of it), but part of the second half appears to imply a very primitive stage of the evolution of the Christian ministry and does not seem entirely consistent with what is written elsewhere in the document. Thus, this too may well be a composite work bringing together a number of earlier written sources.[66]

---

64 See above, p. 5.
65 See David A. Fiensy, *Prayers Alleged to be Jewish: An Examination of the Constitutiones Apostolorum* (BJS 65; Chico, CA 1985). For possible sources for the eucharistic prayer in *Apostolic Constitutions* 8, see below, pp. 108–9.
66 See Adolf Harnack, *Die Quellen der sogenannten apostolischen Kirchenordnung* (TU 2/5, 1886); Faivre, 'Le texte grec de la Constitution ecclésiastique des apôtres 16–20 et ses sources'.

Most scholars subscribe to the view that the *Didache* also evolved by stages, but are divided over the number of redactions, and the relative antiquity of different parts of the work.[67] At the very least, the first part of the document, the 'Two Ways', appears to have had a separate existence: it is also found in a Latin version, the *Doctrina Apostolorum*, and in parallel form in the later chapters of the second-century *Epistle of Barnabas*, though the precise relationship between the three documents is debated. The question is further complicated by the omission of a small section of this part of the *Didache* (1.3b–2.1) both from the *Doctrina Apostolorum* and from the *Apostolic Church Order*. Is this section a later interpolation? And what are we to make of the fact that both Pseudo-Cyprian, *Adversus Aleatores*, and Augustine knew the whole *Didache* in Latin, including this 'interpolation'?[68] The 'Two Ways' material is often thought to be of Jewish origin, but this is less sure than is commonly supposed: although the Qumran Manual of Discipline has shown that there existed a Jewish arrangement of moral teaching in the form of 'Two Ways' (1QS3.13–4.14), this does not prove a direct literary relationship with the material found in the *Didache*.

Since we have suggested above that a similar process of evolution may also be true in the case of the *Apostolic Tradition*, it would perhaps be better to think of the various church orders not as works by a single author at all, but rather as having had a succession of editors who shaped the stream of tradition which came down to them, both before and after it emerges to our sight in documentary form.

Fact or Fantasy?

Viewed in this light, therefore, can any overall trends be discerned in the development of this material? Why were the different editors modifying it?

As A. F. Walls has pointed out,[69] there is a change in the way in which the term 'apostolic' seems to be understood as the literature evolves. In the earlier documents it appears to have a more dynamic sense, meaning 'that which is in accordance with the witness and teaching of the apostles', whereas the later documents become pseudepigraphical, with the various injunctions explicitly attributed to the apostles themselves, either collectively or individually. Thus, beyond the title, 'The teaching of the twelve apostles', the *Didache* makes no other claims concerning the source of its material; and the *Apostolic Tradition*, and even the *Canons of Hippolytus*, while asserting that what they

---

67 See Giet, *L'énigme de la Didachè*; Niederwimmer, *The Didache*, pp. 42ff.
68 See Willy Rordorf, 'Le problème de la transmission textuelle de *Didachè* 1,3b–2,1', in F. Paschke, ed., *Überlieferungsgeschichtliche Untersuchungen* (Berlin 1981), pp. 499–513.
69 'A Note on the Apostolic Claim in the Church Order Literature', *SP* 2 (1957), pp. 83–92.

are teaching is in accordance with the apostolic tradition which has come down to them, do not suggest that it derives verbatim from the mouths of the original 12 disciples.

Not so, however, with the *Didascalia*: although this starts out in a similar way to the other church orders mentioned above, just before the last chapter of the work, and immediately after a robust attack on heretics who pervert the truth, there is inserted an alleged account of the composition of the document by a council of the 12 apostles, who intended it as a defence against heresy. Then follows the final lengthy chapter which argues strongly that Christians are free from any obligation to obey the ritual legislation of the Old Testament, even though they are bound to follow its moral law. This arrangement of material would seem to suggest that this final point was a much controverted issue in the Christian community from which this church order came, and so at this stage in his work the author needed to bring out the biggest weapons he could find – the authority of the 12 apostles themselves – to defend his position against that of his opponents, although he had not found it necessary to do this for the earlier, and presumably less controversial, part of what he had written.

The author of the *Apostolic Church Order* goes one step further, and distributes everything he has to say between the 12 apostles, putting a different injunction into the mouth of each of them in turn – though he appears to regard Peter and Cephas as two separate individuals but manages to keep the total at 12 by excluding both Judas Iscariot and his successor Matthias. Like the *Didascalia*, he places the origin of his work in a meeting of the 12, at which Martha and Mary are also said to be present – the main purpose for this addition being apparently to create an excuse for the apostles to give firm directions about what women are not to be allowed to do in the Church. As we have already mentioned, the *Testamentum Domini* caps the whole process by attributing the teaching not just to the apostles but to Jesus himself.

Not only is there this change of form in the gradual development of the literature, but there is also a change of content. Most of the earlier documents – the *Didache*, the *Didascalia*, and the *Apostolic Church Order* – are principally concerned with the Christian life as a whole, with the moral conduct of the members of the Church. It is only in relation to the welfare of the whole community, therefore, that they deal with those who are its leaders, and consequently are naturally more concerned about the personal qualities which such ministers should display than with the process of their institution. The *Didache* devotes no more than a single sentence to their appointment, the *Apostolic Church Order* scarcely more than that, while the *Didascalia* does not refer to it at all. Indeed the *Apostolic Church Order* contains no strictly liturgical material; the *Didascalia* merely alludes obliquely to liturgical practices; while the *Didache* includes only very brief liturgical directions together with prayer-texts for the Eucharist or *agape*, all of which may be later additions to its original nucleus.

Alexandre Faivre, in an important study of the church order literature, would extend this trajectory further, and see the roots of the genre as being related to writings such as the Pastoral Epistles and the *Letter of Polycarp to the Philippians*, which similarly offer moral exhortations to the community followed by the delineation of the qualities required in its ministers.[70] Indeed, there is another resemblance which should be noted between the Pastoral Epistles and some of the church orders: both are pseudepigraphical. Further parallels might also be drawn with early Christian apocryphal works which not only are similarly pseudonymous but also seem, at least in part, to have an analogous aim: the attempt to bestow legitimacy on contemporary practices by means of apostolic fiction.

With the *Apostolic Tradition*, however, we move into literature of a very different kind. Here, at least in its extant form, exhortations concerning Christian behaviour and the moral qualities required of ordained ministers have almost entirely disappeared, and are replaced by directives about the correct procedure to be adopted in the appointment of ministers, the texts of prayers to be used for ordination and in the celebration of the Eucharist, the ritual to be followed in the administration of baptism, and other such matters. It is the ordering of the church and its liturgy which is now the principal focus. This trend continues in the derivatives of this document, so that, for example, whereas the *Didascalia* was concerned with the proper disposition of different groups of people – ordained, lay, male, female, etc. – within the Christian assembly, the *Testamentum Domini* concerns itself instead with the proper arrangement of the church building and its furniture.

These shifts in form and content suggest that, as time passed, the focus of the church orders changed, and their 'apostolic' pedigree needed to be more firmly underscored and reinforced by more emphatic claims if it were to have any authority. This in turn raises the suspicion that not all editorial hands were necessarily modifying the received text in order to correspond with the actual historical practice of their own churches. At least to some extent, they may have been indulging in an idealizing dream – *prescribing* rather than *describing* – imagining what the organization and liturgy of their community would be like if they were allowed to have their own way and impose their idiosyncratic ideas on the rest of the congregation. Thus, we may sometimes have less of a factual account than a clever piece of propaganda, which required the guise of alleged apostolic prescription to promote its cause. This has long been suspected with regard to at least parts of the later documents,

---

70 'La documentation canonico-liturgique de l'Église ancienne', *RevSR* 54 (1980), pp. 204–19, 237–97: see especially, pp. 287ff.

but there is no reason to think that any of the church orders are free from this tendency, still less that they constitute the official handbook of a local church, as earlier scholars tended to suppose.

On the other hand, this does not mean that they should simply be dismissed as worthless historical sources. Beneath what may be fanciful embroidery in theology and practice, there is undoubtedly some foundation based on the reality either of the local tradition or of influences from other churches. But the evidence needs to be sifted with care, and reliance should not too readily be placed on the unsubstantiated testimony of a church order, without corroboration from other sources.

The change of emphasis in subject-matter also provides some clues as to why certain texts were retained and others dropped in the development of the collections of church orders which we considered earlier. It was not merely that the *Didascalia* did not lend itself easily to division into separate canons, as Botte suggested: the problem was not simply one of form but of content. What the *Didascalia* had to say was not the sort of apostolic material which later generations wanted to preserve. It was no longer relevant to their needs, and so ceases to appear in the later canonical collections. This may also explain why copies of the *Didache* do not exist in the wide variety of languages in which other church orders are found: its moral teaching was no longer important enough for anyone to consider it worthwhile to translate and copy it, and its meagre liturgical provisions were too archaic to be reconciled with the contemporary practice of the translators' world.

Equally, it explains why the *Apostolic Tradition* was translated, copied, amended, and expanded so many times: its subject-matter was exactly what later eyes were looking for – the beginnings of liturgical rubrics and canon law. Similarly, it explains why *Apostolic Constitutions* 8 should have been abstracted from the totality of the work and grafted on to the later collections, even though it partially duplicated the contents of the *Apostolic Tradition*: it too contained just the sort of material people wanted. Finally, it explains why ultimately there were no more church orders[71] and the genre simply died out: eventually apostolic fiction ceased to be used as a source of authority in the mainstream churches of both East and West, and collections

71 In addition to the examples considered within this chapter, however, we should include within the genre at least two other compositions: the Coptic *Canons of Basil*, which in its final form circulated in Egypt in the sixth century and which used the *Canons of Hippolytus* as one of its sources (text in W. Riedel, *Die Kirchenrechtsquellen des Patriarchats Alexandrien* [Leipzig 1900], pp. 231–83); and the Gallican *Statuta Ecclesiae Antiqua*, which was perhaps composed by Gennadius of Marseilles *c.* 490 and which drew on both the *Apostolic Tradition* and the *Apostolic Constitutions* (text in Charles Munier, *Les Statuta Ecclesiae Antiqua*, Paris 1960). For the continuing influence of the *Apostolic Tradition* on ordination practice in the West, see Bradshaw, *Ordination Rites of the Ancient Churches of East and West*, pp. 14–15, 45, 56, 59–60.

of liturgical texts and canon law were produced which derived their authority instead from individual living bishops and genuine synodical assemblies. It was only in the lesser Oriental churches that the pseudo-apostolic directives continued to be respected and carefully preserved, and even came to constitute the foundation of much liturgical practice, while elsewhere the original Greek texts were allowed to disintegrate: they had served their purpose and ceased to be of practical use.

The *Apostolic Church Order*, however, constitutes a fly in the ointment, upsetting the neatness of this theory of development. Although it is not a liturgical document, it continues to make an appearance alongside the *Apostolic Tradition* in every single collection of church orders. Nevertheless, perhaps even this can be explained. The *Apostolic Tradition* refers in its opening words to an earlier work (or to a first part of the same work) on the subject of spiritual gifts. No trace of this has ever been found. But it is possible that someone mistakenly thought that the *Apostolic Church Order* was this missing text and placed the two together in that order to form the nucleus of all other later collections. If they were thereafter looked upon as a single work, then it is less surprising that this short treatise managed to retain its place even when its subject-matter had ceased to be of interest to copyists and translators.

Conclusion

The jigsaw puzzle is far from solved, and other pieces still need to be inserted. For example, published versions and recent critical editions are still lacking for several parts of this literature. Moreover, although what in biblical studies would be called 'source-criticism' has to some extent been done, the equivalent of serious 'form-criticism' and above all 'redaction-criticism' still wait to be tackled, so that we may further comprehend what shaped the material in its development and learn more about the world of the various editors and translators who transmitted and revised it.

Perhaps the whole church order literature is not so much a simple jigsaw puzzle but, as Friedrich Loofs suggested at the end of the nineteenth century,[72] a giant kaleidoscope, capable of being arranged in a variety of patterns wherein each person can see the image that they wish to find. Yet, in spite of the apparent morass which first impressions present, if we are willing to take account of the total complexity of the literature and avoid the practice of simply abstracting pieces without reference to their context – what one might call the 'hit and run' approach to historical sources – we can begin to discern an underlying pattern and a logical progression in its development, which may help us to understand it better.

72 'Die urchristliche Gemeindeverfassung mit spezieller Beziehung auf Loening und Harnack', *Theologische Studien und Kritiken* 63 (1890), p. 637.

5

Other Major Liturgical Sources

This chapter contains a brief introduction to some of the other major documentary resources which need to be used in any attempt at the reconstruction of liturgical practices in the early Church. It is arranged according to geographical provenance and includes both material dating from the second, third, and fourth centuries and also eucharistic prayers and other liturgical texts which in their extant form are of a somewhat later date but which may be able to cast some light on earlier practices. It can make no claim to be a comprehensive listing, for our knowledge comes from a wide variety of texts, many of which supply only one or two incidental details concerning some individual custom. Nonetheless, it does aim to provide background information to the more widely used sources, and especially those which pose critical problems or other difficulties of interpretation.

Rome

Justin Martyr, writing at Rome around 150, provides the earliest substantial description that we have of Christian worship. This occurs in his *First Apology*, which is addressed to the emperor Antoninus Pius and is obviously intended to explain Christianity to those outside the Church. There are two accounts, the first dealing with baptismal procedure, which culminates in the celebration of the Eucharist, and the second outlining a regular Sunday Eucharist.[1] These present us with two principal problems of interpretation. The first is the difficulty in deciding whether Justin is here recounting the specific form of worship practised in Rome at this time, or whether he is offering a more generic description of the sort of worship which might be encountered by his readers in various parts of the world. Indeed, are we in any case justified in thinking that there was a single church in Rome at this

---

1 Chs 61–7. Justin also speaks about the Eucharist in his *Dialogue with Trypho* (a Jew), probably written at Ephesus *c.* 135.

period rather than a loose collection of Christian communities distinguished from one another by significant ethnic and liturgical differences?[2]

The second problem is related to the first. Since Justin's writing is intended for non-Christians, how far has this affected the detail that is given? For example, does his vague expression 'the records of the apostles or the writings of the prophets' really imply that the form of the ministry of the word was very flexible, or is it so phrased because Justin thought the precise details of this part of the service unimportant to his readers?[3] Does the absence of a reference to any post-baptismal ceremonies mean that there actually were none, or only that he did not judge it relevant for his purpose to mention them?[4]

Moreover, it is important that we are aware of what Justin does *not* tell us in his descriptions. We generally read his account as describing an assembly which took place in the morning, because that is what we find in other, later sources, but Justin does not actually say so; it could still have taken place in the evening. We assume that there was a single eucharistic prayer spoken over both bread and wine,[5] but Justin does not actually say so; there could still have been separate short prayers over each, as in the Jewish tradition, and it may be significant that Justin uses the plural, saying that the president 'sends up prayer*s* and thanksgiving*s* to the best of his ability'. Even his next statement that 'the people assent, saying the Amen' could mean that this was done after each prayer and not just once, at the very end. We also assume that the rite no longer involved a full meal but only bread and wine; but while the actions connected with the bread and cup certainly appear to be distinguished from any other eating and drinking here, it is not completely impossible that a more substantial meal still followed the ritual act, and this may even be alluded to in the brief statement which comes after Justin's description of a

2 See further the important study by A. Hamman, 'Valeur et signification des renseigne-ments liturgiques de Justin', *SP* 13 (1975), pp. 364–74; and also G. La Piana, 'The Roman Church at the End of the Second Century', *Harvard Theological Review* 18 (1925), pp. 214–77.

3 M.-E. Boismard, *Le Diatessaron: de Tatien à Justin* (Etudes bibliques, new series 15; Paris 1992) has argued that the 'records of the apostles' were an early gospel harmony rather than the New Testament writings as such. For discussion of other parts of Justin's eucharistic rite, see Everett Ferguson, 'Justin Martyr and the Liturgy', *Restoration Quarterly* 36 (1994), pp. 267–78, and the works cited therein; also G. J. Cuming, 'DI'EUCHES LOGOU (Justin Apology 1.66.2)', *JTS* 31 (1980), pp. 80–2, and the response by Anthony Gelston, *JTS* 33 (1982), pp. 172ff.; Maurice Jourjon, 'Justin', in Willy Rordorf *et al.*, *The Eucharist of the Early Christians* (New York 1978), pp. 71–85; Gordon W. Lathrop, 'Justin, Eucharist, and "Sacrifice": A Case of Metaphor', *Worship* 64 (1990), pp. 30–48; E. C. Ratcliff, 'The Eucharistic Institution Narrative of Justin Martyr's First Apology', *JEH* 22 (1971), pp. 97–102 = A. H. Couratin and David Tripp, eds, *E. C. Ratcliff. Liturgical Studies* (London 1976), pp. 41–8.

4 On this question, see below, pp. 159–61.

5 For the possibility that the reference to wine may actually be an interpolation here, see above, p. 69, n. 108.

baptismal eucharist: 'After this we constantly remind each other of these things. Those who have more come to the aid of those who lack, and we are constantly together. Over all that we receive, we bless the Maker of all things through his son Jesus Christ and through the Holy Spirit.' This is usually taken to be simply a summary of Christian life in general; but if the opening phrase 'after this' (*meta tauta*) is taken more literally, it could be interpreted as an outline of what followed the ritual act with the bread and cup on a Sunday evening – religious discourse between the participants, charitable donations, and a supper with blessings over all that was received – a pattern analogous to rabbinic meals within Judaism.

Apart from Justin's description, a little evidence for baptismal and ministerial practices provided by the **Shepherd of Hermas** (mid-second century),[6] and the very questionable testimony offered by the **Apostolic Tradition** attributed to Hippolytus,[7] there are no other substantial sources of information for ancient Roman liturgy belonging to this early period. We do not, for example, possess a set of fourth-century baptismal catecheses like those belonging to some of the other major centres of early Christianity which might have offered a step-by-step account and explanation of the baptismal and eucharistic rites. We have to make do, therefore, chiefly with attempts at reconstruction of earlier practices based on the evidence provided by somewhat later sources, such as the letter of **Innocent I** to Decentius of Gubbio (416)[8] and the sermons of **Leo the Great** (440–61),[9] as well as the much later liturgical books of the Roman rite.[10] But what these sources cannot tell us is which of the practices they describe go back to the earliest times of the church at Rome, and which are much later developments or importations from elsewhere; and thus their witness is ambiguous.

North Africa

There is always some difficulty in knowing how far writers are expressing their own personal opinions and how far they are reflecting the common

---

6 See Carolyn Osiek, *Shepherd of Hermas : A Commentary* (Minneapolis 1999).
7 See above, pp. 80–3.
8 Critical edition by Robert Cabié, *La lettre du pape Innocent I à Decentius de Gubbio* (Louvain 1973).
9 See also N. W. James, 'Was Leo the Great the Author of Liturgical Prayers?', *SP* 26 (1993), pp. 35–40.
10 For an introduction to these, see John F. Baldovin, *The Urban Character of Christian Worship* (OCA 228, 1987), pp. 119–41; Gordon P. Jeanes, *The Origins of the Roman Rite*, two vols (A/GLS 20 and 42, 1991 and 1998); Eric Palazzo, *A History of Liturgical Books* (Collegeville 1998), pp. 35–56. On the origin of the Roman eucharistic prayer and its possible connection with the Alexandrian tradition, see Mazza, *The Origins of the Eucharistic Prayer*, pp. 240–86.

beliefs of their culture, but the problem is greatly increased when there are virtually no alternative sources against which to check a statement. This dilemma can be clearly illustrated in the case of **Tertullian**, who was a North African lay Christian, converted to the faith *c*. 195. Although at first fiercely opposed to the Montanist movement, which among other things laid great emphasis on the continuing gift of prophecy within the Church, he eventually allied himself with it. Scattered throughout his writings, which cover both the Catholic and Montanist phases of his life, are numerous brief references to various aspects of liturgical practice.[11] But are these always descriptions of what *was* the case; or should at least some of them be treated as expressions of what the author thought *should be* the case?

For instance, Tertullian says that 'Pascha [Easter] provides the day of most solemnity for baptism . . . After that, Pentecost is a most joyful period for arranging baptisms . . . For all that, every day is a Lord's day: any hour, any season, is suitable for baptism' (*De baptismo* 19). On the other hand, he claims elsewhere that lay people may baptize and even preside at the Eucharist when an ordained minister is not available.[12] The majority of scholarly opinion has generally treated the first passage as firm factual evidence that the Easter season was already established as the primary occasion for baptism, certainly in North Africa if not in the whole Church, but has dismissed the claim to lay eucharistic presidency in the second as merely Tertullian's personal opinion, with no basis at all in ecclesiastical practice. There are, however, no real grounds for distinguishing the two statements in this way, apart from the preconceptions that one brings to them, and so it is necessary to look for external confirmation before jumping to one conclusion or another.

Further information about liturgical practices in North Africa is furnished in the writings of **Cyprian**, bishop of Carthage from 248 to 258,[13] and of

---

11 See E. Dekkers, *Tertullianus en de geschiedenis der liturgie* (Brussels 1947).

12 *De exhort. cast.* 7.3. See G. Otrano, 'Nonne et laici sacerdotes sumus? (*Exhort. Cast.* 7.3)', *Vetera Christianorum* 8 (1971), pp. 27–47; C. Vogel, 'Le ministre charismatique de l'eucharistie. Approche rituelle', in idem, *Ministères et célébration de l'eucharistie* (Studia Anselmiana 61; Rome 1973), pp. 198–204; Pierre van Beneden, 'Haben Laien Eucharistie ohne Ordinierte gefeiert? Zu Tertullians "De exhortatione castitatis" 7.3', *ALW* 29 (1987), pp. 31–46. With regard to lay men (but not women!) baptizing in cases of emergency, see also Tertullian, *De baptismo* 17.

13 See A. Coppo, 'Vita cristiana e terminologia liturgica a Cartagine verso la metà del IIIo secolo', *EL* 85 (1971), pp. 70–86; V. Saxer, *Vie liturgique et quotidienne à Carthage vers le milieu du IIIe siècle. Le témoignage de S. Cyprien et de ses contemporains d'Afrique* (Vatican City 1969); G. G. Willis, 'St Cyprian and the Mixed Chalice', *Downside Review* 100 (1982), pp. 110–15.

Augustine, bishop of Hippo Regius from 396 to 430,[14] as well as in various pieces of synodical legislation.[15] Unfortunately, however, because of the Arab conquest of the region at the end of the seventh century and in contrast to other parts of the ancient Christian world, no later sacramentary or other collection of prayers has survived from which earlier practice might have been inferred.

North Italy

Very early sources for this region are lacking, and the writings of the fourth-century bishop, **Ambrose** (*c.* 339–97), provide the chief evidence for liturgical practices at Milan.[16] However, since his audience were generally Christians already familiar with the rituals to which he was alluding, Ambrose is not always very explicit about the precise details, and his extensive use of metaphor also makes it difficult to know if and when references to such things as incense and anointing are to be taken literally. Moreover, the authenticity of *De Sacramentis*,[17] one of the works attributed to him which provides con-

14 See, for example, Albert Gerhards, 'Benedicere/benedictio in Theologie und Liturgie nach den Schriften des hl. Augustinus', *EO* 5 (1988), pp. 53–75; William Harmless, *Augustine and the Catechumenate* (Collegeville 1995); Martin Klöckener, 'Das eucharistische Hochgebet bei Augustinus. Zu Stand und Aufgaben der Forschung', in Adolar Zumkeller, ed., *Signum Pietatis* (Würzburg 1989), pp. 461–95; idem, 'Die *Recitatio nominum* im Hochgebet nach Augustins Schriften', in Andreas Heinz and Heinrich Rennings, eds, *Gratias Agamus* (Freiburg 1992), pp. 183–210; R. de Latte, 'Saint Augustin et le baptême: Étude liturgico-historique du rituel baptismal des adultes chez saint Augustin', *QLP* 56 (1975), pp. 177–223; idem, 'Saint Augustin et le baptême: Étude liturgico-historique du rituel baptismal des enfants chez saint Augustin', *QLP* 57 (1976), pp. 41–55; G. G. Willis, *St Augustine's Lectionary* (ACC 44; London 1962).
15 See E. J. Kilmartin, 'Early African Legislation concerning Liturgical Prayer', *EL* 99 (1985), pp. 105–27.
16 There is a wide range of secondary literature dealing specifically with this. Among more recent works are J. Beumer, 'Die ältesten Zeugnisse für die römische Eucharistiefeier bei Ambrosius von Mailand', *ZKTh* 95 (1973), pp. 311–24; Ansgar Franz, 'Die Tagzeitenliturgie der Mailander Kirche im 4 Jahrhundert: ein Beitrag zur Geschichte des Kathedraloffiziums im Westen', *ALW* 34 (1992), pp. 23–83; W. Ledwich, 'Baptism, Sacrament of the Cross: Looking behind St Ambrose', in Bryan D. Spinks, ed., *The Sacrifice of Praise* (BEL 19, 1981), pp. 199–211; H. M. Riley, *Christian Initiation. A Comparative Study of the Interpretation of the Baptismal Liturgy in the Mystagogical Writings of Cyril of Jerusalem, John Chrysostom, Theodore of Mopsuestia, and Ambrose of Milan* (Washington, DC 1974); Josef Schmitz, *Gottesdienst im Altchristlichen Mailand* (Köln 1975); E. J. Yarnold, 'The Ceremonies of Initiation in the De Sacramentis and the De Mysteriis of St Ambrose', *SP* 10 (1970), pp. 453–63; idem, 'Did St Ambrose know the Mystagogic Catecheses of St Cyril of Jerusalem?', *SP* 12 (1975), pp. 184–9.
17 Editions by Henry Chadwick, *Saint Ambrose: On the Sacraments* (London 1960); Bernard Botte, *Des sacrements; Des mystères* (SC 25, 1961; SC 25bis, 1961); partial ET in E. J. Yarnold, *The Awe-Inspiring Rites of Initiation* (Slough 1971), pp. 97–153; 2nd edn (Edinburgh/Collegeville 1994), pp. 100–49.

siderable liturgical information (and not least sheds light on the early form of the eucharistic prayer of the church at Rome), has been seriously questioned since the sixteenth century. In the 1940s Otto Faller and R. H. Connolly, working independently of one another, succeeded in convincing most scholars of its Ambrosian authorship,[18] but there has been a more recent debate between Klaus Gamber and Josef Schmitz, the former attributing the work to Nicetas of Remesiana.[19]

Some further details of north Italian liturgical practices also emerge from the writings of Ambrose's contemporaries, **Chromatius** (Bishop of Aquileia, *c.* 388–407), **Gaudentius** (who became Bishop of Brescia, *c.* 397), and **Zeno** (Bishop of Verona, 362–*c.* 375),[20] and from the works of the fifth-century **Maximus**, Bishop of Turin, and **Peter Chrysologus**, Bishop of Ravenna.

Gaul and Spain

We are even less informed about early Christian worship in these regions than we are about the practices of northern Italy. Nearly all the sources here date from at least the fifth century and are in any case very meagre, which makes reconstruction of earlier traditions extremely hazardous and speculative. A little insight into the theology of baptism and Eucharist is offered by **Irenaeus**, Bishop of Lyons in the late second century,[21] but little else can be gleaned.

Egypt

The writings of **Clement of Alexandria** (*c.* 150–*c.* 215) and **Origen** (*c.* 185–*c.* 254) make a number of references to liturgical customs in their extensive writings, but they are frequently difficult to evaluate. First, both writers often speak in an allegorical manner about matters pertaining to the Christian faith, and so it is sometimes hard to know whether some allusion is to an

---

18 Otto Faller, 'Ambrosius, der Verfasser von De Sacramentis', *ZKTh* 64 (1940), pp. 1–14, 81–101; R. H. Connolly, *The De Sacramentis a Work of St Ambrose* (Oxford 1942). For a summary of the controversy, see the introduction to Botte's edition, pp. 7–25.

19 Klaus Gamber, *Die Autorschaft von De Sacramentis* (Regensburg 1967) and 'Nochmals zur Frage der Autorschaft von De Sacramentis', *ZKTh* 91 (1969), pp. 587–9; Josef Schmitz, 'Zum Autor der Schrift "De Sacramentis"', *ZKTh* 91 (1969), pp. 58–69. See also Klaus Gamber, 'Eine Frühform des römischen Messkanons zur "Prex Mystica" in den Sermonen "De Sacramentis"', *EL* 103 (1989), pp. 494–502.

20 See the extensive bibliography in Carlo Truzzi, *Zeno, Gaudenzio e Cromazio* (Brescia 1985), pp. 15–29; also Gordon P. Jeanes, 'Early Latin Parallels to the Roman Canon? Possible References to a Eucharistic Prayer in Zeno of Verona', *JTS* 37 (1986), pp. 427–31; idem, *The Day Has Come: Easter and Baptism in Zeno of Verona* (ACC 73; Collegeville 1995).

21 See David N. Power, *Irenaeus of Lyons on Baptism and Eucharist: Selected Texts* (A/GLS 18, 1991).

actual liturgical practice or not. A simple illustration of this difficulty is provided by Clement's comparison of the Christian catechumenate with the directive in the Old Testament Law that after three years the first-fruits of the harvest are to be dedicated to God (*Strom.* 18). Does he mean to imply that the catechumenate lasted for three years, or is the analogy intended in a much less literal sense?[22] Second, both seem to have belonged to a somewhat elitist group of Christians, whose customs may have had relatively little in common with what the vast majority of ordinary people in Alexandria were wont to do. Moreover, in the case of Origen, we cannot be sure whether the liturgical usages to which he alludes were always those of Alexandria or were the observance of Palestine, where he spent a considerable time.[23]

The problems of describing Egyptian liturgy are further exacerbated, as at Rome, by the almost complete absence of substantial fourth-century sources. The **Canons of Hippolytus** present us with difficulties of interpretation: we do not know exactly where the document comes from, nor how far it represents what was really happening in the early fourth century.[24] The authenticity of the only other major witness to the early Egyptian liturgical tradition, the **Sacramentary of Sarapion**, has also been questioned in the past. This collection of 30 prayers attributed to a fourth-century bishop of Thmuis in lower Egypt is extant in a single eleventh-century manuscript in the monastery of the Great Lavra on Mount Athos, which was first published by Aleksej Dmitrievskij in 1894, and again shortly afterwards by Georg Wobbermin.[25] The edition most familiar to English-speaking students, however, was that by F. E. Brightman in 1900, who thought that the contents were not arranged in any proper order, and so he rearranged them in what he considered the most logical form.[26] Unfortunately, Brightman's order was then frequently treated as though it were Sarapion's own, and the only complete English translation of the sacramentary until recently, by John Wordsworth, although at first made from Wobbermin's edition, was also later revised on the basis of Brightman's text.[27]

---

22 Cf. the different conclusions reached by P.-T. Camelot, ed., *Les Stromates* 2 (SC 38, 1954), p. 107, n. 1; Michel Dujarier, *A History of the Catechumenate: The First Six Centuries* (New York 1979), pp. 42–3; A. Mehat, *Étude sur les 'Stromates' de Clément d'Alexandrie* (Paris 1966), p. 221.

23 See further, Werner Schütz, *Der christliche Gottesdienst bei Origenes* (Stuttgart 1984).

24 See above, pp. 83–4.

25 Aleksej Dmitrievskij, *Ein Euchologium aus dem 4. Jahrhundert, verfasst von Sarapion, Bischof von Thmuis* (Kiev 1894); Georg Wobbermin, *Altchristliche liturgische Stücke aus der Kirche Aegyptens nebst einem dogmatischen Brief des Bischofs Serapion von Thmuis* (Leipzig/Berlin 1898).

26 'The Sacramentary of Serapion of Thmuis', *JTS* 1 (1900), pp. 88–113, 247–77. Brightman's text and order were followed by Funk, *Didascalia et Constitutiones Apostolorum* II, pp. 158–95.

27 *Bishop Sarapion's Prayer-Book* (London 1899; 2nd edn 1909 = Hamden, CT 1964).

Bernard Capelle argued that the material in the collection had all been composed by a single author, because of the repetition of certain words, and that the author was an innovator because he attributed to the Logos the role which tradition assigned to the Spirit, and even inserted a Logos-epiclesis in the eucharistic prayer.[28] This latter argument was taken up by Bernard Botte, who concluded that the text was therefore the work of a heretic and not the real Sarapion 'who evoked the letters of Athanasius on the divinity of the Holy Spirit'. He suggested that it belonged to a later date, possibly *c.* 450.[29]

Geoffrey Cuming challenged these conclusions. Against Brightman, he took up a suggestion originally made by Theodor Scherman[30] and contended that – with one simple change – the order of the manuscript was perfectly natural. The change required the assumption that in the process of copying, the second half was accidentally placed before the first. Against Capelle, he argued that there were clear signs of different strata in the material, indicated by features of style and vocabulary; and against Botte, he maintained that, both in the use of the Logos and in his Christology, the author was orthodox and utilized in his eucharistic prayer an earlier and simpler form of the Alexandrine Anaphora of St Mark (for which see below). He concluded that 'it thus becomes increasingly possible that the collecting and editing of these prayers was, after all, the work of Sarapion, Bishop of Thmuis, the friend of Athanasius'.[31] Maxwell Johnson has continued Cuming's approach, and subjected the text to close literary analysis and comparison with other contemporary evidence. His research reveals the existence of several different strata of material within the collection, but nothing which would contradict the traditional attribution and date for its compilation as a collection. He has also argued that behind its present eucharistic prayer can be discerned an older tripartite nucleus akin in shape to the Strasbourg Papyrus (see below), comprising praise, offering, and supplication/intercession.[32]

28 'L'anaphore de Sérapion: essai d'exégèse', *Le Muséon* 59 (1946), pp. 425–43 = idem, *Travaux liturgiques* 2 (1962), pp. 344–58.

29 'L'Euchologe de Sérapion, est-il authentique?', *Oriens Christianus* 48 (1964), pp. 50–6.

30 *Ägyptische Abendmahlsliturgien des ersten Jahrtausends* (Paderborn 1912 = 1967), pp. 102–3.

31 'Thmuis Revisited: Another Look at the Prayers of Bishop Sarapion', *Theological Studies* 41 (1980), pp. 568–75.

32 *The Prayers of Sarapion of Thmuis: A Literary, Liturgical, and Theological Analysis* (OCA 249, 1995). This includes both text and ET. Bryan Spinks has challenged his conclusions, defending the integrity both of Sarapion's anaphora in its present form and of the baptismal material within the collection: 'The Integrity of the Anaphora of Sarapion of Thmuis and Liturgical Methodology', *JTS* 49 (1998), pp. 136–44; 'Sarapion of Thmuis and Baptismal Practice in Early Christian Egypt; The Need for a Judicious Reassessment', *Worship* 72 (1998), pp. 255–70. See Johnson's response, 'The Baptismal Rite and Anaphora in the Prayers of Sarapion of Thmuis: An Assessment of a Recent "Judicious Reassessment"', *Worship* 73 (1999) pp. 140–68; and also his essay, 'The Archaic Nature of the Sanctus, Institution Narrative, and Epiclesis of the Logos in the Anaphora Ascribed to Sarapion of Thmuis', in Paul F. Bradshaw, ed., *Essays on Early Eastern Eucharistic Prayers* (Collegeville 1997), pp. 73–107.

Also important as clues for early Egyptian eucharistic prayers are a number of fragmentary texts discovered during the course of the twentieth century. The most significant of these is **Strasbourg Papyrus 254**, which dates from the fourth or fifth century (although the actual prayer may be older still) and by verbal parallels reveals itself to be an early version of the Anaphora of St Mark. The major controversy which has surrounded the text is whether what survives was the entire anaphora or just a part of something much longer. Its extant contents consist of praise for the work of creation through Christ, thanksgiving for/offering of 'this reasonable and bloodless service' (with a quotation of Malachi 1.11), extensive intercession, and a doxological conclusion.[33] Many recent scholars have concluded that the anaphora was more or less coterminous with the extant material, and that therefore it did not include such elements as the Sanctus or the narrative of institution. A few, however, remain more cautiously agnostic, and regard the case as unproven. The doxology might, for instance, only be the conclusion of one section of the prayer and not of the whole anaphora, as happens in *Didache* 10 and other early texts.[34]

When studied in conjunction with the other fragmentary texts, it is possible to see that the later **Anaphora of St Mark** had substantially assumed its current form, though in a less wordy version, by the time of the Council of Chalcedon.[35] Its shape is distinctive, in that it begins with the elements found in the Strasbourg Papyrus and so only after extensive intercession reaches the Sanctus, epiclesis, institution narrative, anamnesis, and offering, and concludes with a second epiclesis and doxology.

Finally, there is the **Anaphora of St Basil**. Scholars generally assume that this composition did not originate in Egypt because its shape follows the pattern of Antiochene eucharistic prayers, with the intercessions coming towards the end rather than at an earlier point in the prayer as in the Anaphora of St Mark. Its oldest known form, however, is a version in the Sahidic dialect of Coptic. This is extant only in an incomplete manuscript lacking the first third of the later text and dating from somewhere between 600 and 800, although the contents probably belong to the first half of the fourth century or even earlier.[36] It has been thought that it may have been the native Cappadocian anaphora brought by Basil when he visited Egypt *c.* 357,

---

33 Text in M. Andrieu and P. Collomp, 'Fragments sur papyrus de l'Anaphore de saint Marc', *RevSR* 8 (1928), pp. 489–515; ET in Jasper and Cuming, *Prayers of the Eucharist*, pp. 52–4.

34 See the review of scholarship in Walter D. Ray, 'The Strasbourg Papyrus', in Bradshaw, ed., *Essays on Early Eastern Eucharistic Prayers*, pp. 39–56.

35 For full details, see G. J. Cuming, *The Liturgy of St Mark* (OCA 234, 1990).

36 Edition in J. Doresse and E. Lanne, *Un témoin archaïque de la liturgie copte de S. Basile* (Louvain 1960); ET in Jasper and Cuming, *Prayers of the Eucharist*, pp. 67–73.

and subsequently amplified by the saint himself into the longer form underlying the later Armenian, Byzantine, and Syriac versions. On the other hand, the possibility cannot be excluded that the prayer is in fact of Egyptian origin – maybe even actually composed in Sahidic and not Greek – and was later exported to other parts of the East, perhaps through Basil's own agency.[37]

Syria

Apart from the *Didache*,[38] some of the main sources which may shed light on early liturgical practices in this region are the apocryphal scriptures, especially the *Acts of John* (usually dated late second or early third century)[39] and the *Acts of Thomas* (third century, probably from East Syria)[40] and the *Syriac Acts of John* (fourth or fifth century).[41] Yet these present us with a number of problems. There is, first of all, the difficulty of establishing an original text. This material belongs to the category of 'living literature', about which we have spoken earlier,[42] and so was often reshaped by the communities through which it passed. This practice is particularly evident in the case of the *Acts of Thomas*, which exists in two recensions, a Greek and a Syriac, differing markedly from one another in a number of places. Then, too, there is the question of how the narrative form should be interpreted: are descriptions of alleged baptismal and eucharistic activities by apostolic figures, for example, to be taken as reflecting the actual customs familiar to the compilers and editors, or do they bear little resemblance to contemporary liturgical observances? Even if they are held to be based on genuine practices, whose rituals do they represent – what was common to what might be called mainstream

37 See the survey of scholarship in D. Richard Stuckwisch, 'The Basilian Anaphoras', in Bradshaw, ed., *Essays on Early Eastern Eucharistic Prayers*, pp. 109–30.
38 See above, pp. 77–8.
39 Greek text in Eric Junod and Jean-Daniel Kaestli, eds, *Acta Iohannis* (Turnhout, Belgium 1983); ET in J. K. Elliott, ed., *The Apocryphal New Testament* (Oxford 1993), pp. 303–49. Some think this work may have originated in Egypt and not Syria. See also R. H. Miller, 'Liturgical Materials in the Acts of John', *SP* 13 (1975), pp. 377–81; Hans Roldanus, 'Die Eucharistie in den Johannesakten', in Jan N. Bremmer, ed., *The Apocryphal Acts of John* (Kampen, The Netherlands 1995), pp. 72–96.
40 Greek text in R. A. Lipsius and M. Bonnet, *Acta Apostolorum Apocrypha* II.2 (Leipzig 1903 = Hildesheim 1959), pp. 99–291; ET in Elliott, *The Apocryphal New Testament*, pp. 439–511; Syriac text and ET in William Wright, *Apocryphal Acts of the Apostles* (London/Edinburgh 1871 = Amsterdam 1968) I.171–333; II.146–298. See also A. F. J. Klijn, *The Acts of Thomas* (Leiden 1962); Gerard Rouwhorst, 'La célébration de l'eucharistie selon les Actes de Thomas', in Charles Caspers and Marc Schneiders, eds, *Omnes Circumstantes* (Kampen, The Netherlands 1990), pp. 51–77.
41 Text and ET in Wright, *Apocryphal Acts of the Apostles* I.4–65; II.3–60. Junod and Kiestli, eds, *Acta Iohannis*, pp. 705–16, judge it to be independent of the Greek *Acts of John*.
42 See above, pp. 5, 92.

Christianity or what was only the tradition of an esoteric group? It is interesting to note that while there has been a willingness to use the baptismal material as a source for mainstream practice,[43] there has been some reluctance to do the same with the eucharistic material, because it does not fit neatly the form that scholars have decided that early eucharistic prayers are supposed to have taken.

A major source for the liturgy of Antioch in the fourth century is **John Chrysostom** (*c*. 347–407), since his extensive writings, and not least his baptismal homilies,[44] include many references to liturgical practices.[45] On the other hand, whether the anaphora which bears his name should really be ascribed to him has been much debated, as has the nature of the relationship between that anaphora and the Syriac **Anaphora of the Twelve Apostles**. However, both John Fenwick and Robert Taft have argued that the two prayers share a common Greek ancestor, which, in the case of the Anaphora of the Twelve Apostles, was conflated with elements from the Syriac version of the Anaphora of St James (for which see below), and in the case of the Anaphora of St John Chrysostom, was conflated with elements from the Byzantine version of the Anaphora of St Basil. Taft contended that Chrysostom himself was the redactor of this second anaphora, and Fenwick took the argument even further to suggest that the same ancestor lay behind the eucharistic prayer in *Apostolic Constitutions* 8.[46] He was reticent with regard to what additional source or sources might have been used in this latter case, but Raphael Graves has since examined the prayer further and reviewed the various theories about its origin. He concludes that, while there is evidence of

---

43 See below, pp. 146–53.
44 Text partly in Antoine Wenger, *Jean Chrysostome: Huit catéchèses baptismales* (SC 50, 1957), and partly in Auguste Piédagnel, *Jean Chrysostome: Trois catéchèses baptismales* (SC 366, 1990); ET in P. W. Harkins, *St John Chrysostom: Baptismal Instructions* (Westminster, MD 1959). Studies include: A. Cesara-Gestaldo, 'Teoria e prassi nella catechesi battesimale di S. Giovanni Crisostomo', in S. Felici, ed., *Catechesi battesimale e reconciliazione nei Padri del IV secolo* (Rome 1984), pp. 57–63; T. M. Finn, *The Liturgy of Baptism in the Baptismal Instructions of St John Chrysostom* (Washington, DC 1967); Riley, *Christian Initiation*; D. Sartore, 'Il mistero del battesimo nelle catechesi di S. Giovanni Chrisostomo', *Lateranum* 50 (1984), pp. 358–95.
45 For other aspects besides baptism, see Reiner Kaczynski, *Das Wort Gottes in Liturgie und Alltag der Gemeinden des Johannes Chrysostomos* (Freiburg 1974); F. van de Paverd, *Zur Geschichte der Messliturgie in Antiocheia und Konstantinopel gegen Ende des vierten Jahrhunderts. Analyse der Quellen bei Johannes Chrysostomos* (OCA 187, 1970); idem, 'Anaphoral Intercessions, Epiclesis and Communion Rites in John Chrysostom', *OCP* 49 (1983), pp. 303–39.
46 John R. K. Fenwick, *'The Missing Oblation': The Contents of the Early Antiochene Anaphora* (A/GLS 11, 1989); Robert F. Taft, 'The Authenticity of the Chrysostom Anaphora Revisited. Determining the Authorship of Liturgical Texts by Computer', *OCP* 56 (1990), pp. 5–51 = idem, *Liturgy in Byzantium and Beyond* (London 1995), III; idem, 'St John Chrysostom and the Byzantine Anaphora that Bears His Name', in Bradshaw, ed., *Essays on Early Eastern Eucharistic Prayers*, pp. 195–226.

some use of the Anaphora of St Basil, the principal parallels lie with the compiler's own work elsewhere in the *Apostolic Constitutions* rather than with any other known prayer.[47]

Some further light is cast on Antiochene liturgical practices by **Theodore of Mopsuestia**, who was ordained as a presbyter at Antioch about 383, and served there until 392 when he became Bishop of Mopsuestia, a town about 100 miles away but still within the patriarchate of Antioch. Of his 16 baptismal homilies, Nos 1–10 are on the Nicene Creed, 11 is on the Lord's Prayer, 12–14 are on baptism, and 15–16 are on the Eucharist, the first 14 being delivered before the baptism took place and the last two after it. The original Greek text has not been preserved, and all that exists is a Syriac translation made perhaps in the fifth or sixth century. There is just one extant manuscript of this, which dates from the seventeenth century. The only edition (with English translation) is by Alphonse Mingana, and it is not without fault.[48]

While the authorship of these homilies is not disputed, the date and place of composition are. Most scholars believe that they were delivered while Theodore was still a presbyter at Antioch, but some have placed them during his episcopate in Mopsuestia, 392–428.[49] This question also has some relation

---

47 'The Anaphora of the Eighth Book of the Apostolic Constitutions', in Bradshaw, ed., *Essays on Early Eastern Eucharistic Prayers*, pp. 173–94. Other studies of the eucharistic prayer of *Apostolic Constitutions* 8 include: Marcel Metzger, 'Les deux prières eucharistiques des Constitutions apostoliques', *RevSR* 45 (1971), pp. 52–77; idem, 'The *Didascalia* and the *Constitutiones Apostolorum*', in *The Eucharist of the Early Christians*, pp. 194–219; A. Verheul, 'Les prières eucharistiques dans les "Constitutions Apostolorum"', *QLP* 61 (1980), pp. 129–43.

48 *Commentary of Theodore of Mopsuestia on the Nicene Creed* (Woodbrooke Studies 5; Cambridge 1932); *Commentary of Theodore of Mopsuestia on the Lord's Prayer and on the Sacraments of Baptism and Eucharist* (Woodbrooke Studies 6; Cambridge 1933). See also the excellent French translation by R. Tonneau and R. Devreesse, *Les Homélies Catéchétiques de Théodore de Mopsueste* (Vatican 1949); and the ET of homilies 13–16 in Yarnold, *The Awe-Inspiring Rites of Initiation*, pp. 173–263; 2nd edn, pp. 168–250.

49 Liturgical studies of Theodore's sermons include: S. Janeras, 'En quels jours furent prononcées les homélies catéchétiques de Théodore de Mopsueste?', in *Memorial Mgr Gabriel Khouri-Sarkis* (Louvain 1969), pp. 121–3; J. Lécuyer, 'Le sacerdoce chrétien et le sacrifice eucharistique selon Théodore de Mopsueste', *Recherches de science religieuse* 36 (1949), pp. 481–516; J. P. Longleat, 'Les rites du baptême dans les homélies catéchétiques de Théodore de Mopsueste', *QLP* 66 (1985), pp. 193–202; Enrico Mazza, 'La formula battesimale nelle omilie di Teodoro di Mopsuestia', *EL* 104 (1990), pp. 23-34; J. Quasten, 'The Liturgical Mysticism of Theodore of Mopsuestia', *Theological Studies* 15 (1954), pp. 431–9; F. J. Reine, *The Eucharistic Doctrine and the Liturgy of the Mystagogical Catecheses of Theodore of Mopsuestia* (Washington, DC 1942); Riley, *Christian Initiation*; George E. Saint-Laurent, 'Pre-baptismal Rites in the Baptismal Catecheses of Theodore of Mopsuestia', *Diakonia* 16 (1981), pp. 118–26; W. C. van Unnik, 'Parrhesia in the Catechetical Homilies of Theodore of Mopsuestia', in *Mélanges offerts à Mlle Christine Mohrmann* (Utrecht 1963), pp. 12–22.

to the authenticity of a passage in Theodore's description of the baptismal rite which refers to a post-baptismal anointing of the forehead associated with the gift of the Holy Spirit (14.27). Such a ceremony is not mentioned by Theodore's contemporary, John Chrysostom, nor by any other Syrian source in the first five centuries, with the exception of the *Apostolic Constitutions*, and even there it is not connected with the gift of the Spirit (3.16; 7.22; 7.44). Some scholars would therefore regard the passage as a later interpolation, while others would argue that it should not be understood as a reference to a literal anointing with oil, and still others would defend it as the genuine first appearance of an innovation which did eventually become a standard part of later Syrian baptismal rites, usually explaining the divergence from Chrysostom's rite either with the claim that there had been a recent change in Antiochene practice, or with the argument that the description reflects the rite of Mopsuestia.[50]

Enrico Mazza has also claimed that in the homilies we can discern two stages in the evolution of the local eucharistic prayer: the older pattern received by the community and reproduced section by section at the head of each part of the commentary (what Mazza calls the *Ordo*), and the form as currently celebrated there, which Theodore describes in the commentary itself and which seems to differ in some significant respects from the *Ordo*. Mazza finds this apparent later form closer to the Byzantine Anaphora of St Basil than to the Anaphora of St John Chrysostom, while the anaphora in the *Ordo* he sees as similar to that known to Cyril of Jerusalem.[51] However, his arguments are not completely convincing. He does not, for example, allow for the possibility that the preacher may simply have been commenting rather freely on a single text rather than alluding to another form known to him, nor for the possibility that – as Bryan Spinks has suggested – Theodore may have been attempting to make his remarks cover more than one anaphora used in his community, both a version of Byzantine Basil and a version of the Anaphora of St John Chrysostom.[52]

For East Syria, we have the writings of **Aphraates** (early fourth century),[53]

---

50 See C. J. A. Lash, 'L'onction post-baptismale de la 14e homélie de Théodore de Mopsueste: une interpolation syriaque?', in *XXIX Congres International des Orientalistes: Resumés* (Paris 1973), pp. 43–4; Yarnold, *The Awe-Inspiring Rites of Initiation*, p. 208, n. 65; 2nd edn, p. 198, n. 65; J. D. C. Fisher, *Confirmation Then and Now* (ACC 60; London 1978), pp. 115–18.
51 'La struttura dell'Anafora nelle Catechesi di Teodoro di Mopsuestia', *EL* 102 (1988), pp. 147–83 = *The Origins of the Eucharistic Prayer*, pp. 287–331.
52 'The East Syrian Anaphora of Theodore: Reflections upon Its Sources and Theology', *EL* 103 (1989), p. 444 = idem, *Prayers from the East*, p. 49.
53 See E. J. Duncan, *Baptism in the Demonstrations of Aphraates the Persian Sage* (Washington, DC 1945); F. S. Pericoli Ridolfini, 'Battesimo e penitenza negli scritti del "Sapiente Persiano"', in Felici, ed., *Catechesi battesimale e reconciliazione nei Padri del IV secolo*, pp. 119–29; Jaroslav Skira, '"Circumcise Thy Heart": Aphrahat's Theology of Baptism', *Diakonia* 31 (1998), pp. 115–28.

the hymns of **Ephrem** (*c.* 306–73)[54] and of **Cyrillonas of Edessa** (a fourth-century poet and Ephrem's nephew),[55] and the somewhat later evidence of **Narsai** (fifth century),[56] which furnish some information about liturgical customs, and also the important testimony of the **Anaphora of the Apostles Addai and Mari**. Although all the extant manuscripts of this eucharistic prayer are of very late date, the comparative geographical and ecclesiastical isolation of the region and the strong Semitic influence on early Christianity there have encouraged scholars to believe that parts of the prayer may be very ancient indeed, perhaps as early as the second or third century. Furthermore, unlike other early eucharistic prayers, it appears to have been composed in Syriac rather than Greek. The publication by William F. Macomber in 1966 of a critical edition based on a tenth/eleventh-century manuscript from the church of Mar Esa'ya in Mosul[57] – at least 500 years older than any previously known manuscript of the prayer – constituted a significant development for attempts to reconstruct its earlier form, as did the publication by J. M. Sauget in 1973 of a critical text of the **Third Anaphora of St Peter** or *Sharar* of the Maronite rite.[58] Since most of the contents of Addai and Mari are also found in *Sharar*, scholars had long believed that a common source must lie behind the two texts.

Macomber himself attempted to reconstruct the original anaphora from which these extant versions developed as it might have been *c.* 400, and which he thought belonged to the Aramaic-speaking church centred on Edessa. He believed that the whole prayer had originally been addressed to the Son and not the Father, as *Sharar* still is from its post-Sanctus to the final doxology; that the Sanctus, though disputed by some earlier scholars, was original to the text; that the institution narrative, found in *Sharar* but absent from the Mar Esa'ya text, was part of the earlier prayer – as the existence of an anamnesis paragraph in the latter indicated – but had been deleted from Addai and Mari

54 See Sebastian Brock, ed., *The Harp of the Spirit* (2nd edn, London 1983); Joseph P. Amar, 'Perspectives on the Eucharist in Ephrem the Syrian', *Worship* 61 (1987), pp. 441–54; Edmund Beck, 'Le baptême chez St Ephrem', *L'Orient syrien* 1 (1956), pp. 111–36; G. Saber, *La théologie baptismale de Saint Ephrem* (Kaslik 1974); Pierre Yousif, *L'eucharistie chez saint Ephrem de Nisibe* (Rome 1984).

55 See D. Cerbelaud, *Cyrillonas. L'agneau véritable. Hymnes, cantiques, homélies* (Chevetogne 1984).

56 See R. H. Connolly, *The Liturgical Homilies of Narsai* (Cambridge 1909 = Nendeln, Liechtenstein 1967); Marcia Kappes, 'A Voice of Many Waters: The Baptismal Homilies of Narsai of Nisibis', *SP* 33 (1997), pp. 534–47.

57 'The oldest known text of the Anaphora of the Apostles Addai and Mari', *OCP* 31 (1966), pp. 335–71; ET and bibliography of secondary literature, in Bryan D. Spinks, ed., *Addai and Mari – The Anaphora of the Apostles: A Text for Students* (GLS 24, 1980); Anthony Gelston, *The Eucharistic Prayer of Addai and Mari* (Oxford 1992).

58 *Anaphorae Syriacae* II, Fasc. 3 (Rome 1973), pp. 275–323; ET also in Spinks, *Addai and Mari*.

as a result of the reforms of Iso'Yab III in the seventh century; and that the epiclesis was probably a fourth-century accretion to the earlier core.[59]

There is, however, no clear scholarly consensus on the question of its original form. Bryan Spinks, for example, regards the prayer as having a bipartite structure rather than the tripartite shape discerned by many other scholars, and would hold that the institution narrative is an addition to the original core, but the epiclesis is primitive. He also questions whether there ever was a single original written form, and suggests that it may be more accurate to speak simply of common oral tradition shared by the two prayers.[60]

There are also two other East Syrian eucharistic prayers, the **Anaphora of Nestorius** and the **Anaphora of Theodore**, neither of which was actually written by the theologian whose name it bears, although there has been some discussion as to possible connections between the writings of Theodore of Mopsuestia and the Anaphora of Theodore. The Anaphora of Nestorius is largely composed of material drawn from the Byzantine Anaphora of St Basil and the Anaphora of St John Chrysostom, with some elements from Addai and Mari; and Bryan Spinks has argued that the Anaphora of Theodore is made up of material from Addai and Mari and the Anaphora of Nestorius, with some influence from the baptismal homilies of Theodore.[61]

---

59 'The Ancient Form of the Anaphora of the Apostles', in *East of Byzantium: Syria and Armenia in the Formative Period* (Dumbarton Oaks Symposium 1980; Washington, DC 1982), pp. 73–88.

60 See his review of scholarship, 'The Quest for the "Original Form" of the Anaphora of the Apostles Addai and Mari', in idem, *Worship: Prayers from the East* (Washington, DC 1993), pp. 1–20; and his studies, 'The Original Form of the Anaphora of the Apostles: A Suggestion in the Light of Maronite *Sharar*', *EL* 91 (1977), pp. 146–61; 'Addai and Mari and the Institution Narrative: The Tantalizing Evidence of Gabriel Qatraya', *EL* 98 (1984), pp. 60–7; both reproduced in *Worship: Prayers from the East*, pp. 21–45. Other recent studies include: Peter Hofrichter, 'The Anaphora of Addai and Mari in the Church of the East – Eucharist without Institution Narrative', and Sarhad Jammo, 'The Quddasha of the Apostles Addai and Mari and the Narrative of the Eucharistic Institution', both in *Syriac Dialogue No. 1, Pro Oriente* (Vienna 1994), pp. 167–93; Stylianos Muksuris, 'A Brief Overview of the Structure and Theology of the Liturgy of the Apostles Addai and Mari', *Greek Orthodox Theological Review* 43 (1998), pp. 59–83; Walter D. Ray, 'The Chiastic Structure of the Anaphora of Addai and Mari', *SL* 23 (1993), pp. 187–93; Stephen B. Wilson, 'The Anaphora of the Apostles Addai and Mari', in Bradshaw, ed., *Essays on Early Eastern Eucharistic Prayers*, pp. 19–37.

61 'The East Syrian Anaphora of Theodore', pp. 441–55 = idem, *Prayers from the East*, pp. 47–64. Critical edition in Jacob Vadakkel, *The East Syrian Anaphora of Mar Theodore of Mopsuestia* (Vadavathoor, Kottayam, India 1989); ET and bibliography of secondary literature in Bryan D. Spinks, *Mar Nestorius and Mar Theodore the Interpreter: The Forgotten Eucharistic Prayers of East Syria* (A/GLS 45, 1999).

Jerusalem

Although evidence for the very early period of Christian liturgical life in Jerusalem is lacking,[62] we are fortunate in having several substantial sources to illuminate our knowledge of practices in the fourth and fifth centuries.[63] Care needs to be taken, however, not to generalize from this testimony to what might have been the liturgical customs of other places during the same period. Because Jerusalem was the major pilgrimage centre of the fourth-century Christian world, its pattern of worship was necessarily unique in some respects and at least in part hybrid in character, as visiting groups of Christians from other parts of the world imported into it their own local usages as well as exporting from it other practices that were novel to them. The most important sources for its liturgy are as follows.

The Catecheses of Cyril

Cyril was Bishop of Jerusalem from 350 until his death in 387, although exiled several times as a result of the Arian controversy. His 18 catechetical lectures, together with an introductory address (the *Procatechesis*), were delivered while he was still a presbyter.[64] There is in addition a series of *Mystagogical Catecheses*, five post-baptismal homilies which have traditionally been thought to have been preached by Cyril to newly baptized Christians at Jerusalem,[65] but questions have been raised about their authorship.

Since the appearance of an important article on the question by W. J. Swaans in 1942,[66] there has been increasing support for the view that the *Mystagogical Catecheses* were not the genuine work of Cyril, but of some later person, possibly his successor as Bishop of Jerusalem, John. The grounds for this are variations in manuscript attribution (some ascribe authorship to

62 See, however, John Wilkinson, 'Jewish Influences on the Early Christian Rite of Jerusalem', *Le Muséon* 92 (1979), pp. 347–59.

63 For an introductory survey, see John F. Baldovin, *Liturgy in Ancient Jerusalem* (A/GLS 9, 1989), and also his extensive study, *The Urban Character of Christian Worship*, pp. 45–104. There is an exhaustive annotated bibliography of secondary literature from 1960 to 1980 in A. Renoux, 'Hierosolymitana', *ALW* 23 (1981), pp. 1–29, 149–75.

64 Text in Migne, *Patrologia Graeca* 33.331–1064; ET in Leo P. McCauley and A. A. Stephenson, *The Works of St Cyril of Jerusalem* (Washington, DC 1969–70). See Alexis Doval, 'The Date of Cyril of Jerusalem's Catecheses', *JTS* 48 (1997), who argues for 351 as the year of their delivery rather than either 348 or 350 as others have suggested.

65 Text and ET in F. L. Cross, *St. Cyril of Jerusalem's Lectures on the Christian Sacraments: The Procatechesis and the Five Mystagogical Catecheses* (London 1951); text also in A. Piédagnel, *Cyrille de Jerusalem: Catéchèses mystagogiques* (SC 126, 1966); ET in McCauley and Stephenson, *Works of St Cyril of Jerusalem* II; Yarnold, *The Awe-Inspiring Rites of Initiation*, pp. 65–95; 2nd edn, pp. 70–97.

66 'A propos des "catéchèses Mystagogiques" attribuées à S. Cyrille de Jerusalem', *Le Muséon* 55 (1942), pp. 1–43.

Cyril, some to John, some to no one), differences in literary style and theology, and the description of the Jerusalem liturgy, which suggests a more developed form than is likely to have been the case as early as 348. C. Beukers suggested in 1961 that they were by Cyril, but from a date towards the end of his episcopate, and argued that the petition 'for our emperors, soldiers and allies' (5.8) pointed to the years 383–6.[67] Edward Yarnold has also championed the traditional ascription to Cyril, suggesting that they were delivered later in Cyril's episcopate (350–86). This would explain the more developed form of the liturgy, and the differences in style and theological ideas, as Cyril's thought evolved. In any case they show similarities with Cyril's other works, and are unlike the sermon on the Church attributed to John.[68] Yarnold had earlier suggested that Ambrose of Milan knew these catecheses in 391, which also implied that Cyril rather than John was their author.[69]

Quite independently of the issue of the authorship of the *Mystagogical Catecheses*, there has also been a considerable discussion over the structure and contents of the eucharistic prayer to which these addresses allude. In particular, the debate has focused on the question: did the prayer contain the narrative of institution? The narrative is mentioned in the fourth address, but not in the description of the eucharistic prayer which comes in the fifth address. Some have argued that the prayer did include the narrative, but the author did not refer to it because he had already dealt with it in the preceding address or because it was already being recited silently in the eucharistic prayer and so would not have been heard by those to whom he was speaking.[70] Geoffrey Cuming suggested, on the basis of an analogous comment in John Chrysostom, that the author's reference to the spiritual sacrifice being 'perfected' (5.8) was really an allusion to the narrative of institution. If so, it would thus have followed the epiclesis in the prayer, in line with the pattern of eucharistic prayer which evolved in Egypt, rather than have preceded it, as was the West Syrian custom; and from this and other apparent similarities, he argued for an Egyptian origin to the Jerusalem anaphora.[71] Bryan Spinks challenged Cuming's conclusions, pointing out that the reference to the completion of the spiritual sacrifice could just as easily be to the epiclesis itself,[72] and Cuming later modified his claim, arguing only for a

---

67 '"For our Emperors, Soldiers and Allies": An Attempt at Dating the Twenty-third Cate-chesis by Cyrillus of Jerusalem', *VC* 15 (1961), pp. 177–84.

68 'The Authorship of the Mystagogic Catecheses Attributed to Cyril of Jerusalem', *Heythrop Journal* 19 (1978), pp. 143–61.

69 'Did St Ambrose know the Mystagogic Catecheses of St Cyril of Jerusalem?', pp. 184–9.

70 See, for example, Baldovin, *Liturgy in Ancient Jerusalem*, pp. 25–7; Georg Kretschmar, 'Die frühe Geschichte der Jerusalemer Liturgie', *Jahrbuch für Liturgik und Hymnologie* 2 (1956), pp. 30–3.

71 'Egyptian Elements in the Jerusalem Liturgy', *JTS* 25 (1974), pp. 117–24.

72 'The Jerusalem Liturgy of the *Catecheses Mystagogicae*: Syrian or Egyptian?', *SP* 18/2

common shape as the root of both the early Jerusalem anaphora and the Egyptian Anaphora of St Mark, such as we find in the Strasbourg Papyrus.[73]

The Pilgrimage of Egeria

This document is a travel-diary, evidently written by a female pilgrim to the Holy Land some time in the fourth century and intended to provide an account of what she saw for the members of the religious community from which she came. The one surviving manuscript, dating from the eleventh century, was discovered in 1884 and published in 1887.[74] The manuscript is incomplete and may represent only about one-third of the original. A few quotations from the work in medieval writings help to fill in some of its missing pages. Its opening and final pages are lacking, and consequently it has no title or author's name. The work itself says that the author came from 'the other end of the earth', and compares the colour of the Red Sea with that of 'the Ocean'. Its first editor, J. F. Gamurrini, attributed it to a pilgrim from Aquitaine mentioned by Palladius: her name was Silvia, or Silvania. However, in 1903 Dom Marius Férotin recognized that a seventh-century 'Letter in praise of the Blessed Aetheria', written by a monk named Valerius, was in fact about the author of this work.[75] Most scholars accepted this conclusion, but different versions of the name appear in different manuscripts of Valerius' letter, including Egeria, Echeria, Etheria, Heteria, and Eiheria. Subsequently other evidence has been assembled which makes it more likely that Egeria is the correct version, but it is far from certain.[76] From details given in the narrative, it has been calculated that the author was in Jerusalem from 381 to 384.

While the diary gives a wealth of useful information about the Jerusalem liturgy in the late fourth century, it has several limitations. For example, it is

---

(1989), pp. 391–5. See also E. J. Cutrone, 'Cyril's Mystagogical Catecheses and the Evolution of the Jerusalem Anaphora', *OCP* 44 (1978), pp. 52–64; Fenwick, *Fourth Century Anaphoral Construction Techniques*, pp. 13–15.

73 'The Shape of the Anaphora', *SP* 20 (1989), p. 341. See also Kent J. Burreson, 'The Anaphora of the Mystagogical Catecheses of Cyril of Jerusalem', in Bradshaw, ed., *Essays on Early Eastern Eucharistic Prayers*, pp. 131–51, esp. pp. 142ff.

74 The best edition is still that by Pierre Maraval, *Égérie. Journal de Voyage* (SC 296, 1982); and the standard ET is by John Wilkinson, *Egeria's Travels* (London 1971; 2nd edn, Warminster 1981; 3rd edn 1999). Wilkinson includes a select bibliography of secondary literature, and M. Starowieyski, 'Bibliografia Egeriana', *Augustinianum* 19 (1979), pp. 297–318, offers a more comprehensive one, containing 296 entries, to which there is a supplement in S. Janeras, 'Contributo alla bibliografia egerianae', in *Atti del Convegno Internazionale sulla 'Peregrinatio Egeriae' (Arezzo 23–25 ottobre 1987)* (Arezzo 1990), pp. 355–66.

75 'Le véritable auteur de la Peregrinatio Silviae, la vierge espagnole Etheria', *Revue des questions historiques* 74 (1903), pp. 367–97.

76 See Wilkinson, *Egeria's Travels*, pp. 235–6.

inevitably somewhat selective in the liturgical practices the author chooses to report, reflecting no doubt her personal interests, and in particular it supplies no details of customs widely or universally practised at the time, but only of those which would have been unfamiliar to her original readers. Moreover, because it is the work of a visitor to a foreign community, there is some uncertainty concerning how far she correctly understood what was going on. A good example of this is the apparent discrepancy between her description of an eight-week Lenten season, with seven weeks of daily catechetical instruction on both the Scriptures and the Creed, and the evidence of other Jerusalem sources for a six-week Lent, as well as the existence of only 18 lectures of Cyril which are to be delivered in this period and which focus on the Creed alone.[77]

The Armenian and Georgian Lectionaries
The former of these, dating from the first half of the fifth century, reproduces the readings, feasts, and a number of the rubrics of the church at Jerusalem,[78] while the latter represents a later stage of development of the same material.[79] Peter Jeffery has also drawn attention to the value of the Georgian chantbook, the *Iadgari*, in reconstructing Jerusalem liturgical practice.[80]

The Liturgy of St James
The earliest manuscripts of this eucharistic liturgy date from the ninth century, and the rite has obviously undergone a considerable degree of development from earlier times. Its core appears to be a conflation of the eucharistic traditions of Antioch and Jerusalem, perhaps having taken place around the year 400.[81] John Fenwick developed this idea further and argued

77 For further details and attempts at reconciliation of the conflicting evidence, see Maxwell E. Johnson, 'Reconciling Cyril and Egeria on the Catechetical Process in Fourth-Century Jerusalem', in Bradshaw, ed., *Essays in Early Eastern Initiation*, pp. 18–30; and also below, p. 185.

78 Introduction and text in A. Renoux, *Le Codex Arménien Jérusalem 121*, two vols (PO 35/1 and 36/2, 1969, 1971). See also, John F. Baldovin, 'A Lenten Sunday Lectionary in Fourth Century Jerusalem', in J. Neil Alexander, ed., *Time and Community* (Washington, DC 1990), pp. 115–22; S. Janeras, 'A propos de la catéchèse XIVe de Cyrille de Jérusalem', *EO* 3 (1986), pp. 307–18; M. F. Lages, 'The Hierosolymitan Origin of the Catechetical Rites in the Armenian Liturgy', *Didaskalia* 1 (1971), pp. 233–49.

79 M. Tarchnischvili, ed., *Le grand lectionnaire de l'Église de Jérusalem*, two vols (Corpus Scriptorum Christianorum Orientalium 189 and 205; Louvain 1959–60). See also H. Leeb, *Die Gesänge in Gemeindegottesdienst von Jerusalem* (Vienna 1970).

80 'The Sunday Office of Seventh-Century Jerusalem in the Georgian Chantbook (Iadgari): A Preliminary Report', *SL* 21 (1991), pp. 52–75.

81 Text in A. Hänggi and I. Pahl, *Prex Eucharistica* (Fribourg 1968), pp. 244–61, 269–75; ET in Jasper and Cuming, *Prayers of the Eucharist*, pp. 88–99. For other aspects of the later Liturgy of St James, see G. J. Cuming, 'The Litanies in the Liturgy of St. James', *EO* 3 (1986), pp. 175–80; 'The Missa Catechumenorum of the Liturgy of St James', *SL* 17 (1987), pp. 62–71; 'Further Studies in the Liturgy of St James', *SL* 18 (1988), pp. 161–9.

that its anaphora is the result of the amalgamation in the late fourth century of the eucharistic prayer known to the author of the *Mystagogical Catecheses* with an early form of the Anaphora of St Basil.[82] John Witvliet has examined his thesis, and suggested that the story may be a little more complicated than that, with the compiler(s) of the Anaphora of St James drawing on material from the Anaphora of St Basil at two successive stages of the latter's development.[83]

82 *The Anaphoras of St Basil and St James: An Investigation into their Common Origin* (OCA 240, 1992); summary in his *Fourth Century Anaphoral Construction Techniques.*
83 'The Anaphora of St James', in Bradshaw, ed., *Essays on Early Eastern Eucharistic Prayers*, pp. 153–72.

6

The Evolution of Eucharistic Rites

As we saw in Chapter 1, at least up to the middle of the twentieth century the majority of liturgical scholars believed that all extant ancient eucharistic rites were ultimately derived from a single apostolic archetype. But as more and more evidence for early practices emerged, they were forced to qualify their theories to some extent. Thus Louis Duchesne (1843–1922), in what became a standard work for first half of the twentieth century, *Origines du culte chrétien*,[1] maintained that, while there must have been variation in the details of early eucharistic rites and that the celebrant would have had some freedom in improvising the prayers, yet 'at the beginning the procedure was almost identical everywhere'. Even so, he had to admit that it was not long before 'local diversities had crept into the ritual. The uses of Rome, Antioch, and Alexandria must, in the third century, have departed widely from the primitive uniformity.'[2] His approach was echoed by, among others, Adrian Fortescue and F.-J. Moreau.[3] Later in the twentieth century, Josef Jungmann (1889–1975), in his monumental and highly influential work, *Missarum Sollemnia* (Vienna 1948), espoused a broadly similar position: 'the local diversity of the earliest liturgies . . . must be understood only in the sense that, for want of precise legislation, certain minutiae might change from place to place'.[4] However, he too acknowledged that three different types of eucharistic prayer must have developed 'quite early': one represented by the prayer in the *Apostolic Tradition*, one derived from the synagogue, and one 'in which the thoughts of the Christian acknowledgement of God were clothed in the phrases of hellenist philosophy'.[5]

Nevertheless, although belief in a single apostolic parent-liturgy was wide-

1 Paris 1899ff.; ET: *Christian Worship: Its Origins and Evolution* (London 1903ff.).
2 *Christian Worship*, p. 54.
3 Fortescue, *The Mass*, pp. 51–7, 76ff.; F.-J. Moreau, *Les liturgies eucharistiques: notes sur leur origine et leur développement* (Brussels 1924), pp. 31–2.
4 ET: *The Mass of the Roman Rite* (New York 1951) I, p. 22, n. 1. See also ibid., p. 32, n. 20.
5 ibid., I, p. 31. For the *Apostolic Tradition*, see above, pp. 80–3.

spread, it was not universal. There were those who held on dogmatic grounds that Christ had prescribed no particular form of eucharistic rite for the Church to follow,[6] and there were others who opposed the single-origin theory on textual grounds: later eucharistic rites showed such diversity among themselves that it was difficult to see any real evidence to suggest that they were descended from a single archetype.[7] Scholars of this school tended to conclude that in the apostolic age and for a considerable time afterwards liturgical forms were fluid.[8] R. M. Woolley (1877–1931) thought that in the evidence from before the year 200 'there are signs of three or perhaps four different uses, based on different ideas, and yet all expressing the fact that in the Eucharist the Church is doing as her Lord bids her'.[9]

The *Didache*

The publication in 1883 of the *Didache* with its unusual liturgical provisions presented something of a challenge to the majority view.[10] *Didache* 9 contains prayers for what it describes as a *eucharistia*: a short prayer of thanksgiving to be said over 'the cup' followed by a somewhat longer prayer to be said over the 'broken bread' (*klasma*); and *Didache* 10 a lengthy prayer of thanksgiving to be said 'after being filled', ending with the direction that the prophets were to be allowed to give thanks (*eucharistein*) as they wished. Chapter 14 also gave the brief instruction that on the Lord's Day its readers were to 'break bread and give thanks' (*eucharistesate*). Clearly, if Chapters 9 and 10 were describing an actual Eucharist, it was of a very different kind from those otherwise known from Christian antiquity.

Precisely because it did not harmonize with the rest of the evidence (and for some, because it did not include the supposedly consecratory narrative of institution), scholars committed to the single-origin theory therefore generally sought ways to exclude it from consideration. Hence Duchesne was willing to admit that the rite described was a Eucharist, but he still dismissed it as 'an anomaly; it might furnish some of the features which we meet with in later compositions, but it is on the whole outside the general line of

---

6 An early example of this approach can be seen in Charles Wheatly, *Rational Illustration upon the Book of Common Prayer* (London 1710), chapter 6, Introduction, sec. 2.

7 See, for example, William Palmer, *Origines Liturgicae* (Oxford 1832), pp. 5–6; Philip Freeman, *The Principles of Divine Service* II (Oxford 1862), pp. 380ff.; C. A. Swainson, *The Greek Liturgies* (Cambridge 1884), p. xxxii.

8 See, for example, J. H. Srawley, *The Early History of the Liturgy* (Cambridge 1913), pp. xiii–xiv; Armitage Robinson, 'Invocation in the Holy Eucharist', *Theology* 8 (1924), pp. 89–100.

9 *The Liturgy of the Primitive Church* (Cambridge 1910), pp. 45–6.

10 For this document, see above, pp. 77–8.

development both in respect of its ritual and style'.[11] Jungmann, on the other hand, simply stated that it was 'hardly likely' that the meal included 'the sacramental Eucharist'.[12] A more common response was to regard Chapters 9–10 as referring to an *agape* rather than a Eucharist as such. This was the position taken, for example, by both R. H. Connolly and Gregory Dix.[13] A variant hypothesis that became very popular was put forward by Theodor Zahn (1838–1933), who argued that *Didache* 10 constituted a prayer of preparation for the reception of the eucharistic elements following the meal in *Didache* 9.[14] While Eduard Von der Goltz[15] and Theodor Schermann[16] thought that the bread and wine would have been consecrated at a prior celebration of the Eucharist, others regarded *Didache* 10.6 as constituting the point of transition to a eucharistic celebration following the meal.[17] This theory was more recently revived by Willy Rordorf, who asserted that it was 'the most common view today'.[18] While it may still command support from New Testament and patristic scholars, the majority of liturgical scholars in the last 30 years have taken the opposite view, that it is a Eucharist, and modified their theories accordingly, as we shall see.[19]

One way of accommodating the *Didache* was to postulate the existence of two sorts of Eucharist in the primitive Christian community. Thus Paul Drews proposed that there had originally been a 'private' celebration – a daily religious meal which might be presided over by any member of the community, reflected in *Didache* 9–10 – alongside which there developed before the end of the first century a more official form of the celebration of the Eucharist, held only on Sundays and presided over by a bishop, which was

---

11 *Christian Worship*, pp. 52, 53–4.
12 *The Mass of the Roman Rite* I, p. 12.
13 Connolly, 'Agape and Eucharist in the Didache', *Downside Review* 55 (1937), pp. 477–89; Dix, *The Shape of the Liturgy*, pp. 48, n. 2, and 90ff. An earlier example is F. Kattenbusch, 'Messe', in *Realencyclopädie für protestantische Theologie und Kirche* 12 (Leipzig 1903), pp. 671ff.
14 *Forschungen zur Geschichte des neutestamentlichen Kanons und der altchristlichen Literatur* III (Erlangen 1884), pp. 293–8.
15 *Tischgebete und Abendsmahlsgebete in der altchristlichen und der griechischen Kirche* (Leipzig 1905).
16 *Die allgemeine Kirchenordnung, frühchristliche Liturgien und kirchliche Uberlieferung* (Paderborn 1915 = New York 1968) II, pp. 282ff.
17 For examples, see Niederwimmer, *The Didache*, pp. 142–3 (who also shares the view).
18 'The Didache', in *The Eucharist of the Early Christians* (New York 1978), pp. 1–23; see also idem, 'Die Mahlgebete in *Didache* Kap. 9–10. Ein neuer *status quaestionis*', *VC* 51 (1997) pp. 229–46.
19 In addition, Arthur Vööbus, *Liturgical Traditions in the Didache*, pp. 63–74, regarded it as a Eucharist; while both Erik Peterson, *Frühkirche, Judentum und Gnosis: Studien und Untersuchungen* (Rome 1959), pp. 168–71, and Johannes Betz, 'Die Eucharistie in der Didache', *ALW* 11 (1969) pp. 10–39 (ET: 'The Eucharist in the Didache' in Draper, ed., *The Didache in Modern Research*, pp. 244–75), advocated the idea that the prayers had originally been eucharistic, but the redactor had made them *agape* prayers.

referred to in *Didache* 14.[20] And we have seen in an earlier chapter the various theories advanced by Hans Lietzmann and others concerning a duality of eucharistic origins, which were occasioned in part by the need to account for *Didache* 9–10.[21] Edmund Bishop also hinted at a similar possibility, though without specifying exactly what he meant.[22]

Other scholars dealt with the problem by simply ignoring the *Didache* altogether and switching the search for the apostolic liturgy elsewhere. Thus William Lockton, in an article published in 1918, considered that it was from the eucharistic prayer of the 'Egyptian Church Order' (later identified as the *Apostolic Tradition*) that 'every known Eastern liturgy without a single exception is ultimately derived'. Since he found its language to be Johannine and Ephesine, he asked, 'Is it too much to conclude that it represents the liturgy of the church at Ephesus in the later apostolic days, and was in practically its present form the work of St. John – an idea which would explain what would otherwise be very difficult, its almost universal distribution?'[23] The same point of view, although in a much less extreme form, was later advanced by Walter Frere: 'This Hippolytean Anaphora fully corroborates the norm or canon which ... [lies] at the basis of the vast number of later Anaphoras'.[24]

What did come to be generally accepted in the twentieth century, however, was that the ultimate roots of the Christian Eucharist lay in Jewish liturgical practice. Already in the nineteenth century Gustav Bickell (1838–1906) had attempted to show that the first half of the eucharistic liturgy was ultimately derived from the Jewish Sabbath morning service, and the second half from the Passover meal.[25] His hypothesis was at first followed by a number of other scholars,[26] but an alternative theory about the second half of the rite proposed by Paul Drews eventually won greater support. He argued that its source was not the Passover, but the regular Jewish evening meal that inaugurated the Sabbath and festivals, the eucharistic prayer having evolved out of the grace said on such occasions.[27] The notion that the first half of the eucharistic rite

---

20 'Untersuchungen zur Didache', *ZNW* 5 (1904), pp. 74–9. His interpretation was followed by M. Goguel, *L'Eucharistie des origines à Justin Martyr* (Paris 1910), and Rudolf Knopf, *Die Lehre der zwölf Apostel* (Tübingen 1920).
21 See above, pp. 65–6.
22 In an appendix to R. H. Connolly, *The Liturgical Homilies of Narsai*, p. 145.
23 'The Eucharistic Prayer', *Church Quarterly Review* 86 (1918), pp. 309–13.
24 *The Anaphora* (London 1938), p. 48.
25 *Messe und Pascha* (Mainz 1872). His work was translated into English by W. F. Skene in *The Lord's Supper and the Paschal Ritual* (Edinburgh 1891), and popularized in Britain in a series of articles in the periodical *Dawn of Day* (1895–6) entitled 'The Passover and the Holy Communion by E. M.'
26 See, for example, Moreau, *Les liturgies eucharistiques*, pp. 40–1, 58ff.; J. B. Thibaut, *La Liturgie Romaine* (Paris 1924), pp. 11–37.
27 'Eucharistie', in *Realencyklopädie für protestantische Theologie und Kirche* 5 (Leipzig 1898), p. 563.

was descended from the synagogue service and the second half from the Jewish grace at meals came to be pursued in particular by a whole series of Anglican liturgical scholars – Woolley, Lockton, W. O. E. Oesterley (1866–1950), Frank Gavin (1890–1938), Felix Cirlot (1901–56),[28] and eventually Gregory Dix (1901–52).

Gregory Dix

Dix shared the standard scholarly consensus that the first half of the rite was 'in its Shape simply a continuation of the jewish synagogue service of our Lord's time', and declared that its 'original unchanging outline . . . everywhere' was:

1   Opening greeting by the officiant and reply of the church.
2   Lesson.
3   Psalmody.
4   Lesson (or Lessons, separated by Psalmody).
5   Sermon.
6   Dismissal of those who did not belong to the church.
7   Prayers.
8   Dismissal of the church.[29]

This conclusion involves two major presuppositions: first, that the contents of the first-century synagogue Sabbath service were fixed and are known to us; second, that the fact that these eight elements are consistently found in liturgical sources from the fourth century onwards means that they must have been in existence from early times. But all this is far from certain. We have indicated in earlier chapters how little is really known of first-century synagogue practice (and indeed that a Sabbath liturgy as such may not even have existed then), and that the relative uniformity of later Christian liturgical customs may be the result of a fourth-century movement towards standardization rather than the faithful adherence to a primitive norm.[30]

28 Woolley, *The Liturgy of the Primitive Church*, pp. 48–53; Lockton, 'The Eucharistic Prayer', pp. 309–10; Oesterley, *The Jewish Background of the Christian Liturgy*, esp. pp. 172–4, 187–91; Gavin, *The Jewish Antecedents of the Christian Sacraments*, pp. 59–97; Felix L. Cirlot, *The Early Eucharist* (London 1939), esp. pp. 61ff.

29 *The Shape of the Liturgy*, pp. 36, 38. Dix regarded the kiss of peace as constituting the beginning of the second half of the Eucharist (ibid., pp. 103–10), but it is attested rather as forming the conclusion of congregational prayer in several early sources. In any case, Dix was mistaken in thinking that it was something inherited from Judaism. See further, L. Edward Phillips, *The Ritual Kiss in Early Christian Worship* (A/GLS 36, 1996), pp. 5–25.

30 See above, pp. 6–8, 36–7.

Dix himself was prepared to admit that the opening greeting was only 'probably' an inheritance from the first days of Christianity. In fact, there is no hard evidence for its use either in early Judaism or in Christian worship before at least the third century, and then only in the dialogue preceding the eucharistic prayer in the *Apostolic Tradition* and not as an initial greeting.[31] Moreover, while Dix believed that the custom of singing psalms between the readings 'must have been familiar to our Lord and His apostles, since it was universal in the synagogues of their day',[32] we have already seen that more recent scholarship has cast serious doubts on this.[33] There is only one piece of firm evidence for the practice among Christians before the fourth century, from Tertullian in North Africa (*De anima* 9), and that is in relation to a Montanist service. As I have remarked elsewhere,[34] this is a very uncertain foundation upon which to make any assertion about the catholic practice of the day. While it *may* have been a common custom to begin the service with a greeting of some sort or to include a psalm between the readings in the second or third century, we do not *know* that this was so.[35] And since the 'dismissal of those who did not belong to the church' is a purely Christian development, what we are left with in terms of alleged similarities between the worship of the synagogue and that of the early Church is simply that both apparently had readings from their Scriptures, preaching, and prayers. These are not particularly striking parallels.[36]

Nor have we any reason to suppose that this development must have involved an 'unchanging outline . . . everywhere'. Our oldest source, the *First Apology* of Justin Martyr written at Rome in the middle of the second century, merely says that 'the records of the apostles or the writings of the prophets are read for as long as time allows. Then, when the reader has finished, the president in a discourse admonishes and exhorts [us] to imitate these good things. Then we all stand up together and offer prayers . . .' (67.3–5).[37] Apart from a few additional details provided by Tertullian and Cyprian in North Africa,[38] we have no other direct evidence for this half of

31 See van Unnik, '*Dominus vobiscum*: The Background of a Liturgical Formula', pp. 270–305.
32 *The Shape of the Liturgy*, p. 39.
33 See above, p. 38.
34 'The Liturgical Use and Abuse of Patristics', in Kenneth Stevenson, ed., *Liturgy Reshaped* (London 1982), p. 136.
35 On the origin of this psalm in the Eucharist, see the suggestion by James W. McKinnon, 'The Fourth-Century Origin of the Gradual', *Early Music History* 7 (1987), pp. 91–106 = idem, *The Temple, the Church Fathers and Early Western Chant*, IX.
36 See also, Thomas J. Talley, 'Word and Sacrament in the Primitive Eucharist', in Ephrem Carr *et al.*, eds, *Eulogêma: Studies in honor of Robert Taft, S.J.* (Studia Anselmiana 110; Rome 1993), pp. 497–510.
37 On the interpretation of Justin's testimony, see above, p. 99.
38 Even this evidence needs to be treated with some care. Just because, for example, Tertullian speaks of the church at Rome, like that of North Africa, as uniting 'the law and the prophets with the writings of evangelists and apostles, from which she drinks in her faith' (*De praescript.* 36), this does not *necessarily* mean that the liturgical ministry of the word always included four readings: Law, Prophets, Epistle, and Gospel.

the rite in the ante-Nicene period, and no justification at all for concluding that what these authors describe as practices familiar in their region were necessarily the universal customs of the time. Once again, this is not to deny that some of the features found in fourth-century sources may not also have existed in the third – or even the second – century, but only to say that we cannot know with any certainty which they were, nor when or where they were practised.

According to Dix, the shape of the second half of the rite was constituted by a modification of the 'seven-action scheme' of the Last Supper, when Jesus is said to have: taken bread; given thanks over it; broken it; distributed it; and after the meal to have taken a cup; given thanks over it; and handed it to his disciples.

> With absolute unanimity the liturgical tradition reproduces these seven actions as four: (1) The offertory; bread and wine are 'taken' and placed on the table together. (2) The prayer; the president gives thanks to God over bread and wine together. (3) The fraction; the bread is broken. (4) The communion; the bread and wine are distributed together.
>
> In that form and in that order these four actions constituted the absolutely invariable nucleus of every eucharistic rite known to us throughout antiquity from the Euphrates to Gaul.[39]

Dix believed that the transition from the sevenfold to the fourfold shape 'must have been very solidly established everywhere as the invariable practice before the first three gospels or 1 Corinthians began to circulate with authority . . . or some tendency would have shown itself somewhere to assimilate current practice to that recorded as original'; and he connected this development with the severance of the Eucharist from the context of a genuine meal.[40] Again, we have questioned earlier whether there ever was an early eucharistic pattern in which the bread and cup rituals were separated by a meal, and suggested that the later pattern, in which thanksgivings were offered over bread and cup together, or in immediate succession, may have been there from the first.[41]

In spite of his insistence that it was the overall shape of the rite rather than

39 *The Shape of the Liturgy*, p. 48. Dix has been criticized for his introduction of the term 'offertory' in relation to the first of the four actions and for confusing here the preparatory 'bringing up' of the bread and wine to the president with the president's taking of them into his hands in order to give thanks over them: see further Colin O. Buchanan, *The End of the Offertory* (GLS 14, 1978), esp. pp. 3ff. and 28ff.
40 *The Shape of the Liturgy*, pp. 49–50.
41 See above, pp. 70–2.

the specific contents of any prayer which constituted the common core of the Eucharist, Dix nevertheless thought that it was possible to reconstruct the general outline of the early eucharistic prayer. Like earlier Anglican scholars, he believed that it had evolved out of the standard Jewish grace after meals, the *Birkat ha-mazon*, the first two paragraphs of which 'in substantially their present form were in use in Palestine in our Lord's time'.[42] He also asserted that part of the opening dialogue to the eucharistic prayer found in the *Apostolic Tradition* ('Let us give thanks to the Lord; It is meet and right') was 'clearly derived' from the invitation preceding the Jewish grace, and concluded that its survival there 'would alone suffice to identify the christian eucharistic prayer with the jewish *berakah*'.[43] We have indicated earlier the uncertainty that exists as to whether the Jewish grace did have a standardized form in the first century, and also noted that what eventually came to be its regular opening dialogue is actually significantly different from the Christian version,[44] which suggests that, if indeed there was a Jewish prototype behind this part of the eucharistic prayer, then either Christian usage had modified it significantly or there were variant forms of the introductory dialogue in existence in first-century Judaism.

Dix thought that the second paragraph of the *Birkat ha-mazon* in particular, which contained a series of thanksgivings, offered parallels to the thanksgiving themes in Justin Martyr and the *Apostolic Tradition*. Moreover, since 'the same themes, in approximately the same order, are found too in other traditions', he judged that

> those who believe that there was an original authoritative outline of the prayer could make out (by a comparison of traditions) an overwhelmingly strong case for regarding this series of 'Thanksgivings' as the original opening of the prayer (after the preliminary 'Naming' of God), especially if its derivation from the second paragraph of the *berakah* be admitted.

He went on to insist, however, that 'the connection – if such there be – between the jewish and christian thanksgiving is one of ideas and form only, not of phrasing. The *berakah* has been entirely re-written in terms of the New Covenant.'[45]

Nevertheless, he was aware of difficulties in suggesting this line of evolution. One was the question of the 'thanksgiving for creation', which was

42 *The Shape of the Liturgy*, pp. 53–4.
43 ibid., p. 127.
44 See above, pp. 45–6.
45 *The Shape of the Liturgy*, pp. 216–17.

present in one form or another in the Christian prayers but had no parallel in the second paragraph of the Jewish prayer. While he thought that it could be argued that this was a later addition, resulting from 'disputes at Rome over the Gnostic doctrine that creation was in itself evil', he believed that 'these controversies might have led only to a change or increase of emphasis on this point in the Roman prayer, not to the insertion *de novo* of the idea itself into the scheme everywhere'. Another difficulty was that there were eucharistic prayers which did not have an opening sequence of thanksgivings as such, but he argued that in these cases it had been eliminated by the later prefixing of the preface and Sanctus.[46]

Since he was unable to detect any similar shared pattern in the second half of ancient eucharistic prayers, 'the inference is that any original material common to them all covered only the first half and the concluding doxology', and so he was inclined to conclude that these elements constituted the earliest shape of the eucharistic prayer, and that the second half was formed by subsequent expansion of the primitive nucleus during the second century.[47] This conclusion was, of course, strongly influenced by his methodological presupposition that only what was common could be regarded as primitive.

Sanctus and *Berakah*

The 1950s saw two further influential – though flawed – contributions to the debate about eucharistic origins. E. C. Ratcliff (1896–1967) expressed his conviction that the eucharistic prayer of the *Apostolic Tradition* had been extensively reworked so as to make it conform to the norms of a later age. In his view, the original version had been closer to the pattern to which he believed Justin Martyr and Irenaeus witnessed, and consisted of more extensive thanksgiving for the work of creation and redemption, the absence of any epiclesis, and the inclusion of a final thanksgiving for the admission of the worshippers to the worship of heaven, culminating in the singing of the Sanctus.[48] He developed a similar theory in relation to a eucharistic prayer outlined in the homilies of Narsai.[49] Though Ratcliff's drastic reconstruction drew support from a few other English scholars, notably A. H. Couratin and

---

46 ibid., pp. 217–19.
47 ibid., pp. 220–37.
48 'The Sanctus and the Pattern of the Early Anaphora', *JEH* 1 (1950), pp. 29–36, 125–34 = *Liturgical Studies*, pp. 18–40. Dix had already acknowledged that the invocation of the Spirit on the oblation was likely to have been a fourth-century interpolation: see *The Shape of the Liturgy*, p. 158, n. 1.
49 'A Note on the Anaphoras Described in the Liturgical Homilies of Narsai', in J. N. Birdsall and R. W. Thompson, eds, *Biblical and Patristic Studies in Memory of Robert Pierce Casey* (Freiburg/New York 1963), pp. 235–49 = *Liturgical Studies*, pp. 66–79.

G. A. Michell,[50] it did not ultimately succeed in convincing the majority. In particular, it seemed unlikely that the Sanctus had once formed the climax of the prayer and was then later omitted from it altogether, especially as W. C. van Unnik forcefully argued in 1951 that there was no clear evidence for any liturgical use of the Sanctus in early Christianity.[51]

Jean-Paul Audet (1918–93), in a paper read at the International Congress on the Four Gospels held at Oxford in 1957, attempted to examine the literary genre of the *berakah*, distinguishing what he called 'the spontaneous original benediction' (made up of two literary elements, the blessing itself and the motive for the blessing), and a supposed later development, 'the cultual benediction', which now had three elements:

> a) the 'benediction' proper, always rather short, more or less stereotyped in its forms, leaning towards the invitatory genre, an enthusiastic call to divine praise; b) a central element which I would call the anamnesis of the *mirabilia Dei*; this second element is nothing else than a more or less protracted development of the motive as it already existed in the original spontaneous 'benediction' . . . ; c) lastly, the return of the initial 'benediction' by way of *inclusio*, or doxology . . . [52]

This short article has been very frequently cited as authoritative,[53] but its analysis of Jewish liturgical forms is quite unsatisfactory. It was criticized in 1968 by Robert Ledogar for grouping the variety of first-century praise formulae into a single classification, and in particular for translating *eucharistein*

---

50 A. H. Couratin, 'The Sanctus and the Pattern of the Early Anaphora: A Note on the Roman Sanctus', *JEH* 2 (1951), pp. 19–23; idem, 'The Sacrifice of Praise', *Theology* 58 (1955), pp. 285–91; G. A. Michell, 'Firmilian and Eucharistic Consecration', *JTS* 5 (1954), pp. 215–20; idem, *Landmarks in Liturgy* (London 1961), pp. 84–9. Building upon the work of these scholars, W. E. Pitt, 'The Origin of the Anaphora of St Basil', *JEH* 12 (1961), pp. 1–13, argued that the original form of that anaphora had consisted of preface and Sanctus alone.

51 '*1 Clement* 34 and the Sanctus', *VC* 5 (1951), pp. 204–48. See also the critique of Ratcliff's theory in Bryan D. Spinks, 'A Note on the Anaphora Outlined in Narsai's Homily XXXII', *JTS* 31 (1980), pp. 82–93 = *Worship: Prayers from the East*, pp. 111–24; idem, 'The Cleansed Leper's Thankoffering before the Lord: Edward Craddock Ratcliff and the Pattern of the Early Anaphora', in Spinks, ed., *The Sacrifice of Praise*, pp. 161–78.

52 'Literary Forms and Contents of a Normal Eucharistia in the First Century', *Studia Evangelica* 1 (1959), pp. 643–62, here at pp. 646–7. An expanded version appeared as: 'Esquisse historique du genre littéraire de la "bénédiction" juive et de l'"eucharistie" chrétienne', *Revue biblique* 65 (1958), pp. 371–99; and he returned to the subject again in 'Genre littéraire et formes culturelles de l'Eucharistie "Nova et Vetera"', *EL* 80 (1966), pp. 353–85.

53 See, for example, the use made of it by Aidan Kavanagh, 'Thoughts on the Roman Anaphora', *Worship* 39 (1965), pp. 516ff.

as 'to bless',[54] and in 1975 by Thomas Talley for failing to examine the *berakot* in the context of the liturgical groupings in which they are found.[55] The article's shortcomings should be even more apparent in the light of our earlier survey of first-century Jewish liturgical forms.[56]

Louis Bouyer (1913–)

In his major work, *Eucharistie*, published in 1966,[57] Bouyer examined the use of the *berakah* in Judaism more broadly than Dix had done and considered not just the meal-prayers but also other liturgical formularies, with the aim of demonstrating the Jewish roots of the whole of the eucharistic prayer, and not merely of its first half. Like Dix, he subscribed to the view that Jewish prayer-forms were already fixed in the first century,[58] and pointed out that the grace after meals possessed a threefold structure: a blessing for creation, to which he gave the designation (D); a blessing for redemption (E); and a supplication for the eschatological fulfilment of the people of God (F). He compared this with a similar threefold pattern which he claimed to find in the synagogue liturgy in the two *berakot* before the *Shema* – which he designated as (A) and (B) – and the following *Tefillah* (C).[59]

Bouyer argued that the oldest forms of the eucharistic prayer followed the DEF pattern, but that because the eucharistic rite came to be situated immediately after a synagogue-type service, containing the ABC pattern, later prayers show a fusion between the two schemas, which he characterized as AD-BE-CF.[60] He believed that 'the first formulas of the Christian eucharist ... are but Jewish formulas applied by means of a few added words to a new content', and regarded the prayers of *Didache* 9–10 as reflecting a primitive Christian Eucharist.[61] The other examples which he cited as still following the DEF schema were the Anaphora of Addai and Mari (in its original version) and that of the *Apostolic Tradition*. While he regarded the first as 'an archaic formula of indisputable authenticity', he held the second to be 'the work of an archaizer' attempting to resurrect the liturgy of an earlier time before the Eucharist had become joined to a synagogue-type service.[62] The Alexandrian

54 *Acknowledgment: Praise-Verbs in the Early Greek Anaphora* (Rome 1968), p. 124. His own analysis, however, fails adequately to distinguish all the varieties of praise formulae.

55 See below, n. 71.

56 See above, pp. 43–4.

57 ET: *Eucharist* (Notre Dame 1968).

58 See especially, in the English edition, pp. 52–3.

59 ibid., pp. 88–9.

60 ibid., pp. 89–90.

61 ibid., p. 106, 115–19.

62 ibid., pp. 146–82. For Addai and Mari, see above, pp. 111–12.

Liturgy of St Mark, on the other hand, he believed showed evidence of a remodelling of the ABC schema combined with the older DEF pattern, because of the presence of the Sanctus and of extensive intercessions, both characteristic of the synagogue liturgy but not of the meal-prayers. He even claimed to detect a correspondence between the themes of the intercessions and those of the Jewish *Tefillah*.[63]

Bouyer's ingenious theory has the advantage of offering an explanation for a puzzling development in eucharistic prayers: the emergence of an element which was seemingly of Jewish origin – the Sanctus – but surprisingly late in the evolutionary process, when one might have imagined Jewish influence to have long since waned, and also in a context – in association with meal-prayers – in which it had apparently not belonged in the Jewish tradition. Yet his theory has not won much favour. It presupposes that one part of Christian worship, that derived from the synagogue, remained remarkably stable and conservative for the first few centuries of the Church's history (for which there is no firm evidence at all), while the eucharistic prayer itself evolved very freely, retaining only the broadest outline of its Jewish ancestor, until a sudden desire arose to try to fuse the two parts into a single whole. Though he may have been pointing in the right general direction in some respects, especially with regard to the later migration of the Sanctus from non-eucharistic to eucharistic use, Bouyer attempted to prove too much and with too great a precision.

Louis Ligier (1911–89)

Bouyer was also criticized by the Jesuit scholar Louis Ligier, the next major contributor to the debate, for being more attentive to similarities than to differences, and for analysing the material more in a theological fashion than from the literary and liturgical viewpoint. Ligier believed that the principal weakness of Bouyer's approach lay in the variety of extant Christian anaphoras, since this inevitably tempted one to select those documents which were most favourable to one's thesis. In particular, he questioned the use of the Liturgy of St Mark as a starting-point, since there was too much uncertainty about its primitive text to justify any firm reflection on it. He also criticized Bouyer's tendency to make a superficial abstraction of ideas and themes from Jewish *berakot* without due consideration of their literary form, place in the liturgical structure, and original context.[64] In this respect he made a passing reference to Joseph Heinemann's important work on Jewish prayer-

---

63 ibid., pp. 192–9. For the Liturgy of St Mark, see above, p. 106.
64 'Les origines de la prière eucharistique', *QLP* 53 (1972), pp. 181–202 = 'The Origins of the Eucharistic Prayer: From the Last Supper to the Eucharist', *SL* 9 (1973), pp. 161–85.

forms, apparently the first Christian liturgical scholar to do so.[65] He was also the first to recognize that the introductory dialogue of the Christian eucharistic prayer ('Let us give thanks . . .') was not exactly identical with the standard invitation preceding the Jewish grace after meals.[66]

The main advantage of his own approach, on the other hand, Ligier believed, was that he was initially concerned not to explain the origins of the whole eucharistic prayer, but instead to concentrate on the presence of the narrative of institution within it, which he compared to the festal narrative embolisms found in some Jewish prayers.[67] He admitted, however, that two main objections could be raised to his line of argument: one was the claim that there was really no need to have to explain the presence of the narrative, as it had always been there; the other was the more serious question as to the antiquity of the Jewish embolisms which he cited. He attempted to answer the latter objection by pointing out that the rabbinic authorities who were said to have discussed the use of festal embolisms in the grace after meals were all figures of the first to the fourth century CE, and hence 'it can be maintained that the practice of embolisms goes back to the first, or at latest the second century'. He also noted that, while the usual place for an embolism was in the thanksgiving section of the grace, it could also be inserted into the supplication, which was significant in view of the two different positions in which the narrative of institution was found in eucharistic prayers.[68]

Finally, he proceeded to combine his approach with that of Dix and Bouyer to suggest the process of evolution of the whole eucharistic prayer. Even though he had earlier acknowledged that in the first century 'the Jewish liturgy allowed the president to adapt and even to invent his own prayer',[69] he still believed that the tripartite *Birkat ha-mazon* constituted the origin of the eucharistic prayer, but that the first section devoted to creation had in Christian usage become integrated into the second and absorbed by it, as was confirmed by *Didache* 10. Then the narrative of institution, together with the anamnesis section ('having in remembrance . . .'), with which it formed a unity, had been inserted into the centre of the prayer, on the model of the Jewish embolisms. Finally the Sanctus, the commemoration of salvation-

---

65 'The Origins of the Eucharistic Prayer', p. 170. He had already made a similar reference in 'De la cène du Seigneur à l'Eucharistie', *Assemblées du Seigneur* 1 (1968) = 'From the Last Supper to the Eucharist', in L. C. Sheppard, ed., *The New Liturgy* (London 1970), p. 135, n. 83. For Heinemann, see above, pp. 27–9.
66 'From the Last Supper to the Eucharist', p. 144.
67 See his earlier articles: 'Autour du sacrifice eucharistique. Anaphores orientales et anamnèse juive de Kippur', *Nouvelle revue théologique* 82 (1960), pp. 40–55; 'Anaphores orientales et prières juives', *Proche-Orient chrétien* 13 (1963), pp. 3–20; 'De la cène de Jésus à l'anaphore de l'Eglise', *La Maison-Dieu* 87 (1966), pp. 7–49.
68 'The Origins of the Eucharistic Prayer', pp. 171–6.
69 'From the Last Supper to the Eucharist', p. 117, n. 15.

history following it in certain Eastern traditions, and extensive intercession were added to complete the classical shape. All of these latter elements appeared to Ligier to show Jewish influence, but he did not think it possible to offer a clear explanation for their appearance.[70]

What is most interesting about Ligier's work is why he thought it necessary to look for a *Jewish* precedent at all for the presence of the narrative of institution in eucharistic prayers. Why is it not sufficient to accept this as a purely *Christian* development, brought about entirely by the current needs of the worshipping community? It would seem that the only reasons for seeking a Jewish background for this phenomenon are that it is being assumed either that Jewish prayer-traditions continued to exercise a strong influence on the Gentile Church of the second and third centuries or even later (which receives little confirmation from other sources), or that the insertion of the narrative happened very early in the evolutionary process, when Jewish influence was still determinative. If the latter is the true motivating force, does one detect here the long shadow of the traditional Western theory of eucharistic consecration as being effected by the recitation of the words of institution? Are Ligier, and other scholars like him, subconsciously influenced by the need to show that the use of the narrative really does go back to very early times, even if not to the absolute beginnings of Christianity?

Thomas Talley (1924–)

Talley's first major contribution to the question of the origins of the eucharistic prayer came in a paper delivered at the 1975 congress of Societas Liturgica.[71] There he criticized Audet's treatment of the Jewish *berakah* and pointed out that the threefold pattern of the Jewish grace after meals was blessing–thanksgiving–supplication, and not blessing–anamnesis–doxology as visualized by Audet. He followed Louis Finkelstein in seeing parallels between the structure of the *Birkat ha-mazon* and the prayer in *Didache* 10, and in noting the inversion of the first two paragraphs from the traditional Jewish order (thanksgiving now preceding the reference to God's gift of food) and the substitution of a doxology for a concluding benediction. Observing that the common tendency among Christian scholars to identify *eulogein* with *eucharistein* and to equate both with the Hebrew verb *barak* had obscured recognition of the priority given to thanksgiving by the early Christians, he suggested that the link between the term *eucharistia* and *zebah*

---

70 'The Origins of the Eucharistic Prayer', pp. 179–85.
71 'The Eucharistic Prayer of the Ancient Church according to Recent Research: Results and Reflections', *SL* 11 (1976), pp. 138–58. This also appeared in a slightly expanded form as 'From Berakah to Eucharistia: A Reopening Question', *Worship* 50 (1976), pp. 115–37 = Kevin Seasoltz, ed., *Living Bread, Saving Cup* (Collegeville 1987), pp. 80–101.

todah, 'the sacrifice of praise', in the Old Testament alleged by Henri Cazelles,[72] might provide a clue to the reason why the *Didache* had made this inversion. He then went on to see in the anaphora of the *Apostolic Tradition* an emendation of the threefold blessing–thanksgiving–supplication pattern to a twofold thanksgiving–supplication pattern, and in the Anaphora of Addai and Mari the retention of the threefold structure (praise for creation, thanksgiving for redemption, supplication) 'though still giving a prominence to thanksgiving'. He also found this threefold pattern 'in such classic anaphoras as those of James and Basil'.

By 1982 Talley was able to say that the main outlines of the history of the eucharistic prayer 'seem much clearer now than they did a decade ago'.[73] He put forward the hypothesis that out of the tripartite pattern of the Jewish grace after meals the primitive Christian anaphora had for some reason focused on thanksgiving, even to the extent of subsuming to it the creation-theme of the first section of the Jewish prayer, and so given rise initially to a bipartite structure of thanksgiving–supplication; but that a prayer of praise of the Creator which culminated in the Sanctus had been adopted from the synagogue as an element in Christian morning prayer and was subsequently prefixed – possibly in the third century – to the anaphora itself 'especially in East Syria where Christianity remained most strongly Jewish', thus restoring the tripartite structure found in later eucharistic prayers. While the East Syrian pattern placed the institution narrative and anamnesis in the final section, further west (possibly in Antioch) it formed the conclusion of the thanksgiving, as it also did in the *Apostolic Tradition*. With regard to Alexandria, he took up Cuming's theory (which will be described more fully below), that since the theme of creation was already included in the original nucleus of the eucharistic prayer there, the Sanctus was not prefixed to the beginning but appended at the end, after the supplicatory section.

Talley took these ideas further in a 1984 article,[74] where he gave considerable attention to a recent book by Cesare Giraudo, which had categorized the Old Testament euchological form *todah* as having a bipartite structure of anamnesis–epiclesis, together with an embolism which served as the *locus theologicus* of the entire formula.[75] That this embolism might occur in either part

---

72 See above, p. 64, n. 85.
73 'The Eucharistic Prayer: Tradition and Development', in Stevenson, ed., *Liturgy Reshaped*, pp. 48–64.
74 'The Literary Structure of the Eucharistic Prayer', *Worship* 58 (1984), pp. 404–19.
75 *La struttura letteraria della preghiera eucaristica* (Rome 1981). See also idem, 'Irrepetibilita dell'evento fondatore e iterazione del rito: la mediazione del segno profetico. Prospettivae teologiiche sul rapporto tra Ultima cena, Morte-Risurrezione ed Eucaristia', *Rivista di teologia* 24 (1983), pp. 385–402; 'Le récit de l'institution dans la prière eucharistique a-t-il des précédents?', *Nouvelle revue théologique* 106 (1984), pp. 513–35. For the *todah*, see above, pp. 64–5.

of the formula was important to Giraudo, since his principal concern was with the narrative of institution, which some anaphoras put in the first half and some in the second. Giraudo's classification is much too rigid to encompass the diversity of its forms evidenced in Old Testament and Jewish sources, and one is led once again to wonder why a *Jewish* archetype was thought so important for the narrative of institution. Talley, however, while querying the division of eucharistic prayers into two fundamental types on this basis, and also the forcing of the Syrian anaphoras into a bipartite model when they really reflect a tripartite division, believed that Giraudo's work could throw valuable light on the early development of the eucharistic prayer by pointing to biblical roots for the bipartite structure.[76]

Talley also noted a reconstruction of the original version of the Anaphora of Addai and Mari by William Macomber[77] in which it was possible to see a bipartite form, beginning after the Sanctus, that might pre-date the opening section. This would make it similar in structure to the eucharistic prayer of the *Apostolic Tradition*, except for the position of the institution narrative, though Talley was forced to admit that 'there is no indication of a seam after Sanctus in Macomber's reconstructed text, and that text . . . may very well present to us the earliest appearance of Sanctus in a Christian anaphora', which he thought could belong to the third century.[78]

Bryan Spinks (1948–)

Bryan Spinks responded to Talley in an important and challenging article in 1985.[79] First, he questioned the assumption that Jesus used the *Birkat ha-mazon* at the Last Supper, and suggested that some Jewish groups may have used other forms of meal-grace, while Jesus himself may have radically transformed the Jewish prayers. Second, referring to a recent study by Allan Bouley on the improvization of eucharistic prayer in the early Church,[80] he suggested that 'the models upon which different celebrants drew as a basis for

---

76 In a revised version of this article, 'Sources and Structure of the Eucharistic Prayer', in T. J. Talley, *Worship: Reforming Tradition* (Washington, DC 1990), pp. 11–34, although still affirming the same conclusion, the author was more critical of Giraudo's work, as were J. Briend in a review in *La Maison-Dieu* 181 (1990), pp. 155–9, and Albert Gerhards, 'Enstehung und Entwicklung des Eucharistischen Hochgebets im Spiegel der neueren Forschung. Der Beitrag der Liturgiewissenschaft zur liturgischen Erneuerung', in Heinz and Rennings, eds, *Gratias Agamus*, p. 80.

77 See above, p. 111, n. 57.

78 'The Literary Structure of the Eucharistic Prayer', p. 415.

79 'Beware the Liturgical Horses! An English Interjection on Anaphoral Evolution', *Worship* 59 (1985), pp. 211–19.

80 *From Freedom to Formula: The Evolution of the Eucharistic Prayer from Oral Improvisation to Written Texts* (Washington, DC 1981).

their anaphoras may have varied widely'. Third, he questioned the 'absolute priority' which Talley gave to *eucharistein*, and pointed to the work of Robert Ledogar,[81] who had suggested that this verb may not have featured in the earliest form of the Anaphoras of St Basil, St John Chrysostom, or St Mark; Addai and Mari too displayed variants. He also questioned Talley's claim that the creation section of the Jewish grace was first dropped by Christians and then reintroduced: was it abandoned everywhere or retained in some anaphoras from their conception? Finally, he observed how extremely limited was the evidence upon which to construct any hypothesis concerning early anaphoral development: we have hardly any examples from the countless prayers which must have been used in the first three centuries, and concerning most of these – *Didache* 10, the *Apostolic Tradition*, Addai and Mari, and the Strasbourg Papyrus – there were still serious uncertainties.

Geoffrey Cuming (1917–1988)

In a paper delivered at the 1979 Oxford Patristic Conference, Cuming sketched out the way in which he thought that the Anaphora of St Mark had developed out of the primitive nucleus of thanksgiving for creation, offering, intercession, and doxology found in the Strasbourg Papyrus by adopting features from eucharistic prayers elsewhere. First the Sanctus was added, but appended here to the conclusion of the prayer, replacing the original doxology, and so creating the unusual pattern in which intercession preceded it. At the same time, or shortly afterwards, a first epiclesis was added after the Sanctus; then the narrative of institution and anamnesis section were appended; and finally a second epiclesis which reflected a more developed eucharistic doctrine and prayed for the change of the elements into the body and blood of Christ, the whole anaphora being rounded off with prayer for the fruits of communion.[82]

Cuming also indicated in the paper his further belief that something like the Strasbourg Papyrus was also the ancestor of the Jerusalem Anaphora of St James, that prayer too having been built up by similar additions, but with the Sanctus and everything that followed it in this case being inserted at the end of the preface and before the intercessions. As indicated in the previous chapter,[83] John Fenwick, one of his students, explored this suggestion further and argued that the Anaphoras of St Basil and St James (which show marked similarity to one another) each constituted an independent reworking in the

81 See above, n. 54.
82 'The Anaphora of St Mark: A Study in Development', *Le Muséon* 95 (1982), pp. 115–29 = Bradshaw, ed., *Essays on Early Eastern Eucharistic Prayers*, pp. 57–72.
83 Above, pp. 116–17.

late fourth century of a common original, which was most closely represented by the Egyptian version of the Anaphora of St Basil, and which in the case of the Anaphora of St James had been conflated with the anaphora reflected in the *Mystagogical Catecheses* attributed to Cyril of Jerusalem.[84]

In a short paper at the 1983 Patristic Conference, Cuming took the question of early anaphoras a stage further. Following a suggestion made by Ligier, he thought that behind the longer texts of later centuries were signs of very brief, simple, and ancient eucharistic prayers which had consisted of nothing but the expression of praise for what God had done. Even the Strasbourg Papyrus might once have lacked the elements of offering and intercession found in the extant version. Some of these prayers seem to have ended with a doxology, while others – the more developed ones – appear to have led into the Sanctus as their conclusion. The later versions of the prayers would thus have evolved by the addition of further elements to the end of the original nucleus, as in the case of the Anaphora of St Mark, or by inserting them at appropriate points within it; and this conclusion was supported by the clear evidence which existed in numerous cases of a general process of piecemeal construction by the insertion of prefabricated passages into pre-existent prayers.[85]

In a subsequent paper delivered at the 1987 conference, Cuming continued to pursue his theory, but also suggested that, while the *Birkat ha-mazon* was an important source for the Christian anaphora, biblical examples of prayer and other Jewish prayers also needed to be taken into account. He went on to point out that no extant anaphora exactly reproduced the tripartite structure or the content of the *Birkat ha-mazon*: some anaphoras had two thanksgivings and a supplication; others had originally a single thanksgiving later divided into two by the Sanctus (as he thought was the case with Addai and Mari); some had lengthy intercessions from the start; others probably had none, but acquired them later; others had only an epiclesis.[86]

The Sanctus Again, and the Epiclesis

Bryan Spinks, who had already made an important contribution to the study of the Jewish background of the Sanctus in 1980,[87] returned in 1991 to a more thorough exploration of its history. He rejected two common theories of its point of entry into Christian eucharistic prayers – the so-called 'Egyptian theory' strongly advocated by Gregory Dix and Georg Kretschmar, which

---

84 *The Anaphoras of St Basil and St James.*
85 'Four Very Early Anaphoras', *Worship* 58 (1984), pp. 168–72.
86 'The Shape of the Anaphora', pp. 333–45.
87 'The Jewish Sources for the Sanctus', *Heythrop Journal* 21 (1980), pp. 168–79.

maintained that its appearance can be traced to the writings of Origen in the early third century,[88] and the 'climax theory' developed by E. C. Ratcliff and discussed earlier in this chapter.[89] He pointed out that while in some early eucharistic prayers the Sanctus certainly appeared to be a later addition, in others it seemed instead to be an integral part of the original nucleus, which could perhaps best be explained by positing a variety of early models of eucharistic prayer rather than a single archetype. He thought that its use may have been derived by Christians from the synagogue liturgy, or from the Jewish tradition of *merkavah* mysticism, or perhaps directly from biblical phraseology without a Jewish intermediary. It might even be that it originated in a different way in different places, which could account for regional differences in its form.[90]

At the same time as Spinks, but independently of him, Robert Taft was also investigating the emergence of the Sanctus in early eucharistic prayers. Although in some respects reaching broadly similar conclusions, he argued that the Egyptian form of the Sanctus, which lacked the conclusion 'Blessed is he who comes in the name of the Lord', appeared more primitive than the Antiochene version, and furthermore only in Egypt was the Sanctus integral to the structure of all extant eucharistic prayers, with the possible exception of the Strasbourg Papyrus. He was inclined to conclude, therefore, that it had begun to be incorporated into Egyptian anaphoras probably in the second half of the third century. But, while the *idea* of adding the Sanctus to the eucharistic prayer had later spread from there to Antioch, the *form* adopted at Antioch was instead a Christianization of the version found in the Jewish synagogue.[91]

Although it has often been assumed that the Sanctus may have migrated to the eucharistic prayer from an earlier usage within patterns of daily prayer, Gabriele Winkler has put forward the interesting argument, based on liturgical material found in the apocryphal scriptures, that it first emerged in Christian usage within Syrian initiatory rites, along with the epiclesis, both forming part of prayers for the consecration of oil and water. In these sources, as in Egypt, it occurs without the concluding *Benedictus qui venit*. Building upon earlier work done by Sebastian Brock, she also argued that in the earliest Syrian tradition the customary form of the epiclesis was an imperative, 'Come', addressed to the Messiah and/or his Spirit, although she later

---

88 Dix, 'Primitive Consecration Prayers', *Theology* 37 (1938), pp. 261–83; idem, *The Shape of the Liturgy*, p. 165; Kretschmar, *Studien zur frühchristlichen Trinitätstheologie* (Tübingen 1956), pp. 180, 182.
89 See above, pp. 126–7.
90 *The Sanctus in the Eucharistic Prayer* (Cambridge 1991), pp. 1–121.
91 'The Interpolation of the Sanctus into the Anaphora: When and Where? A Review of the Dossier', *OCP* 57 (1991), pp. 281–308; 58 (1992), pp. 83–121.

modified this conclusion slightly to claim that the very oldest form was addressed to 'the name of the Messiah', by which the Spirit was always meant. Other forms of epiclesis addressed either to Christ, such as 'May the spirit of holiness come and dwell', or to the Father, such as 'May the Spirit come and rest and abide', or imperatives addressed to the Father, as in 'Send your Holy Spirit', or petitions to the Father to send the Spirit reflected later stages of development.[92] Studies by Robert Taft and Maxwell Johnson also suggested that, while in the Syrian tradition the Holy Spirit was most often seen as the agent of the action, in Greek circles it tended instead to be the Son as Logos: the only two apparently pre-fourth-century references to the Holy Spirit in Greek texts come from the *Didascalia Apostolorum*, which doubtless reflects the Syrian tradition, and from the *Apostolic Tradition*, the date and provenance of which are very uncertain.[93]

Attractive as Winkler's hypothesis is, it perhaps needs to be qualified in two respects. First, there may not have been a single original form of Syrian epiclesis. If we take into account the complete range of early Syrian epicletic material in the apocryphal scriptures, it includes invocations addressed not only to the Spirit and to Christ but also directly to the heavenly counterparts of earthly elements, as for example to 'waters from the living waters' in *Acts of Thomas* 52 and to oil (ibid. 121). This implies that a much wider primitive diversity of imperative epicleses only gradually narrowed down to those found in later liturgical texts. Second, the baptismal context may not have been the ultimate source of the Sanctus or the epiclesis, from which they then migrated to the eucharistic prayer. It is at least possible that these were already standard prayer units in the tradition, and in parallel developments then became part both of the consecration of baptismal oil and water and of eucharistic prayers at around the same time, rather than moving from the one to the other.

Enrico Mazza

After producing a series of articles relating to various aspects of early eucharistic prayers in the 1970s and 1980s, Enrico Mazza gathered them all up

92 'Nochmals zu den Anfängen der Epiklese und des Sanctus im Eucharistischen Hochgebet', *Theologische Quartalschrift* 174 (1994), pp. 214–31; 'Weitere Beobachtungen zur frühen Epiklese (den Doxologien und dem Sanctus). Über die Bedeutung der Apokryphen für die Erforschung der Entwicklung der Riten', *OC* 80 (1996), pp. 1–18. See also Sebastian Brock, 'The Epiklesis in the Antiochene Baptismal Ordines', in *Symposium Syriacum 1972* (OCA 197, 1974) , pp. 183–218; Maxwell E. Johnson, 'The Origins of the Anaphoral Sanctus and Epiclesis Revisited: The Contribution of Gabriele Winkler', in Hans-Jürgen Feulner *et al.*, eds, *Crossroad of Culture: Studies in Liturgy and Patristics in Honor of Gabriele Winkler* (OCA 260, 2000), pp. 405–42.
93 Taft, 'From Logos to Spirit: On the Early History of the Epiclesis', in Heinz and Rennings, eds, *Gratias Agamus*, pp. 489–502; Johnson, *The Prayers of Sarapion of Thmuis*, pp. 233–52.

into one volume, published in Italian in 1992 and translated into English in 1995 as *The Origins of the Eucharistic Prayer*. His fundamental thesis was to reassert the claim that the eucharistic prayer originally possessed a tripartite structure, comprising two thanksgivings and a petition, which can be seen to underlie all later texts.[94] This contention, however, is as difficult to sustain as is Giraudo's theory of an original bipartite structure, and Mazza has to exercise considerable ingenuity to force all ancient extant forms to fit within this particular framework.[95] Yet, although his overall thesis may be dubious, his work did contribute at least two important insights to the question of eucharistic origins.

First, he was prepared to widen the perspective somewhat further than many recent scholars when searching for the Jewish ancestry of Christian prayers. Although he did see some as emanating from the grace after meals, the *Birkat ha-mazon*, he traced the roots of the eucharistic prayer in *Apostolic Constitutions* 7 through its source in the *Didache* to the Jewish blessings over cup and bread earlier in the meal, and he proposed that the *Yotzer,* one of the blessings before the *Shema* in Jewish morning prayer, was the ultimate source of the eucharistic prayer of the Strasbourg Papyrus.[96]

Second, and more importantly, he questioned the normal assumption that early eucharistic prayers would always have been a single seamless whole, flowing from initial dialogue to final doxology. The Jewish tradition knew nothing of a composite blessing over bread and wine, but separate prayers were said over each item of food and drink, and even the *Birkat ha-mazon* is made up of three quite distinct units, as also is *Didache* 10. Moreover, in the account of the Eucharist given by Justin Martyr, while it seems clear that the bread and cup were brought at the same time to the one presiding, separate prayers could still have been used over each, and it may be significant that Justin says that the president 'sends up prayer*s* and thanksgiving*s* to the best of his ability'. The persistence of such separate prayers may also explain the otherwise enigmatic direction in the third-century Syrian *Didascalia Apostolorum* that if a visiting bishop does not wish to accept the invitation to

---

94 He also continued the argument in 'La structure des anaphores alexandrine et antiochienne', *Irénikon* 67 (1994), pp. 5–40.

95 See my critique of his efforts to regard the eucharistic prayer of the *Apostolic Tradition* as having developed out of the tripartite pattern of the *Birkat ha-mazon* via a form such as is found in *Didache* 10: 'The Evolution of Early Anaphoras', in Bradshaw, ed., *Essays on Early Eastern Eucharistic Prayers*, pp. 12–13.

96 Mazza, *Origins of the Eucharistic Prayer*, 12–61, 194–6. Both Jacob Vellian, 'The Anaphoral Structure of Addai and Mari compared to the Berakoth Preceding the Shema in the Synagogue Morning Service contained in Seder R. Amram Gaon', *Le Muséon* 85 (1972), pp. 201–23, and Bryan Spinks, 'The Original Form of the Anaphora of the Apostles', had earlier suggested that the Anaphora of Addai and Mari may also have its roots in these blessings preceding the *Shema*.

preside over the whole eucharistic offering, he should at least 'say the words over the cup'. Mazza even went on to suggest that the unusual form of the narrative of institution in the *Sacramentary of Sarapion* – where the account of the ritual of the bread is separated from that of the cup by the petition for the gathering of the Church drawn from *Didache* 9 – may be the remnant of an archaic structure of the eucharistic rite itself, in which a thanksgiving over the bread was followed by this short petitionary prayer and then by a thanks-giving over the cup.[97] In his detailed analysis of the *Sacramentary of Sarapion*, Maxwell Johnson has endorsed Mazza's theory in this regard.[98]

Conclusion

This chapter has revealed that there have been three main obstacles to real progress in the search for the origins and development of early Christian eucharistic practices. First, there has been a widespread belief that it is necessary to trace both the overall pattern of the rite and the prayer used in it back to a standard, fixed Jewish liturgy. Thus it has become a more or less universal assumption that the rite was formed by the combination of two originally distinct elements – a service of readings, preaching, and prayer owing its origin to the Jewish synagogue, and the stylized remains of a community meal which similarly had its roots in Jewish practice. While this conclusion may contain a considerable element of truth, it needs to be remembered that we do not know the precise form of either of these Jewish institutions nor how much they were subject to variation in the first century. Nor do we know exactly when that pattern became universal in Christian practice: what is described by Justin Martyr may not have been observed everywhere at that time. And we need to remember that the Jewish meal tradition itself seems to have included what might be called 'an informal ministry of the word', the custom of surrounding the repast with religious discourse and the singing of hymns.[99] Hence it is at least possible that the first half of the later eucharistic rites may be as much an outgrowth from that tradition as a legacy from the synagogue.

Similarly, the attempt to track Christian eucharistic prayers back to the Jewish grace after meals has been affected by the unwarranted assumption of the fixed character of the text and universal use of the *Birkat ha-mazon* in the first century, although the difficulties involved in this operation have to some extent been masked by the failure by most scholars to distinguish between *berakah* and *hodayah* forms of prayer and their tendency to look instead

97 Mazza, *Origins of the Eucharistic Prayer*, pp. 59–60, 221–30.
98 Johnson, *The Prayers of Sarapion of Thmuis*, pp. 224–6.
99 See Bradshaw, *Daily Prayer in the Early Church*, pp. 21–2, 44–5.

merely for a broad congruence of themes. With the notable exception of Bryan Spinks, even the few scholars who have acknowledged the possibility of fluidity in Jewish prayer-patterns in the first century have still tended to see the *Birkat ha-mazon* as the starting-point for comparison. Furthermore, no one in the last 50 years seems to have seriously questioned whether Jewish patterns of praying would have predominated at Gentile Christian eucharistic meals. Jewish prayer is certainly one significant influence on Christian eucharistic practices, but not the only one.

A second major obstacle to seeing the picture clearly has been the general desire (to which Spinks has again been one of the few exceptions) to situate all extant examples of later Christian rites and prayers within a single line of development. Not only has this involved an unnatural forcing of the facts to fit the theory (whether that has been in terms of trying to find a universal bipartite structure of eucharistic prayer, as in the case of Giraudo, or a tripartite shape of the prayer, as in the case of Mazza, or in some other way), but it has usually resulted in giving attention only to material which conforms, broadly speaking, to that which later became standard in the mainstream Christian tradition, and in excluding from consideration all indications of practices that have a very different appearance, especially if they are known to us solely from sources that appear to reflect less conventional forms of early Christianity, such as Syrian apocryphal texts. But to pick from the debris of history only those pieces that fit our preconceived pattern and to ignore those that do not is to distort the picture. It may well be true that it is the pieces which most closely resemble the later forms that are best able to explain where those particular shapes came from, but they do not necessarily tell the whole story, nor do they accurately portray the situation in the earlier centuries.

Thus, the assertion by Gregory Dix that the fourfold shape 'constituted the absolutely invariable nucleus of every eucharistic rite known to us throughout antiquity from the Euphrates to Gaul'[100] can only be sustained by very selective use of the evidence – by denying that primitive Christianity was as pluriform as modern New Testament and historical scholarship suggests and by ignoring meals that were patterned otherwise, for instance, with water instead of wine or with a cup–bread sequence or some other variation. Such a monolinear perspective also causes the misrepresentation of other pieces of evidence. So, for example, *Didache* 9–10 has either been forced to fit somehow into the single trajectory or rejected from consideration altogether on the grounds that what it describes is not a Eucharist, defended by the circular argument that it cannot be one because it does not fit into the pattern! Similarly, the anaphora of the *Apostolic Tradition* has tended to be

100 *The Shape of the Liturgy*, p. 48.

treated as an example of the stage of evolution that all eucharistic prayers had reached by the beginning of the third century, and consequently any 'more primitive' types (for example, those lacking a narrative of institution and anamnesis section) often regarded as belonging to the second century or even earlier. But to assume that eucharistic traditions everywhere were marching in step and exhibiting similar characteristics and changes at roughly the same time as each other seems unwarranted in itself, and to use this particular text as a fixed marker of progress even more so, in the light of the doubts that have been raised about its date and provenance. Moreover, like other parts of the *Apostolic Tradition*, it seems to have undergone expansion in the course of time, especially with regard to the institution narrative, anamnesis, and epiclesis.[101]

The third obstacle that may well have sent us on a wild-goose chase has been the unquestioned assumption that an early Christian community's eucharistic prayer, whether in written form or orally transmitted, would always have been a single, flowing, seamless whole. Here Mazza has done us a great service, by reminding us that Jewish prayers were composed of short, individual units which might be combined together, and that there are signs of similar patterns in early Christianity. If this was more widespread than we have previously supposed, and early eucharistic praying was at first commonly in the form of a number of small discrete prayer units, then the short acclamations and/or invocations which make up eucharistic-type prayers in the apocryphal scriptures (which we have usually ignored as peripheral to the tradition) may after all not be far from the forms practised by many Christians in at least the first two centuries;[102] and the various communal acclamations that we find emerging at a number of points within later Eastern eucharistic prayers, and especially 'Amen' in connection with the narrative of institution,[103] may not have been completely new creations at that time, but simply the continuation and development of a practice which we find as early as the *Didache*, of punctuating the eucharistic praying with an 'Amen' response at the end of each individual prayer unit rather than just at the conclusion of the whole oration. The fact that there is only limited documentary evidence of this in texts of the intervening period does not count against the theory, since those who wrote down those prayers would have felt

101 See Bradshaw, Johnson, and Phillips, *Apostolic Tradition: A Commentary*, on chapter 4; Paul F. Bradshaw, 'A Paschal Root to the Anaphora of the *Apostolic Tradition*? A Response to Enrico Mazza', *SP* 35 (2001), pp. 257–65.

102 See *Acts of John* 85, 109 (a series of short expressions of praise); *Acts of Thomas* 50 (a series of short epicleses), 133 (naming 'the name' over the bread); and 158 (a series of short petitions).

103 See Marc Schneiders, 'Acclamations in the Eucharistic Prayers', in Caspers and Schneiders, eds, *Omnes Circumstantes*, pp. 78–100.

no particular need to remind themselves in the text where they expected the congregation to make a response.

This suggests that the connecting links which can certainly be seen between parts of later prayers are unlikely to have belonged to their earliest stratum, but were more probably introduced at a later stage in order to smooth out the original roughness of the juxtaposition of individual prayer units, thus often resulting in the impression of a single continuous whole.[104] It also implies that the process of adding further components – such as the Sanctus and narrative of institution – that we encounter from the fourth century onwards does not represent an alien intrusion into what were formerly unified creations, but is simply continuing a tradition of combining smaller units together that was at the heart of the most ancient compositions.

In the light of all this, it should not be surprising to find a diversity of patterns of anaphoras in the evidence of early Christianity, originally formed more often by the combination of small pre-existent units as the situation required than by the creation of unitary compositions. While some of these may well have their roots in Jewish meal-prayers, others are likely to have arisen out of quite different contexts, both Jewish and Christian, especially once Christianity had moved away from its Jewish roots and perhaps no longer distinguished so sharply between euchological forms which had originally been used in relation to meals and those which had formerly been used for other purposes. Thus the ancestors of the later extant written texts probably included some that originally had a simple unitary structure of praise alone, or a sequence of short praise units; there would certainly have been those with a bipartite structure of praise and petition (anamnesis–epiclesis); while others appear to have had a tripartite structure, some along the lines of the Jewish grace with two acts of praise coupled with a single petitionary unit (as, for example, in *Didache* 10) and some with the sequence, praise–offering–petition/intercession, which underlies the Strasbourg Papyrus and apparently also the anaphora in the *Sacramentary of Sarapion*.

In most cases, these prayers probably circulated orally rather than in written form until perhaps the late third or even the early fourth century, when the relatively fluid prayer traditions began to crystallize, and more stable, written texts began to appear. The increasing use of written texts at that time would have been encouraged both by pressures towards doctrinal conformity and by the desire to provide more elevated and polished forms

104 For example, the phrase in the Strasbourg Papyrus which links the petitionary material in the second half of the prayer to what precedes it, 'over this sacrifice and offering we pray and beseech you', is unlikely to be as old as what follows it, 'remember your holy and only catholic Church', especially when we recall that the petitionary prayer in *Didache* 10 began simply: 'Remember, Lord, your Church'.

appropriate to the new surroundings created by the building of large city churches, in place of what had no doubt often been short and simple formulas used in the relatively domestic settings experienced by many – though not necessarily all – earlier Christian communities. Thus those responsible for leading prayer are likely then to have cast around for what they regarded as suitable models, regardless of whether these originally belonged to eucharistic or non-eucharistic contexts,[105] and to have discarded some traditional forms that did not meet contemporary needs. In other words, a measure of selective evolution took place. Then apparently began a phase of standardization and cross-fertilization, as Cuming and Fenwick have suggested, with units which had emerged in one tradition (like the Sanctus, the narrative of institution, the epiclesis, and extensive intercession) being copied and adapted into the anaphoras of other traditions – sometimes at the same point in the order, sometimes in a different place – to complete the classical shape of the eucharistic prayer with its different regional variants which characterized later Christian history.[106]

---

105 The Strasbourg Papyrus, for example, seems remarkably devoid of specific eucharistic reference for a prayer that has supposedly been used in a eucharistic context for several generations, and has much more the appearance of a prayer of blessing for creation and general intercession that might originally have belonged to a non-eucharistic context, perhaps that of daily prayer, and was only much later adapted for eucharistic use. See further Bradshaw, 'The Evolution of Early Anaphoras', pp. 5–7.

106 On all these later developments, see below, pp. 211–30.

7

Christian Initiation:
A Study in Diversity

Prior to the late 1950s scholars paid considerably less attention to the history of rites of initiation than to the evolution of eucharistic rites. One of the principal reasons for this imbalance was that baptism and confirmation had, in the practice of most churches, generally been relegated to the status of 'pastoral offices' – rites performed more or less in private for individuals as the need arose – rather than being seen as part of the mainstream of the liturgical life of the Church. Consequently, until the later phases of the twentieth-century liturgical movement began to have an impact on initiation rites, there was not the same sensitivity to their theological and liturgical shortcomings nor the same pressure for their revision as was felt in the case of the Eucharist, and it was these things that provided the main stimulus for historical research. What little exploration of the origins of Christian initiation there was mostly occurred among Anglicans, for whom the nature and purpose of confirmation, and to a lesser extent the question of baptismal regeneration, were hotly debated issues during the nineteenth and early twentieth centuries.[1]

We have seen that the dominant tendency in scholarly research into the origin and early history of the Eucharist has been to attempt to understand the evidence largely in terms of a monolinear development from a supposed single archetypal ritual structure in the first century. We can also observe a similar tendency towards a single harmonized picture in the study of early baptismal rites. Admittedly, in this instance the nature of the data has made this approach somewhat more difficult than in the case of the Eucharist, and scholars have gradually been forced to acknowledge some marked differences between the major geographical regions of Christian antiquity. Nevertheless, there has been a clear preference for emphasizing as far as

---

1 See, for example, Colin O. Buchanan, *Anglican Confirmation* (GLS 48, 1986); Peter J. Jagger, *Clouded Witness: Initiation in the Church of England in the Mid-Victorian Period, 1850–1875* (Allison Park, PA 1982).

possible the similarity of the various traditions to one another rather than their diversity, so as to encourage the impression that the early Church initiated new converts everywhere in basically the same manner, with only very minor differences of ceremonial being observable.

A major trait which can be observed in early-twentieth-century studies was the tendency to treat evidence from one geographical region as representing the custom of the Church universal, in the absence of any clear testimony to the contrary from other sources, and to regard later Western practice as the normative standard against which to measure any deviations. Thus, Duchesne, in his survey of early Christian worship, affirmed that 'the ceremonies of Christian initiation, such as they are described in authorities from the end of the second century onwards, consisted of three essential rites – Baptism, Confirmation, and First Communion'. This tripartite ritual was preceded by a catechumenate and 'ordinarily administered' at Easter 'from the earliest times'.[2] Similarly, Thomas Thompson, in a 1914 study of baptism and confirmation which was widely used as a standard textbook in the English-speaking world for the next few decades, stated that 'Easter was the general time for baptism throughout the Church, at least from the time of Tertullian.'[3]

More recent studies have often adopted a similar harmonizing approach: the chapter on baptism in Josef Jungmann's *The Early Liturgy to the Time of Gregory the Great* is a good example of the tendency,[4] and even Edward Yarnold's otherwise excellent edition of extracts from fourth-century baptismal homilies, *The Awe-Inspiring Rites of Initiation*, catalogues the elements of early initiatory rites in his introduction in such a way as to give the impression that a standardized shape existed. Indeed, he explicitly states that the initiation ceremonies 'conform in essentials to a common pattern' (p. 3; 2nd edn, p. 1). On the other hand, Georg Kretschmar and Robert Cabié present notable exceptions to this rule. In a survey of early initiatory practices presented at the 1977 congress of Societas Liturgica, Kretschmar observed that 'in the matter of the essential rites at the core of the action . . . the diversity is greater than we have hitherto been willing to admit' and so it was 'hard to go on speaking of a single original and therefore normative form of baptism'.[5] Cabié similarly stated that when the ritual of baptism did begin to become organized in the middle of the second century, 'it took appreciably different forms in the various churches and underwent many changes in the space of four centuries', adding a footnote that 'it must be kept in mind that each document provides information only for the place and time of its

2 *Christian Worship*, pp. 292–3.
3 *The Offices of Baptism and Confirmation* (Cambridge 1914), p. 19.
4 (Notre Dame 1959/London 1960), pp. 74–86.
5 'Recent Research on Christian Initiation', *SL* 12 (1977), pp. 93, 102 = Johnson, ed., *Living Water, Sealing Spirit*, pp. 21, 32.

origin. Even neighbouring churches might have different customs.'[6]

As we shall see as this chapter unfolds, the traditional claim that early initiation practice was fundamentally identical in every place cannot really be sustained. Not only are there differences in the ritual structures between East and West, but these external variations also reflect important divergences in their underlying theology. Furthermore, there are some significant variations within the supposed Eastern and Western patterns themselves which suggest that even this basic twofold division presents a false perspective. The major centres of early Christianity were not nearly so uniform in the elements of their baptismal practice as many others have tended to conclude, and a very different picture emerges if we observe not what appears to have been common but what was distinctive or unique about the baptismal process in each place.

Early Syrian Practice: Older Scholarship

In 1909 R. H. Connolly laid out the evidence for the apparent absence from early Syrian practice of any post-baptismal ceremonies which could be considered the equivalent of the Western rite of confirmation.[7] This observation created a major difficulty for attempts to paint a harmonized picture of initiation practice, and two principal solutions were offered to this inconvenient obstacle to the standard theory that confirmation was of apostolic origin and had been universally practised in the early Church. One solution was to assume that it must originally have been part of the Syrian tradition, but had simply fallen out of use in the course of time. This approach was adopted, for instance, by Joseph Ysebaert in 1962, who went even further and tried to find traces of the retention of confirmation in *Didascalia* 16, where the unction of female baptismal candidates involved a twofold action, first of the head by the bishop and then of the whole body by a woman deacon. Other scholars have understood both actions to be pre-baptismal and to have been divided from one another in the case of female candidates only for reasons of propriety. Ysebaert claimed, however, that the second action was meant to take place after the baptism, but that it had to be performed under cover of the water for the sake of modesty, and this eventually led to its fusion with the first and so to the complete disappearance of a post-baptismal anointing in the Syrian tradition.[8]

---

6 'L'Initiation chrétienne', in A. G. Martimort, ed., *L'Eglise en prière III: Les Sacrements* (new edn, Paris 1984), p. 27 = *The Church at Prayer III: The Sacraments* (Collegeville 1988), p. 17.

7 *The Liturgical Homilies of Narsai*, pp. xlii–xlix.

8 *Greek Baptismal Terminology* (Nijmegen 1962), pp. 312, 360f. For a critique of his position, see E. C. Whitaker, *Documents of the Baptismal Liturgy* (2nd edn, London 1970), pp. xix–xx. For the *Didascalia*, see above, pp. 78–80.

Ysebaert and Joseph Lécuyer also interpreted John Chrysostom's reference to the bishop's imposition of the hand on baptismal candidates during their immersion and his remark, 'It is at this moment that through the words and hands of the priest the Holy Spirit descends on you', as meaning that the two sacraments of baptism and confirmation were being conveyed at the same time.[9] This interpretation, however, has not been accepted by other scholars, especially in the light of other passages in Chrysostom's writings which suggest rather that the Holy Spirit was seen as being present in the whole baptismal action.[10]

The other solution to the problematic absence of any post-baptismal ceremonies in the early Syrian tradition was to regard the pre-baptismal anointing as really being the unction of confirmation. Although this involved conceding the existence of a difference in the structure of the rites, it was able to hold on to the notion of an identity of significance: even if both patterns were somewhat unalike in form, they still had the same meaning. This line was followed by a number of scholars, although with interesting variations between them.

Some, like Thompson[11] and Joseph Coppens (1896–1981),[12] simply noted the difference in structure without offering an explanation for it. Others, however, sought to salvage the idea that there had once been a single prototypical rite. F. E. Brightman (1856–1932) believed that the Syrians had 'apparently transformed what was elsewhere an exorcism into the unction of Confirmation',[13] while Gregory Dix on the other hand produced the ingenious theory that 'Confirmation was in the Apostolic age regularly administered *before* Baptism in water', that it consisted of the affusion of oil, and that it originated as the Christian equivalent of Jewish circumcision;[14] only later was it transferred to a post-baptismal position, although this move was made in the West much earlier than in the East.[15] T. W. Manson

9 Ysebaert, *Greek Baptismal Terminology*, pp. 376–9; Lécuyer, 'San Juan Crisostomo y la Confirmacion', *Orbis Catholica* (Barcelona 1958), pp. 365–87.
10 See, for example, Finn, *The Liturgy of Baptism in the Baptismal Instructions of St John Chrysostom*, p. 180.
11 *The Offices of Baptism and Confirmation*, p. 31.
12 *L'imposition des mains et les rites connexes dans la Nouveau Testament et dans l'église ancienne* (Paris 1925), p. 281.
13 'Terms of Communion and the Ministration of the Sacraments in Early Times', in H. B. Swete, ed., *Essays on the Early History of the Church and the Ministry* (London 1918), p. 350.
14 *'Confirmation or the Laying on of Hands'?* ('Theology' Occasional Papers, No. 5; London 1936), p. 1 (emphasis in original). The notion that confirmation was the Christian counterpart of Jewish circumcision had already been put forward by earlier scholars: see Lampe, *The Seal of the Spirit*, pp. 82ff.
15 ibid., pp. 5, 8–9, 15f. See also Dix, *The Theology of Confirmation in Relation to Baptism* (London 1946), p. 15.

(1890–1969) adopted a fundamentally similar position, citing Galatians 4.6f., Romans 8.15f., 1 Corinthians 12.3, 2 Corinthians 1.21f., and above all the reference in 1 John 5.7f. to 'the Spirit, the water, and the blood' as possible allusions to the sequence: unction, baptism, and communion.[16]

E. C. Ratcliff at first sought to play down the importance of the Syrian pattern: 'the remote and isolated church of Eastern Syria' was an exception to the 'all but universal' rule that confirmation followed baptism, and so 'we may reasonably assume that the Romano-Byzantine pattern of initiation represents the main stream of Christian tradition, as we can clearly trace it to the middle of the second century'.[17] Later, however, he acknowledged that 'the old Eastern liturgical usage of baptism differed markedly from that which obtained in the West'[18] and argued that the Syrian anointing was 'not a confirmation or completion, but an inception; the giving of the Spirit is the beginning of initiation'. On the basis of Acts 9.17–18; 10.44–8 and the passages from the Epistles cited by Manson, where the gift of the Spirit seems to precede baptism, it could be said that

> Syrian baptismal usage has its roots in the Apostolic past. In the earliest period, we may suppose, the laying-on of the bishop's hand was unaccompanied by anointing with oil. From teaching catechumens about the non-material unction of the Spirit, it is but a short step to representing that unction by an anointing with material oil. The next step is to explain the material anointing as the means of effecting spiritually that which it represents. The practice of consecrating the oil is the corollary of the explanation.[19]

While thus claiming an apostolic origin for the Syrian pattern, Ratcliff did not make it clear whether he thought that it was the sole shape that the rite then

---

16 'Entry into Membership of the Early Church', *JTS* 48 (1947), pp. 25–33; 'Baptism in the Church', *SJT* 2 (1949), p. 394. In 'Miscellanea Apocalyptica III', *JTS* 48 (1947), pp. 59–61, he also added to the list a Christian interpolation in the *Testament of Levi* 8.4–10, which spoke of unction, baptism, and communion, in that order. Cf., however, the criticism in Lampe, *The Seal of the Spirit*, pp. 87–91; R. E. Brown, *The Epistles of John* (Garden City, NY 1982/London 1983), pp. 583f. Manson's explanation was adopted by L. L. Mitchell, *Baptismal Anointing* (ACC 48; London 1966), pp. 49–50; and G. G. Willis, 'What was the Earliest Syrian Baptismal Tradition?', *Studia Evangelica* 6 (1973), pp. 651–4, argued that 1 Corinthians 10.1–2, mentioned by Dix, also lent support to that same sequence as being the original Christian practice.

17 'The Relation of Confirmation to Baptism in the Early Roman and Byzantine Liturgies', *Theology* 49 (1946), p. 264 = *Liturgical Studies*, p. 125.

18 'The Old Syrian Baptismal Tradition and its Resettlement under the Influence of Jerusalem in the Fourth Century', *Studies in Church History* 2 (1965), p. 19 = *Liturgical Studies*, p. 135.

19 ibid., p. 27 = p. 141.

took, with the Western structure a later development, or whether the two patterns had coexisted from the earliest days. However, he did draw attention to another important difference from the West in the ancient Syrian tradition: Christian baptism was understood here as a *mimesis* ('imitation') of the baptism of Christ. 'What was done at Jordan is done again, *mutatis mutandis*, in the water of the font. A man comes out of that water reborn as a "son" of God . . .' So it was that, in allusion to the concept of rebirth, some ancient commentators referred to the font as a womb, but never as a grave, and the idea of Romans 6.3–5 (of Christians being baptized into the death and resurrection of Christ) made no mark upon early Syrian thought about baptism.[20]

On the other hand, not all scholars were determined to find an equivalent of confirmation in the Syrian tradition. The central thesis of Geoffrey Lampe's book, *The Seal of the Spirit*, written as a response to Dix, was that in New Testament times the gift of the Spirit had been mediated through baptism in water alone and that all other external signs of the coming of the Spirit were later developments, probably derived from Gnostic circles.[21] Others, notably Benedict Green[22] and E. C. Whitaker[23] argued that the pre-baptismal unction in the Syrian documents was intended to be exorcistic, just as it was in Western sources. Thus, these scholars also managed to retain the notion of a single primitive pattern of Christian initiation, but they did so by claiming that any separate ceremony denoting the giving of the Spirit was a secondary development in all regional traditions.

Early Syrian Practice: the Contribution of Gabriele Winkler

In the late 1970s important contributions to the debate were made by Gabriele Winkler. In a paper delivered at the second Symposium of Syriac Studies in Paris in 1976 she built upon a suggestion made by Juan Mateos at the first Symposium in 1972[24] and argued forcefully that, in the light of early Armenian evidence, the original Syrian practice did not involve an anointing of the head and the whole body, as other scholars had concluded,[25] but an

---

20 ibid., p. 28 = p. 142.
21 He dealt with the Syrian evidence briefly on pp. 186–9.
22 'The Significance of the Pre-Baptismal Seal in St John Chrysostom', *SP* 6 (1962), pp. 84–90.
23 'Unction in the Syrian Baptismal Rite', *Church Quarterly Review* 162 (1961), pp. 176–87; *Documents of the Baptismal Liturgy*, pp. xv–xxii; *Sacramental Initiation Complete in Baptism* (GLS 1, 1975), pp. 24–9.
24 'Théologie du baptême dans la formulaire de Sévère d'Antioche', *Symposium Syriacum 1972* (OCA 197, 1974), pp. 135–61.
25 See, for example, A. F. J. Klijn, 'An Ancient Syriac Baptismal Liturgy in the Syriac Acts of John', *NovT* 6 (1963) pp. 216–28.

anointing of the head alone, to which was gradually added the anointing of the body.[26]

In a further study she examined the significance of the Syrian pre-baptismal anointing and concluded that in the oldest stratum of the tradition

> Christian baptism is shaped after Christ's baptism in the Jordan. As Jesus had received the anointing through the divine presence in the appearance of a dove, and was invested as the Messiah, so in Christian baptism every candidate is anointed and, in connection with this anointing, the gift of the Spirit is conferred. Therefore the main theme of this prebaptismal anointing is the entry into the eschatological kingship of the Messiah, being in the true sense of the word assimilated to the Messiah-King through this anointing.[27]

This, she believed, explained why at first oil was poured only over the head (this was the custom at the anointing of the kings of Israel), why the coming of the Spirit was associated with it (the Spirit of the Lord came over the newly nominated king), and why the anointing and not the immersion in water was regarded as the central feature of baptism in the early Syrian sources (this was the only visible gesture for what was held to be the central event at Christ's baptism – his revelation as the Messiah-King through the descent of the Spirit).

Winkler argued that the subsequent introduction of the anointing of the whole body led to the loss of its original impact and its reinterpretation as a healing ritual. The conferring of the Spirit together with the themes of royal and sacerdotal anointing were transferred to the immersion itself in the thought of John Chrysostom, and to a newly introduced post-baptismal unction at Jerusalem in the late fourth century, while the older pre-baptismal anointing was now understood as a cathartic and apotropaic ritual. This change also led to the reinterpretation of the rite as a death/resurrection event, in accordance with Romans 6, rather than a birth event, in accordance with John 3. She therefore held that the two descriptions of baptism in the third-century *Acts of Thomas* which mention the anointing of both the head and the whole body, focus on the theme of healing, and include a prayer for the blessing of the oil (Chapters 121 and 157), constitute a later stratum than the two descriptions which refer to an anointing of the head alone, associate this with the Messiah, and have no blessing prayer (Chapters 27 and 132).[28]

---

26 'The History of the Syriac Prebaptismal Anointing in the Light of the Earliest Armenian Sources', *Symposium Syriacum 1976* (OCA 205, 1978), pp. 317–24. See also her more detailed study, *Das armenische Initiationsrituale* (OCA 217, 1982).

27 'The Original Meaning of the Prebaptismal Anointing and its Implications', *Worship* 52 (1978), p. 36 = Johnson, ed., *Living Water, Sealing Spirit*, p. 71.

28 ibid., pp. 36–45 = 71–81. For the *Acts of Thomas*, see above, p. 107.

Similarly, while A. F. J. Klijn attempted to harmonize the two somewhat different accounts of baptisms in the *Syriac Acts of John*,[29] Winkler again saw in them two chronological stages of the development of the baptismal ritual.[30] In one case – the baptism of Tyrannus, the procurator of Ephesus, together with a multitude of people – there is a confession of faith by the crowd after the consecration of the oil and the water, and a confession of faith by Tyrannus after he is anointed. In the other case, the baptism of the priests of Artemis, again with a crowd of people, a renunciation of Artemis and a confession of faith by the multitude precede the consecration of the oil and the water, and the confession of faith by the priests follows the consecration but precedes the anointing.

Further Signs of Syrian Diversity

Winkler's interpretation of the early Syrian evidence has subsequently become widely accepted.[31] But it may need some adjustment. While it is obviously true that Christ's baptism in the Jordan was increasingly adopted as the model for Syrian baptismal practice, it is unlikely to have been its original archetype, or we would have expected to see the immersion followed by the anointing, rather than the other way round. And her division of the evidence for anointing practices into two chronological strata is not the only possible explanation for the differences between the descriptions in the *Acts of Thomas*. Ruth Meyers, for example, suggested that the discrepancies might be capable of reconciliation, pointing out that explicit mention of the anointing of the body occurs only when female candidates are involved, who require the services of a woman to perform the action. In the other instances the body-anointing may have been presumed without necessitating detailed description, the oil perhaps simply being allowed to run down from the head over the body, or the apostle Thomas himself performing the service.[32]

On the other hand, these differences in the descriptions could instead be pointers to a diversity of baptismal practices within the Syrian region that was only slowly disappearing. Even in fourth-century Syrian sources, where a greater element of standardization is apparent, there are still signs of some continuing variation in baptismal rituals which seem to be remnants of an older diversity. Thus Theodore of Mopsuestia records the strange practice of

---

29 'An Ancient Syriac Baptismal Liturgy in the Syriac Acts of John', pp. 220–1. For the *Syriac Acts of John*, see above, p. 107.

30 *Das armenische Initiationsrituale*, pp. 154–6.

31 It has, for example, been supported by Baby Varghese, *Les onctions baptismales dans la tradition Syrienne* (Louvain 1989), p. 12.

32 'The Structure of the Syrian Baptismal Rite', in Bradshaw, ed., *Essays in Early Eastern Initiation*, p. 41.

the sponsor spreading a linen stole on the candidate's head after the anointing of the head and before the anointing of the body, which he says symbolizes 'the freedom to which you are called, for this is the decoration that free men wear both indoors and out'.[33] This certainly looks like the survival of an ancient local custom, as it is not mentioned in other early Syrian literature, although it is found in a different position – as a post-baptismal ceremony – in later Syrian rites and in some Western sources.[34] Coupled with other evidence, it supports the possibility that Syria once knew an inherently multi-farious practice, which only later became more uniform.[35]

First, it is not certain that unction of any sort was everywhere always part of the Syrian baptismal ritual. There is a further description of a baptism in the *Acts of Thomas*, that of a woman possessed by a devil (Chapters 49–50), where no mention is made in the Syriac version of anything other than the use of water, and also the similar evidence of the *Didache*, which we shall consider in a moment. On the other hand, the importance accorded to the anointing in relation to water baptism in sources which know of both, together with its position before rather than after the immersion in water, as one might have expected from the pattern of Jesus' own baptism, imply that it should not be dismissed simply as a later elaboration of an original practice of water baptism alone. There are also two instances in the Greek version of the *Acts of Thomas* where there is no reference to water: Chapter 27, which speaks only of oil, and Chapter 49, which does not mention either water or oil explicitly but only the 'seal' (*sphragis*, translated as *rushma*, 'sign', in the Syriac). While it has sometimes been argued that this word here refers to the rite as a whole, both anointing and immersion, its more usual import in the Syrian tradition is simply to denote anointing.[36] We have already suggested in an earlier chapter the possibility that water baptism and anointing with oil may once have been two alternative ways in which different primitive Christian communities might have initiated new converts before they became combined in a single composite ritual, and indeed that a third pattern of initi-ation may have involved merely the washing of the feet rather than of the

33 *Baptismal Homily* 14.19.
34 See Sebastian P. Brock, 'Some Early Syriac Baptismal Commentaries', *OCP* 46 (1980), p. 45; Yarnold, *The Awe-Inspiring Rites of Initiation*, p. 30; 2nd edn, p. 33.
35 On the other hand, Winkler's interpretation of *Didascalia* 9 ('The Original Meaning of the Prebaptismal Anointing and its Implications', p. 36 = Johnson, ed., *Living Water, Sealing Spirit*, p. 71) followed by Johnson (*The Rites of Initiation*, p. 42) as meaning that the baptismal rite included the bishop quoting Psalm 2.7 ('You are my son . . . ') while he performed the pre-baptismal hand-laying/anointing, does seem to suggest an improba-ble variation, and the text is more likely the author's interpretation of the act rather than a description of actual practice.
36 See further, Susan E. Myers, 'Initiation by Anointing in Early Syriac-Speaking Chris-tianity', *SL* 31 (2001), pp. 150–70.

whole body.[37] The early Syrian evidence would seem to lend support to that hypothesis, and the tendency towards the duplication of the pre-baptismal anointing found in later Syrian rites, with both an anointing of the forehead alone and a quite separate anointing of the head and whole body,[38] also seems to strengthen the view that, rather than the one being an – admittedly quite natural – evolution out of the other, as oil from the head flowed down upon the person's body, the two were at one time parallel traditions with somewhat different meanings, which in some places coalesced into a single anointing of head and body together quite early and in others remained distinct for much longer.

Baptism in the *Didache*

The *Didache* seems to be of Syrian provenance and yet appears to make no reference to a baptismal anointing. While some scholars have simply ignored this inconvenient exception to the general practice, others have put forward a variety of suggestions to explain the omission. Some have argued that the document was a manual for presbyters and deacons and so made no reference to liturgical actions which only the bishop could perform[39] – over-looking the fact that the *Didache* does not seem to presuppose a threefold ministerial order. Dix thought that it was meant for the laity, and therefore only gave instructions about the rites which they could perform in the absence of the clergy[40] – overlooking the fact that the East has always been much more hesitant than the West about accepting lay administration of baptism. Others have regarded the prayer over 'perfume' or 'ointment' found in the Coptic fragment of the *Didache* and in *Apostolic Constitutions* 7 as being part of the original text, and so as indicating the existence of a baptismal anointing after all.[41] Theophile Lefort, however, argued that the Coptic word was not a translation of the Greek word *myron* nor was the prayer baptismal in context,[42] and Stephen Gero suggested, somewhat

---

37 See above, p. 61.
38 See Sebastian P. Brock, 'The Transition to a Post-Baptismal Anointing in the Antioch-ene Rite', in Spinks, ed., *The Sacrifice of Praise*, pp. 215–25, esp. 215–19; idem, 'Studies in the Early History of the Syrian Orthodox Baptismal Liturgy', *JTS* 23 (1972), pp. 16–64, esp. 24–40.
39 A. T. Wirgman, *The Doctrine of Confirmation* (London/New York 1897), p. 102; Charles Gore, *The Church and the Ministry* (London 1919), p. 252.
40 '"The Seal" in the Second Century', *Theology* 51 (1948), p. 9. Fisher, *Confirmation Then and Now*, p. 3, was uncertain whether the omission was to be explained along these lines or not, but he rejected the suggestion that the baptism rite was 'complete in itself and regarded by its author as such'.
41 See the critical evaluation of earlier literature in Vööbus, *Liturgical Traditions in the Didache*, pp. 41–60; Niederwimmer, *The Didache*, pp. 165–7.
42 *Les Pères apostoliques en copte* (Louvain 1952), pp. 32–4.

improbably, that the original word was incense, which was burned at the meal described in *Didache* 9–10, and this was then changed to *myron* by the tradition lying behind *Apostolic Constitutions* 7, which arose in Egypt and was unfamiliar with the practice of burning incense.[43]

Alastair Logan has recently returned to this Coptic text as the chief support for his argument that one of the varied patterns that existed in early Syrian practice did include a post-baptismal anointing. He is led in this direction in large part by his interpretation of certain ambiguous texts circulating in Gnostic circles as reflecting a post-baptismal anointing there,[44] and his supposition that they would have been paralleled by a similar practice in more orthodox Christian groups. While this cannot be ruled out as a possibility, he is unable to adduce any convincing testimony that it actually was so.[45] All the other evidence he cites is of an anointing in connection with baptism, but says nothing about its position within the rite,[46] and even if the Coptic version is a witness to the original form of the *Didache* (which seems unlikely, for it is difficult to explain why it should have dropped out of the Greek) and does refer after all to *myron*, neither the text itself nor its location in the document (after the meal-prayer of Chapter 10) hints at any baptismal association, let alone a post-baptismal one.

Characteristics of Syrian Practice

Whatever may be the case with regard to the original diversity within early Syrian baptismal practice, the extant sources reveal that the baptismal practices of this region prior to the fourth century differed from the picture which was traditionally painted of the classic pattern of Christian initiation in more ways than just the absence of a post-baptismal anointing. There is no sign of Easter having been the preferred baptismal season, and indeed one would not expect such a connection to have been made in a tradition which did not understand initiation in terms of Romans 6. There is also nothing to imply the existence of a lengthy, highly formalized and strongly ritualized catechumenate, such as we find in the fourth-century evidence, and no mention of pre-baptismal exorcisms nor even of sponsors.[47]

---

43 'The So-called Ointment Prayer in the Coptic Version of the Didache: A Re-evaluation', *Harvard Theological Review* 70 (1977), pp. 67–84.
44 'The Mystery of the Five Seals: Gnostic Initiation Reconsidered', *VC* 51 (1997), pp. 188–206.
45 See below, p. 228, however, for one later factor that might support his case.
46 'Post-Baptismal Chrismation in Syria: The Evidence of Ignatius, the "Didache" and "Apostolic Constitutions"', *JTS* 49 (1998), pp. 92–108.
47 Cf. the unconvincing efforts of Dujarier, *A History of the Catechumenate*, pp. 64–8, to read a formal catechumenate into the earlier Syrian evidence, culminating in the assertion that 'in the third century, catechumenal practice had the same structure everywhere'.

Moreover, there are strong indications that initiation was once a two-stage affair in Syria, with the profession of faith, in the form of an act of adherence to Christ or *syntaxis* (preceded by a renunciation of evil, if that is not a later development), taking place on a separate occasion prior to the baptism. The primary evidence for this is provided by the *Didascalia*, which says that 'when the heathen desire and promise to repent, saying "We believe", we receive them into the congregation so that they may hear the word, but do not receive them into communion until they receive the seal and are fully initiated'.[48] Although it may seem odd that converts were expected to express their faith before they were allowed to hear the word, what is meant here seems to be that, while there would have been some preliminary moral instruction designed to bring them to repentance and faith, certain teachings were reserved until after they had made their expression of commitment to Christ. Although this final pre-baptismal instruction disappeared in the fourth century, being replaced by post-baptismal mystagogy, its earlier existence is confirmed both by evidence of comparable practice in other regions, as we shall see later, and by the persistence of at least a short interval between the profession of faith and the baptism itself in later Syrian rites: John Chrysostom in the late fourth century and the Constantinopolitan rite of the fifth century seem to have known the renunciation and act of adherence as still occurring on the day before the baptism, and the testimony of Theodore of Mopsuestia and of the later Syrian baptismal *ordines* show traces of this two-part structure, even though both parts now take place on the same occasion.[49]

If we can generalize at all from the early Syrian evidence – and that may be a dangerous thing to do – we could perhaps describe the dominant understanding and practice of initiation here as being primarily *Christological* in character, i.e., centred around the person of Christ. The act of commitment to Christ seems to mark the key turning-point in the process, and what followed articulated ritually the positive consequences of that act: the candidate was then admitted to receive Christ's teaching, and subsequently anointed with the priestly/kingly/messianic spirit which Christ had received at his baptism in the Jordan, and born to new life through immersion in the water in the name of the Lord Jesus Christ (later changed to Father, Son and Holy Spirit).[50]

48 II.39; cited from Brock and Vasey, *The Liturgical Portions of the Didascalia*, p. 12.
49 For further details, see Meyers, 'The Structure of the Syrian Baptismal Rite', pp. 31, 34-8.
50 Not only does New Testament evidence suggest that the earliest baptisms were in the name of Jesus, but Vööbus claimed (*Liturgical Traditions in the Didache*, pp. 35-9) that the Trinitarian baptismal formula in the *Didache* was a later addition to the text, the original being simply 'in the name of the Lord', as it is still in the reference to baptism in *Didache* 9.5. See also the apocryphal *Acts of Paul*, where Thecla immerses herself, saying 'In the name of Jesus Christ I baptize myself . . . ' (Elliott, ed., *The Apocryphal New Testament*, p. 370) and *The Shepherd of Hermas*, *Vis.* 3.7.3 (below, p. 164). Willy Rordorf, 'Baptism according to the Didache', in Draper, ed., *The Didache in Modern Research*, p. 217, takes a similar view to Vööbus, but Niederwimmer (*The Didache*, pp. 127–8, nn. 8, 11, and 12) disagrees.

North Africa

From the references to the rites of Christian initiation which are scattered throughout the writings of Tertullian,[51] the order of the baptismal rite known to him around 200 CE seems to have been:

- Preparation, 'with frequent prayers, fastings, bendings of the knee, and all-night vigils, along with the confession of all their sins' (*De baptismo* 20);
- Prayer over the water, invoking the Holy Spirit to sanctify it (*De baptismo* 4);
- Renunciation of the devil (*De corona* 3.2; *De spectaculis* 4);
- Threefold interrogation about the Christian faith 'in the words of its rule' and triple immersion (*De corona* 3.2; see also *Ad martyras* 3.1; *Adversus Praxean* 26; *De baptismo* 6; *De praescriptione haereticorum* 36; *De pudicitia* 9.16; *De spectaculis* 4);
- Anointing (*De baptismo* 7.1; *De resurrectione carnis* 8.3); (?Sign of the cross;)[52]
- Imposition of hands (*De baptismo* 8.1; *De resurrectione carnis* 8.3);
- Prayer for the first time with other Christians (*De baptismo* 20.5);
- Eucharist, including the partaking of milk and honey (*De corona* 3.2).

Because Tertullian nowhere gives a systematic account of the whole rite, it is of course quite possible that there were other elements which he does not mention. Yet, from what he does say, it is clear that, as in Syrian practice, there was here both immersion and an anointing with oil associated with the priestly anointing of Aaron and with Christ's anointing with the Spirit; but unlike Syria, the anointing followed rather than preceded the immersion. There are also various other features which are not mentioned in the early Syrian sources.

1 The invocation of the Holy Spirit over the water probably arose as a result of the change in the location of baptisms, from rivers and lakes to indoor baths or tanks. While the naturally flowing character of the former could enable them to be seen as 'living' and already imbued with God's spirit, the water in the latter would have seemed deficient in this respect, and

---

51 ET of many in Whitaker, *Documents of the Baptismal Liturgy*, pp. 7–13. See also Alistair Stewart-Sykes, 'Manumission and Baptism in Tertullian's Africa: A Search for the Origin of Confirmation', *SL* 31 (2001), pp. 129–49, esp. 130–40.

52 Stewart-Sykes, 'Manumission and Baptism in Tertullian's Africa', pp. 136–7, queries the usual interpretation of a statement in *De resurrectione carnis* 8.3 ('flesh is signed that the soul may be protected') that the rite included a consignation, and suggests that it should rather be understood as a more general reference to baptism as a sign.

hence in need of investing with the power that it lacked.[53] We have already seen this happening with regard to the oil used in Syria, and it is interesting to note that Tertullian describes the power bestowed on the sanctified water as that of healing, as is also the case with the Syrian oil.

2 The renunciation is said by Tertullian to be a repetition of one made earlier, perhaps a week before,[54] 'under the hand of the bishop'. Could this interval perhaps have been the equivalent of the time of 'restricted' instruction after the profession of faith found in the *Didascalia*?

3 The threefold interrogatory profession of faith in conjunction with the immersion is a clear difference from Syrian practice, where a profession of faith in Jesus Christ was made some time before the baptism and the immersion accompanied instead by the indicative formula. This interrogatory procedure seems to have been shaped by the mode of making a contract under Roman law,[55] and dipping three times rather than just once would be a natural development from the Trinitarian form of the questions.

4 The post-baptismal imposition of hands is also different from Syrian practice. Most scholars assume that it included a prayer for the Holy Spirit on the basis of Tertullian's description of it as being 'in benediction, inviting and welcoming the Holy Spirit', but it is at least possible that Tertullian was here offering his personal interpretation of a gesture that might at this time have been performed in silence or only with words of blessing. Alistair Stewart-Sykes has recently offered the interesting suggestion that this ceremony may have been derived from the manner of the manumission of slaves in the ancient world.[56]

5 The giving of milk and honey at first communion of the newly baptized is another variation from Syrian practice, otherwise attested only in later Roman, Egyptian, and Ethiopic sources.[57]

Perhaps surprisingly, Cyprian in his extensive writings 50 years later, adds very little to Tertullian's testimony. There is mention in one of his letters (*Ep.* 69.15–16) of exorcism before baptism, but that appears to be for individuals who were seen as violently possessed rather than a general requirement for all candidates, although the latter seems to have been the practice in at least

---

53 See J. D. C. Fisher, 'The Consecration of Water in the Early Rites of Baptism', *SP* 2 (1957), pp. 41–6.
54 See Stewart-Sykes, 'Manumission and Baptism in Tertullian's Africa', p. 132–3.
55 See J. Albert Harrill, 'The Influence of Roman Contract Law on Early Baptismal Formulae (Tertullian, *Ad Martyras* 3)', *SP* 35 (2001), pp. 275–82.
56 'Manumission and Baptism in Tertullian's Africa', pp. 141–9.
57 See further, Johannes Betz, 'Die Eucharistie als Milch in frühchristlicher Sicht', *ZKTh* 106 (1984), pp. 1–25, 169–85; Edward Kilmartin, 'The Baptismal Cups Revisited', in Carr *et al.*, eds, *Eulogêma*, pp. 249–67.

some parts of the region, because at a council in Carthage in 256 (over which Cyprian presided) one bishop apparently refers to it.[58] In another letter (*Ep.* 70.1) Cyprian refers to the sanctification of the baptismal water by the bishop, and later (70.2) to the consecration of the oil (apparently taking place during a celebration of the Eucharist and not within the baptismal rite itself[59]) and to the post-baptismal anointing, and he also quotes part of the text of the baptismal interrogation, indicating that it included reference to belief in ever-lasting life and the forgiveness of sins. Finally, in a further letter (*Ep.* 73.9) he indicates that the newly baptized are presented to bishops so that 'by our prayer and the imposition of our hands they receive the Holy Spirit and are made perfect with the Lord's seal'. He thus maintains Tertullian's interpreta-tion of this gesture and appears to confirm that it was at least by his time accompanied by a specific prayer for the Holy Spirit. Scholars have commonly interpreted 'seal' (*signaculum*) here and elsewhere in Cyprian's writing as meaning the making of the sign of the cross in addition to the impo-sition of hands, but perhaps the phrase may not be intended quite so literally as a distinct ritual act.

It is often claimed that the general pattern of initiation in North Africa is very similar to that found in the later Roman rite. Nevertheless, there is some divergence in detail, the most notable differences being in the post-baptismal ceremonies. In North Africa there was seemingly only one anointing followed by the imposition of hands and prayer associated with the gift of the Spirit, whereas the later Roman tradition knew a double post-baptismal anointing, the first performed by presbyters and the second performed by the bishop and associated with the gift of the Spirit.

Other scholars have often sought to minimize the importance of these vari-ations. J. D. C. Fisher, for example, claimed that, although the gift of the Spirit was associated by Tertullian with the imposition of hands and not the unction, 'yet unction cannot be altogether separated from the giving of the Spirit, because it conferred membership in Christ, the anointed one, so called because he was anointed with the Holy Spirit'.[60] Ysebaert argued that the imposition of the hand, the anointing, and the sign of the cross should not be regarded as three distinct rites but rather as one 'complicated liturgical act',[61] and Whitaker accepted his argument, claiming that its effect was to show that

---

58 See Henry Ansgar Kelly, *The Devil at Baptism* (Ithaca, NY 1985), pp. 109–10.
59 On the obscurities of this passage, see G. W. Clarke, *The Letters of St Cyprian* 4 (New York 1989), pp. 201–3.
60 *Confirmation Then and Now*, p. 31.
61 *Greek Baptismal Terminology*, pp. 264, 289f.

if some later documents appear to connect the gift of the Spirit with the imposition of the hand, and others with the anointing; if some areas have retained only one post-baptismal anointing although others have two; then the differences arise from differences in the way in which one basic and complex act has developed and disintegrated in response to circumstances.[62]

But such a conclusion remains to be proved. It is at least equally possible that the differences arise both from the independent addition of further ritual elements to an originally simple nucleus and also from quite distinct interpretations of their significance.

Not only is Tertullian our first clear witness to a post- rather than pre-baptismal anointing, but as we noted in an earlier chapter, he is also the first to speak of Easter as the preferred occasion for baptism. This suggests that there is here a quite different concept from what we encountered in Syria. In contrast to the primarily *Christological* character that we ascribed to initiation there, this might perhaps best be described as *soteriological*: the biblical model is not Christ's baptism in the Jordan, but rather his passage from death to resurrection, in which the candidates symbolically share, by renouncing this evil world and going down into the water, where they proclaim their faith and come up again to be anointed as God's priestly people, to receive the Spirit of the risen Lord through the imposition of hands, and to enter the promised land by feeding on milk and honey. It is interesting to note that it is about this time in Alexandria that we encounter for the very first time the interpretation of the celebration of Easter as the passage of Christ from death to life rather than as the commemoration of his saving death.[63] Did the change in understanding of the feast bring about the connection of baptism to Easter, or was it the other way around?

Rome: Justin Martyr

The evidence for early Roman initiation practice is extremely limited. We do not possess a set of fourth-century baptismal catecheses from this city such as we have from other places, and of the few sources from earlier centuries, the two principal ones – the *First Apology* of Justin Martyr and the *Apostolic Tradition* attributed to Hippolytus – both present problems of interpretation.

Justin's account is very brief and mentions only that converts 'are taught to pray and ask God, while fasting, for the forgiveness of their sins, and we pray and fast with them'. They are then 'led by us to a place where there is water,

62 *Documents of the Baptismal Liturgy*, p. xv.
63 See below, p. 181.

and they are reborn' in the name of the Father, Son, and Holy Spirit. Justin also describes this process as being 'washed' and 'enlightened', and says that 'after we have thus washed him that is persuaded and declares his assent, we lead him to those who are called brethren, where they are assembled', and common prayer, the exchange of a kiss, and the celebration of the Eucharist follow.[64]

Many things are not said here. There is, for example, no reference to a formally structured catechumenate, though some pre-baptismal instruction is certainly implied; no indication whether baptism was restricted to a specific season of the year; no allusion to exorcism or other pre-baptismal ceremonies; no roles assigned to specific ministers; and above all, no mention of either a post-baptismal prayer with imposition of hands and/or anointing such as is found at Rome in later centuries. Of course, it can be argued that since Justin is writing a brief account for pagans, we should not expect a very detailed description of every element of Christian practice, and there may well have been many other ceremonies which were included in the rite besides those explicitly mentioned. This argument certainly has some force. But the fact remains that we do not actually know which of the features of later Roman practice, or of other Western centres of Christianity, were being practised at Rome in the middle of the second century and which were not. If we assume a large measure of continuity and stability, then we can argue that it is likely that what we find later at Rome and elsewhere was already known to Justin. But this assumption precisely begs the questions at issue: how alike was the practice of the early centres of Christianity, and how much change and development took place in the first three or four centuries?

Attempts were made by a few scholars of a previous generation, most notably the Anglo-Catholics Dix, Ratcliff, Arthur Couratin, and L. S. Thornton,[65] to read between the lines of Justin's writings and discern there evidence to suggest that Justin did not regard water baptism as the whole of Christian initiation, but also knew of a post-baptismal rite which effected the gift of the Holy Spirit. Their arguments however, failed to convince many,[66] and most modern scholars accept that such a rite cannot be read out of Justin's testimony. Some would want to say that Justin is only giving a generic account of Christian baptismal practices and not a specific description of what

---

64 *I Apol.* 61, 65. ET in Whitaker, *Documents of the Baptismal Liturgy*, p. 2.
65 Dix, '"The Seal" in the Second Century', pp. 7–12; Ratcliff, 'Justin Martyr and Confirmation', *Theology* 51 (1948), pp. 133–9 = *Liturgical Studies*, pp. 110–17; A. H. Couratin, 'Justin Martyr and Confirmation – A Note', *Theology* 55 (1952), pp. 458–60; L. S. Thornton, *Confirmation: Its Place in the Baptismal Mystery* (London 1954), pp. 34–51. See also Fisher, *Confirmation Then and Now*, pp. 11–21.
66 See, for example, Lampe, *The Seal of the Spirit*, pp. 109–11; Mitchell, *Baptismal Anointing*, pp. 13–15.

was done at Rome. Whether that is so or not, it is indisputable that his description has much in common with what we have encountered in early Syrian practice in general and more especially the witness of the *Didache*, with its lack of mention of specific ministers and of ceremonies other than immersion in water.[67]

Rome: The *Apostolic Tradition*

Reference has been made earlier in this book to the difficulties inherent in interpreting the evidence supplied by the *Apostolic Tradition*: it is very doubtful whether the document really originates from Rome, and even if it does, whether it represents what was the actual practice of the period and not merely the unfulfilled desires of some individual or group.[68] But while there are signs throughout the work that the text as we now have it has been subjected to a measure of later revision, this is particularly the case with regard to the baptismal material.

As early as 1968 Jean-Paul Bouhot had suggested that this section of the document was in reality a fusion of two distinct rites, the older of which was Roman in origin and the later of which was African and had been interpolated into the former in the second half of the third century.[69] Robert Cabié later examined Bouhot's claim and, while judging his precision as to their provenance to be premature, cautiously accepted the idea that there were indeed two sources here,[70] a conclusion with which Victor Saxer also concurred.[71] My own examination of the text suggests that there are no fewer than three strata – an original core; additional episcopal directives; and detailed instructions concerning the roles of presbyters and deacons.[72] The original core is not unlike the description given by Justin Martyr, and may well date from the same period.[73] It describes the action in impersonal or passive terms without defining any specific ministerial roles (e.g., 'Let prayer be made over the water'). At the outset of the process candidates were required to have sponsors who could attest to their capacity to 'hear the

---

67 See Johnson, *The Rites of Christian Initiation*, pp. 37–41.

68 See above, pp. 80–3.

69 *La confirmation, sacrement de la communion ecclésiale* (Lyons 1968), pp. 38–45.

70 'L'ordo de l'Initiation chrétienne dans la "Tradition apostolique" d'Hippolyte de Rome', in *Mens concordet voci, pour Mgr A. G. Martimort* (Paris 1983), pp. 543–58.

71 *Les rites de l'initiation chrétienne du IIe au VIe siècle* (Spoleto 1988), pp. 118–19.

72 For further details, see Paul F. Bradshaw, 'Redating the *Apostolic Tradition*: Some Preliminary Steps', in John Baldovin and Nathan Mitchell, eds, *Rule of Prayer, Rule of Faith: Essays in Honor of Aidan Kavanagh, OSB* (Collegeville 1996), pp. 10–15; Bradshaw, Johnson, and Phillips, *The Apostolic Tradition: A Commentary*, on chapters 20–1.

73 For a reconstruction of the text, see Johnson, *The Rites of Initiation*, pp. 80–1.

word' and also to their way of life; and at the end their lives were again examined to determine whether they were ready for baptism. If so, 'then let them hear the gospel'. The baptism itself was preceded by two days of fasting, and began at cockcrow after a night-long vigil. Prayer was made over the water, and the candidates removed their clothes and went down into it. There they answered three brief questions about their belief in Father, Son, and Holy Spirit, and were immersed after each response. Then they came up out of the water, put on their clothes, and joined the congregation for prayer and the Eucharist.

It is unlikely that the reference to daily exorcism in the final period of preparation before baptism was part of the original core, as it is only in the fourth century that *daily* pre-baptismal exorcism is otherwise attested, and then only at Antioch and Jerusalem and not in the West.[74] The oblique statement, 'Let them hear the gospel', is reminiscent of the pattern we saw in the Syrian *Didascalia*, where certain teachings were reserved until the final period before baptism, though here it follows an examination of the lifestyle of the candidates rather than their confession of faith in Jesus Christ. The reference to a Trinitarian credal interrogation at the moment of immersion, on the other hand, rather than that prior confession and an indicative formula said in the water ('I baptize you . . . '), reveals a clear difference from Syrian practice, but is consistent with North African practice and with what appears to be similar credal language about the immersion in Justin's description: 'in the name of the Father and Lord God of all things, and of our Saviour Jesus Christ . . . who was crucified under Pontius Pilate, and in the name of the Holy Spirit, which through the prophets foretold all things concerning Jesus' (*I Apol.* 61). Of course, it is also possible that Justin was here merely drawing on credal language that was familiar to him in order to refer to a Trinitarian indicative formula.

To this core rite in the *Apostolic Tradition* were added at some later date references to specific ceremonies performed by a bishop, including exorcism on the day before the baptism, the blessing of baptismal oils, and a post-baptismal imposition of hands with prayer followed by an anointing of the head using a Trinitarian formula and a kiss. A third stage came when detailed instructions about the role of presbyters and deacons in baptism (which also included a presbyteral post-baptismal anointing in the name of Jesus Christ) were interpolated into this composite text. Subsequent translators and copyists also inserted expanded credal material and other variations, making the text very obscure.[75] The character of the presbyteral and diaconal instruc-

---

74 Cyril of Jerusalem, *Baptismal Catechesis* 1.5–6; Egeria, *Peregrinatio* 46.1; John Chrysostom, *Baptismal Homily* 2.12.

75 See Bradshaw, Johnson, and Phillips, *The Apostolic Tradition: A Commentary*, on chapter 21.

tions points to a date in the early fourth century rather than the third for their addition. When the episcopal material was added is harder to define, but it was almost certainly sometime in the third century, perhaps later rather than earlier. Yet there is no reason to surmise that any of these subsequent additions necessarily reflect Roman practice, even if the core rite does. As indicated above, it has been thought that at least the third stratum may possibly be from North Africa. Above all, we must not suppose that the final version constitutes a rite which was ever used as it stands: it appears to be an artificial blending of material from different liturgical traditions.

Nevertheless, for earlier scholars who did think that this was an actual rite used at Rome in the third century, it was the post-baptismal ceremonies which generated most debate, chiefly with regard to whether or not they envisaged a bestowal of the Holy Spirit at this point. The Latin version of the bishop's prayer reads: 'Lord God, who has made them worthy to receive the remission of sins through the laver of regeneration of the Holy Spirit, send upon them your grace . . .' In the oriental-language versions, however, the phrase 'of the Holy Spirit' is replaced by 'make them worthy to be filled with the Holy Spirit and . . .' While both Dix and Botte in their editions of the text generally preferred to adopt the readings of the Latin version as coming closest to the original, at this point both of them opted for oriental-language versions as reflecting the original. Dix described the Latin version as 'corrupt' here, and Botte thought that a line had accidentally fallen out of the Latin text.[76] Their conclusions have been accepted by a number of scholars,[77] but others have argued that there is nothing to suggest that the Latin is not the original reading and the oriental versions a subsequent amplification made under the influence of later doctrine which associated the gift of the Spirit with the episcopal post-baptismal anointing rather than with the immersion.[78]

Anthony Gelston suggested a third possibility, and proposed a more complicated textual history for the prayer. The Greek original, he believed, had referred to the Holy Spirit twice, once in relation to the immersion (as in the Latin text) and again in connection with the petition for grace (as in the oriental texts), and the Latin and oriental versions had each accidentally left out one of the references but retained the other.[79] Geoffrey Cuming responded to this by pointing out the improbability of two different errors being made by two copyists in the same place, and put forward a fourth hypothesis, that there was no reference at all to the Holy Spirit in the original,

76 Dix, *The Treatise on the Apostolic Tradition*, p. 38; Botte, *La Tradition apostolique*, p. 53, n. 1.
77 See, for example, Fisher, *Confirmation Then and Now*, pp. 52–5.
78 See, for example, Lampe, *The Seal of the Spirit*, pp. 136–42. But cf. p. xvii of the second edition where he appears to retract his argument.
79 'A Note on the Text of the *Apostolic Tradition* of Hippolytus', *JTS* 39 (1988), pp. 112–17.

and that it was later added to the subordinate clause by the textual tradition underlying the Latin and to the main clause in the oriental tradition.[80]

Aidan Kavanagh has taken an even more novel approach to the passage. While accepting the Latin text as authentic, he argued that the whole liturgical unit of prayer and the imposition of hands was originally nothing more than a *missa* – the dismissal ceremony with which ancient liturgical services generally seem to have ended – and it was only later reinterpreted as an invocation of the Holy Spirit.[81] Paul Turner has questioned this conclusion and suggested that the rite should be viewed instead as 'the first public gesture of ratification for the bishop and the faithful who did not witness the pouring of water';[82] in other words, as an act of welcome into the assembly, since the rest of the baptismal rites had taken place in private because of the nudity of the candidates.

Rome: Other Evidence

Apart from Justin's testimony (if that really is specifically about Rome) and the core text of the *Apostolic Tradition* (if that too is of Roman origin and not, for example, from North Africa), there are very few references to baptismal practice in Roman sources of the first three centuries. The mid-second-century *Shepherd of Hermas* speaks of some who have heard the word and wish to be baptized into the name of the Lord, but change their minds and go again after their evil lusts (*Vis.* 3.7.3). This indicates not only that there were already catechumens who did not persevere but also that it was still customary to think of baptism as 'into the name of the Lord', even if a Trinitarian form had already come into the actual practice, just as Justin too can speak of baptism as being in the name of Christ (*Dial.* 39.2) while knowing a Trinitarian interrogation or formula. Elsewhere the *Shepherd* speaks of the baptismal water, and not an anointing, as 'the seal' (*Sim.* 9.16.4). And in the early third century the real Hippolytus in his *Commentary on Daniel* 13.15 speaks of baptism as then regularly (though not necessarily exclusively) taking place at Easter and as including a post-baptismal anointing which was associated with the Holy Spirit.

More than this we cannot say with certainty. It is possible to look at the much later Roman evidence and conjecture what its earlier form might have been, but that is to assume a high degree of continuity and does not allow for

---

80 'The Post-baptismal Prayer in the *Apostolic Tradition*: Further Considerations', *JTS* 39 (1988), pp. 117–19.

81 *Confirmation: Origins and Reform* (New York 1988), esp. pp. 41–52.

82 'The Origins of Confirmation: An Analysis of Aidan Kavanagh's Hypothesis', *Worship* 65 (1991), pp. 320–38, here at p. 336 = Johnson, ed., *Living Water, Sealing Spirit*, pp. 238–58, here at p. 255.

significant changes having taken place in the late fourth and early fifth centuries, which was certainly the case in other major centres of early Christianity. So, for example, while the later Roman rite certainly knew of a double post-baptismal anointing, which was – as far as we know – unparalleled elsewhere, we cannot state that it was an ancient practice and not something that emerged in the post-Constantinian evolution. For after Hippolytus, our next sources of evidence for Rome come from the late fourth century onwards, when an episcopal post-baptismal laying-on of hands and/or second anointing are certainly mentioned, but appear to be innovations designed to enhance the prestige of the episcopal office, which were only accepted slowly, rather than traditional features of the rite.[83]

Northern Italy

We also lack evidence for the pattern(s) of Christian initiation practised in northern Italy prior to the late fourth century. Our principal witness, Ambrose of Milan, takes great pains in his writings to stress the close similarity between liturgical practices in his city and those at Rome, but of course this is no guarantee of the antiquity in either tradition of elements which are not corroborated by some older source. On the other hand, there are at least some variations from both the North African and Roman patterns as we know them. Since we may safely assume that Ambrose would not have introduced new customs which differed from those that were then found at Rome nor have willingly perpetuated any existing customs which were at variance with Roman ones if he had been able easily to abolish them, this suggests that any practices he describes which are peculiar to northern Italy must have been long established there to resist his Romanizing tendency. The major elements of the baptismal process are as follows:

1   The enrolment of candidates for Easter baptism, which took place on the feast of the Epiphany instead of at the beginning of Lent, as had now become usual elsewhere.[84] The same custom also appears to have obtained in nearby Turin,[85] and Thomas Talley would see here a connection with the early Alexandrian baptismal pattern, which we shall examine shortly.[86] There is nothing to suggest that this day was also part of Roman practice.
2   A ceremony which he calls 'the opening' (*apertio*) on Saturday, the day before the baptism. In this, the bishop touched the ears and nostrils of the

---

83   On this, see Johnson, *The Rites of Christian Initiation*, pp. 125–30.
84   Ambrose, *Expos. in Ev. Luc.* 4.76.
85   Maximus addresses two sermons preached on the days immediately after Epiphany (13 and 65) to catechumens apparently preparing for baptism at Easter.
86   *The Origins of the Liturgical Year* (New York 1986; 2nd edn, Collegeville 1991), p. 217.

candidate, and Ambrose links it to the action of Jesus in opening the ears and mouth of a death and dumb man recorded in Mark 7.32–7. It is usual to explain this ceremony by saying that Ambrose has misinterpreted what was originally meant to be part of a pre-baptismal exorcistic ritual, but I have argued[87] that it is more likely the remnant of the transition to a period of 'restricted' teaching, such as we find in the *Didascalia* in Syria and in the *Apostolic Tradition*. As a similar ceremony of 'the opening of the ears' is found in later Roman sources, it was probably part of Roman practice as well at this time.

3   A pre-baptismal anointing of the body, which is the first clear instance of this in a Western rite, apart from the *Apostolic Tradition* with its uncertain provenance. It is located before the renunciation of the devil rather than after it, as in fourth-century Eastern sources; and while the latter all clearly regard the rite as an exorcism, as does the *Apostolic Tradition*, Ambrose instead treats it as a source of strength for combat with the devil, a theme also found alongside that of exorcism in the explanations of baptism given by John Chrysostom and Theodore of Mopsuestia. The Roman 'Canones ad Gallos' of *c.* 400 also mentions an anointing before baptism, but performed at the final scrutiny of the candidates rather than the baptismal rite itself, and gives no explanation as to its precise meaning.[88]

4   A triple renunciation followed by a triple interrogation and immersion, the latter as in both Tertullian and the *Apostolic Tradition*. This recurs in later Roman sources.

5   A single post-baptismal unction performed by the bishop himself, in contrast to both the *Apostolic Tradition* and later Roman practice, where there were two such anointings, the first done by a presbyter and the second by the bishop.

6   The washing of the feet of the newly baptized. This is the most striking difference from the practices of the other regions we have examined, and Ambrose himself reveals considerable embarrassment about this particular deviation from Roman custom.[89] There are, however, possible allusions to this ceremony in some East Syrian sources (Aphraates, Ephrem, and Cyrillonas of Edessa); a prohibition of the practice in canon 48 of the Spanish Council of Elvira (305); and provision for it in later Gallican liturgical books, as well as evidence of its observance elsewhere in northern Italy at this period (although at Aquileia it was apparently a pre-baptismal rite); and so it may once have been more widespread, and even (as we

---

87   'The Gospel and the Catechumenate in the Third Century', *JTS* 50 (1999), pp. 143–52.
88   ET in Whitaker, *Documents of the Baptismal Liturgy*, p. 229.
89   *De Sacramentis* 3.5–7.

have suggested earlier) been practised in place of immersion in some places and only became an adjunct to it as a later compromise.[90]

7   A 'spiritual sealing'. Some scholars have seen this as being the counterpart of the second post-baptismal anointing found in later Roman usage, but while Ambrose does refer to an invocation of the Holy Spirit, he makes no explicit mention of the use of oil, which has led other scholars to conclude that the only gesture was a sign of the cross or an imposition of hands.[91] Maxwell Johnson has recently suggested that the Roman rite too at this time had no second anointing but only an imposition of hands with prayer for the Holy Spirit, and it is the parallel to this to which Ambrose is here referring.[92]

Gaul and Spain

Although the Council of Elvira (305) and the First Council of Toledo (398) supply some information about early Spanish baptismal practice,[93] we lack any really detailed sources for liturgical customs in these regions prior to the fifth century, as we have indicated in an earlier chapter, and can only conjecture what older traditions might have been on the basis of the later evidence. However, Gabriele Winkler has shown that the later Gallican texts suggest that there was originally only one post-baptismal ceremony in this region – an anointing – and that there are also signs in the material of what are usually considered as being Syrian characteristics – Johannine rather than Pauline baptismal theology, allusions to the Jordan event in the blessing of the baptismal water, and references to the conferral of the Spirit in the pre-baptismal anointing.[94]

Egypt

As I have indicated elsewhere,[95] the traditional assumption that early initiatory practice in Egypt was fundamentally Western in character will not stand

---

90   See above, p. 61; and also Pier Franco Beatrice, *La lavanda dei piedi* (BEL 28, 1983).
91   See Fisher, *Confirmation Then and Now*, p. 57; Pamela Jackson, 'The Meaning of the "Spiritale Signaculum" in the Mystagogy of Ambrose of Milan', *EO* 7 (1990), pp. 77–94; Mitchell, *Baptismal Anointing*, pp. 87–91; Riley, *Christian Initiation*, pp. 353ff.
92   *The Rites of Christian Initiation*, pp. 135–41.
93   See Whitaker, *Documents of the Baptismal Liturgy*, pp. 222–4.
94   'Confirmation or Chrismation? A Study in Comparative Liturgy', *Worship* 58 (1984), pp. 2–16 = Johnson, ed., *Living Water, Sealing Spirit*, pp. 202–18.
95   'Baptismal Practice in the Alexandrian Tradition: Eastern or Western?', in Bradshaw, ed., *Essays in Early Eastern Initiation*, pp. 5–17 = Johnson, ed., *Living Water, Sealing Spirit*, pp. 82–100.

up to close scrutiny. Although it is true that there is some resemblance to Western practice, other features seem to have more in common with what we find in Syria, while still other characteristics appear to be unique to this region. The most notable of these is the baptismal season, which seems originally to have been situated at the end of a 40-day period of fasting which began immediately after 6 January in imitation of Christ's fasting in the wilderness.[96] Only in the fourth century was this fast and the baptismal season transferred to a pre-Easter position. The 40 days of this fast appear to have constituted the totality of the pre-baptismal preparation, and its liturgical features seem to have been an enrolment of the candidates at the beginning and a final examination of their suitability for baptism towards the end.

The initiation rite itself appears to have included on the one hand a pre-baptismal anointing to which considerable importance was attached and which shows some parallels to Syrian usage, but on the other hand a credal interrogation resembling that found in North African and Roman evidence rather than an act of adherence of a Syrian kind. It is this latter feature which has chiefly been responsible for scholars describing the rite as 'Western'. However, the interrogatory form of the baptismal confession of faith did not last but was soon replaced by a declaratory form in fivefold shape. There are some signs that this may have existed as a variant to the interrogatory form from early times and perhaps became more common after the indicative baptismal formula, 'I baptize you in the name . . .' (which was apparently introduced from Syria in the fourth century), forced the profession of faith to become detached from the threefold immersion itself.[97] Finally, various pieces of evidence point to the conclusion that the post-baptismal unction with chrism found in the *Canons of Hippolytus*, the *Sacramentary of Sarapion*, and the later Coptic rite may well be a fourth-century innovation, and that, like the early Syrian tradition, ancient Egyptian initiation practice may not have known any post-baptismal ceremonies.[98] Maxwell Johnson's recent analysis of the *Sacramentary of Sarapion* lends support to this thesis, since he has discerned that the prayer accompanying the post-baptismal anointing belongs to a different stratum of material from that accompanying the pre-baptismal anointing. Bryan Spinks has subsequently challenged this

---

96 For further details of the Egyptian post-Epiphany fast, see below, pp. 183–4.
97 See E. Lanne, 'La confession de foi baptismale à Alexandrie et à Rome', in A. M. Triacca and A. Pistoia, eds, *La liturgie expression de la foi* (BEL 16, 1979), pp. 213–28.
98 See Bradshaw, 'Baptismal Practice in the Alexandrian tradition', pp. 12–17; Georg Kretschmar, 'Beiträge zur Geschichte der Liturgie, inbesondere der Taufliturgie, in Ägypten', *Jahrbuch für Liturgik und Hymnologie* 8 (1963), pp. 1–54.

conclusion and attempted to defend the integrity of the whole initiation rite in Sarapion, but his arguments are not convincing.[99]

Conclusion

What seems to emerge from this review is that we cannot really talk of a standard or normative pattern of early initiation practice in primitive Christianity. Nor can we simply classify the various rites as being fundamentally either Eastern or Western in shape. Not only does Egypt not fit into this neat division, but if Winkler's assessment of the Gallican evidence is accurate, then the traditional distinction between 'Eastern' and 'Western' initiation rites may only be marking off Romano-African rites from the rest, and even this latter group exhibit some variations among themselves, especially with regard to the particular post-baptismal ceremony with which the giving of the Holy Spirit is associated: the imposition of hands (Tertullian and Cyprian in North Africa, and perhaps also Ambrose in Milan) or an anointing (Hippolytus and the later Roman evidence). This is not of course to deny that there are some features which are common to many or all of the local rites known to us, and that still more may be capable of discovery. Maxwell Johnson has, for example, demonstrated that an older three-week period of final pre-baptismal preparation can be discerned beneath the layers of many later texts from various parts of the world;[100] and in addition to the evidence already cited in this chapter, I have collected other testimony from later sources that seems to point to a once widespread existence of a short period of 'restricted' teaching of the central truths of Christianity immediately prior to the rite itself and following the more general ethical instruction in the earlier part of the catechumenate.[101]

What can be said to have emerged as common to rites by the time that the third century is reached, out of the apparent diversity of practice of earlier times, are certain fundamental ritual elements – preparatory instruction, renunciation and act of faith, anointing, immersion, and perhaps also imposition of hands – but each of these still tends to take a different form and, at least to some extent, a different meaning in the various local or regional traditions, and they have been combined with one another in differing sequences, with the result that there are just too many variations in structure

---

99 See his article, 'Sarapion of Thmuis and Baptismal Practice in Early Christian Egypt; The Need for a Judicious Reassessment', and Johnson's response, 'The Baptismal Rite and Anaphora in the Prayers of Sarapion of Thmuis: An Assessment of a Recent "Judicious Reassessment"'.

100 'From Three Weeks to Forty Days: Baptismal Preparation and the Origins of Lent', *SL* 20 (1990), pp. 185–200 = Johnson, ed., *Living Water, Sealing Spirit*, pp. 118–36.

101 'The Gospel and the Catechumenate in the Third Century'.

and theology to allow us to construct a single picture in anything but the very broadest terms. To emphasize what is common and to ignore what is distinctive of individual churches – or worse still, to force that evidence to fit some preconceived notion of a normative pattern – is seriously to distort our understanding of the variety of primitive Christian practice, and to lay a false foundation for the modern revision of initiation rites.

8

Liturgy and Time

This chapter explores two distinct but related areas of early Christian liturgical practice, and considers how changing interpretative frameworks adopted by scholars have opened up quite different ways of viewing the various pieces of evidence. In the first part we look at attempts to reconstruct the custom of regular prayer at certain fixed hours of the day – whether practised individually or collectively – otherwise known as the Divine Office or the Liturgy of the Hours. In the second part of the chapter we shall go on to discuss the evolution of the liturgical year.

Daily Prayer

The Office as a Fourth-century Creation

For earlier generations of scholars, the Divine Office was generally understood as being essentially a new development of the fourth century. They were of course aware that Christians in the second and third centuries had been encouraged to pray regularly at fixed hours of the day, but they sharply distinguished such 'private prayer' from the office itself. Louis Duchesne, for example, believed that it was the adoption of these times of prayer as communal exercises by the congregations of ascetics in the fourth century which led to 'the introduction of daily prayers into ecclesiastical use proper'.[1] Pierre Batiffol (1861–1929), Suitbert Bäumer (1845–94), and Gregory Dix all adopted similar positions.[2]

E. C. Ratcliff, in his contribution to the 1932 collection of essays entitled *Liturgy and Worship*, maintained that attempts to trace the origin of the offices to 'the observance by the Apostles and first Christians of the Jewish

---

1 *Christian Worship*, pp. 448–9.
2 Batiffol, *Histoire du Bréviaire Romain* (Paris 1893), pp. 14–15 = *History of the Roman Breviary* (London 1898), pp. 14–15; Bäumer, *Geschichte des Breviers* (Freiburg 1895), pp. 69ff. = *Histoire du Bréviaire* (Paris 1905) I, pp. 100ff.; Dix, *The Shape of the Liturgy*, pp. 319–32.

hours of prayer' was 'a mistake, because such observances were in no sense public acts of worship on the part of the Church; they were the private prayers of one or more individuals'.[3] Ratcliff, however, thought that the roots of the transformation from private to public prayer lay further back in Christian history than the fourth-century ascetics: he ascribed an important place to the *Apostolic Tradition* in the third century, where, although prayer still remained private, 'regimen has replaced recommendation'.[4]

Continuity with Judaism

Eventually scholars were persuaded to take much more seriously the possible Jewish roots of the office, and credit for this development must chiefly go to C. W. Dugmore in *The Influence of the Synagogue upon the Divine Office*, first published in 1944. He argued that two daily services, morning and evening, had been celebrated publicly from the very beginning of the Christian Church and were a continuation of the custom of the Jewish synagogue. He was not the first to propound this theory – nearly a century earlier Philip Freeman (1818–75) had advanced a similar claim[5] – but Dugmore's presentation was persuasive and was subsequently cited with approval by many other scholars.[6]

More recent scholarship, however, has undermined much of his case for the public celebration of these hours of prayer before the fourth century. We have already seen above in Chapter 2 that Jewish worship was much less regimented in the first century than Dugmore supposed, and that contemporary evidence for daily synagogue services is lacking. The foundation for his claims concerning early Christian practice has also proved unreliable, since he failed to distinguish assemblies for the purpose of instruction and occasional services of the word from the regular hours of prayer themselves, and so cited evidence for the former as proof of the public nature of the latter.

The Distinction Between 'Cathedral' and 'Monastic' Offices

The study of the early history of the office took a significant step forward in the middle of the twentieth century when Anton Baumstark drew attention to the fact that there were two quite distinct forms of daily worship in the fourth century, which he labelled as 'cathedral' and 'monastic'.[7] His insight has subsequently been taken up and fruitfully explored by other scholars, most notably by Juan Mateos,

---

3 'The Choir Offices', in W. K. Lowther Clarke, ed., *Liturgy and Worship* (London 1932), p. 257.

4 ibid., p. 259.

5 *The Principles of Divine Service* I (Oxford 1855), pp. 59–78.

6 See, for example, Benedict Steuart, *The Development of Christian Worship* (London 1953), pp. 195ff.

7 *Liturgie comparée* (3rd edn), pp. 123ff. = *Comparative Liturgy*, pp. 111ff.

Gabriele Winkler, and Robert Taft,[8] who have further refined his classification. Mateos divided the monastic type into 'desert monastic' (originating in Egypt) and 'urban monastic' (arising in Cappadocia and Syria and being a hybrid of the other two types), and Taft suggested that within the 'urban monastic' it was possible to distinguish between offices which were fundamentally monastic in character but had absorbed some cathedral elements, and those which had their origin in a cathedral pattern and had added certain monastic elements.[9]

'Cathedral' and 'monastic' were perhaps not the best choice of adjectives to distinguish the worship of the local Christian church assembled under the leadership of its bishop and other clergy on the one hand, from the daily devotions of individual ascetics and early religious communities on the other. But the labels have stuck and become the standard technical terms of later research. The differences between the types of worship, however, relate not merely to the people who participated in them but to their external forms and ultimately to their inner spirit and purpose.

The cathedral office, which was usually celebrated only twice each day, morning and evening, was characterized primarily by praise, in the form of a very selective use of psalmody and hymnody, usually repeated every day;[10] by extensive intercessions; and by the absence of Scripture-reading on most occasions. The ascetics who made their homes in the Egyptian deserts, on the other hand, attempted to fulfil more literally the apostolic injunction to 'pray without ceasing' (1 Thessalonians 5.17), and so occupied nearly all their waking hours with individual meditation. The emergence of the cenobitic life gave rise to more formal rules, which still expected the monk to persevere in prayer throughout the day but also came to include prescribed occasions of prayer at the beginning and the end of the day.[11] In the Pachomian communities of

8 For a full bibliography of the works on these scholars in this area, see Robert F. Taft, *The Liturgy of the Hours in East and West* (Collegeville 1986; 2nd edn 1993), pp. 376–80.

9 ibid., p. 84.

10 Psalms 148–50 seem to have constituted the primitive nucleus of the morning service apparently everywhere, with Psalms 51, 63, and the *Gloria in Excelsis* forming a second stratum in many places. The canticle *Benedicite*, with its strong emphasis on creation, was also commonly used on Sunday mornings. With regard to the evening, the hymn *Phos hilaron*, 'Hail, gladdening light', was widely used at the lighting of the evening lamp, and Psalm 141 is found in virtually all later Eastern rites, but is not so clearly evidenced in the West, where at least in some areas Psalm 104 seems to have been used instead (see above, p. 17, n. 42).

11 One of the main sources which has generally been used to reconstruct the nature of this pattern of daily prayer has been the account given by John Cassian in his *Institutes*, but as Robert Taft has indicated (*The Liturgy of the Hours in East and West*, pp. 58ff.), Cassian was here not simply writing as a disinterested observer: he was using the example of the Egyptian monks as an ideal to promote a reform of monasticism in his native Gaul. Hence, discrepancies between his description and evidence obtained from other sources may be signs of a desire, whether conscious or unconscious, to furnish Egyptian precedents for the Gallican practices which he favoured, and so his testimony needs to be treated with great caution.

Upper Egypt these hours were observed in common and consisted of the alternation of biblical passages read aloud by one of the brothers with the recitation of the Lord's Prayer and silent meditation by the rest of the community.[12] By contrast, in the monasticism of Lower Egypt the daily prayers were said by the monks individually in their cells (except on Saturdays and Sundays), with the morning prayer apparently being at an earlier hour than in Upper Egypt, at cock-crow. The content seems to have been the alternation of psalms (the Psalter being recited in full in its biblical order) and silent prayer.[13] It should be noted that the psalms here were not understood as being prayer themselves – the sources often speak of prayer *and* psalmody – but as readings, as the fount of inspiration for the meditative prayer which followed each psalm.[14]

Although these two traditions – the cathedral and the desert monastic – are similar in terms of the number of times of formal daily prayer, their contents are strikingly different and indicate a radically different concept of the nature of that prayer. The cathedral office had a strong ecclesial dimension: here was the Church gathered for prayer, exercising its royal priesthood by offering a sacrifice of praise and thanksgiving on behalf of all creation and interceding for the salvation of the world. The monastic office, on the other hand, was centred around silent meditation on the word of God and supplication for spiritual growth and personal salvation. Its ultimate aim was spiritual formation: the monk meditated on Christ[15] in order to grow into his likeness, and prayed for the grace necessary for that. It was thus essentially individualistic, and the presence or absence of other people was a matter of

---

12 See Armand Veilleux, *La liturgie dans le cénobitisme pachômien au IVe siècle* (Rome 1968), pp. 307ff.; Taft, *The Liturgy of the Hours in East and West*, pp. 62–5. But cf. Frans Kok, 'L'office pachômien: *psallere, orare, legere*', *EO* 9 (1992), pp. 69–95, who argued that their daily services included psalmody in addition to other biblical readings and prayer.

13 Cassian's claim that 12 psalms were recited on each occasion cannot be accepted uncritically as the original practice. As Veilleux and Taft have shown, the more ancient tradition was that 12 prayers be offered each day and 12 each night; in other words, that one should pray 'every hour', i.e., constantly. The grouping of these prayers into two daily synaxes of 12 psalms each thus appears to be a later development. See Veilleux, *La liturgie dans le cénobitisme pachômien au IVe siècle*, pp. 324ff.; Taft, *The Liturgy of the Hours in East and West*, p. 72.

14 See further Adalbert de Vogüé, 'Psalmodier n'est pas prier', *EO* 6 (1989), pp. 7–32.

15 On the Christological interpretation of the whole Psalter, apparently derived by the desert tradition from the exegetical method adopted by Origen from classical literature, see Marie-Josèphe Rondeau, *Les Commentaires patristiques du Psautier (IIIe-Ve siècles)* II (OCA 220, 1985), pp. 39ff.; Paul F. Bradshaw, 'From Word to Action: The Changing Role of Psalmody in Early Christianity', in Martin Dudley, ed., *Like a Two-Edged Sword: The Word of God in Liturgy and History* (Norwich 1995), pp. 21–37; Graham W. Woolfenden, 'The Use of the Psalter by Early Monastic Communities', *SP* 26 (1993), pp. 88–94.

indifference. There was nothing inherently corporate in the worship, nothing which might not be done equally as well alone as together. It was the same prayer which was performed in the cell as in the community gathering, and neither setting was viewed as superior to the other.[16]

The urban monastic communities display some variation in the details of their prayer-patterns but they usually prayed at least five times during the day – early in the morning, at the third, sixth, and ninth hours, and in the evening – and again at some point in the night. These hours of prayer were generally observed in common, but might be kept individually if circumstances prevented a corporate assembly. In most cases the offices seem to have used psalms selectively, as in the cathedral tradition, but included prayer for spiritual growth instead of intercession for others, just as we find in the desert monastic tradition.

Daily Prayer Before the Fourth Century

My own contribution to this subject has chiefly been to reconsider the connection of these fourth-century patterns of worship with what preceded them in the Christian tradition. Although rejecting Dugmore's conclusions concerning daily public worship, I have argued that a line of continuity can be traced from early Jewish patterns of daily prayer through primitive Christianity to the post-Constantinian practices examined by other scholars.

Because morning and evening prayer emerge as pre-eminent in the fourth century, other scholars have tended to follow Dugmore in assuming that it is these hours which must be of greatest antiquity and that there had always been a greater obligation to observe these particular times of prayer than any others. I challenged this presupposition, however, and pointed out that the early Eastern sources (*Didache*, Clement of Alexandria, and Origen) refer to praying not twice a day but three times – morning, noon, and evening – and to prayer again in the night, and that the early Western sources (principally Tertullian and Cyprian) speak of prayer five times during the day – morning, third hour, sixth hour (= noon), ninth hour, and evening – as well as prayer at night. When their statements are correctly interpreted, none of these sources makes any distinction between the importance of observing some of these hours rather than others. I concluded, therefore, that the oldest Christian pattern of daily prayer seems to have been threefold – morning, noon, and evening – together with prayer at night, and that there are even signs that something like this may already have been current in some Jewish circles in the first century.[17]

Subsequently, one of my former doctoral students, Edward Phillips,

---

16 See Taft, *The Liturgy of the Hours in East and West*, pp. 66–73.
17 *Daily Prayer in the Early Church*, chapters 1–3.

suggested a modification to my theory which seems to fit the facts better. He made a detailed analysis of the prescriptions concerning daily prayer in the *Apostolic Tradition*, which exhibit a number of peculiarities, among them the absence of a true evening hour of prayer. On the basis of this study, he argued that an older tradition of threefold daily prayer does underlie it, but at the third, sixth, and ninth hours, together with prayer at night.[18] His thesis seems to point to the conclusion that threefold daily prayer was indeed a wide-spread, if not universal, custom in the early Church, but that while some communities may have structured it according to the natural rhythm of the day and prayed in the morning, noon, and evening, other communities adopted the major divisions of the day of the Roman Empire and prayed at the third, sixth, and ninth hours. These two traditions seem later to have been conflated into the fivefold pattern that we first encounter in third-century North Africa.

The Urban Monastic Office

I have also argued that in the light of this earlier history we should not view the urban monastic prayer-cycle of the fourth century merely as a hybrid of cathedral and desert monastic usages. Rather, these religious communities were faithfully preserving what had been common practice among ordinary Christians in the third century. They were not innovators, but conservatives in a world which had changed.[19] The cathedral office was a departure from earlier tradition in one direction, formalizing daily worship under clerical presidency and generally reducing the hours of prayer to two, morning and evening, influenced by the Old Testament prescription of morning and evening sacrifices. The desert monastic office was a departure in the opposite direction, making ceaseless meditation the ideal and dispensing with every-thing which did not accord with this vision.

Such was the magnetic attraction of the spirituality of the Egyptian desert tradition, however, that the urban monastic office was rapidly drawn towards it and began to incorporate, to a greater or lesser extent, features from it into its own pattern. At the same time, as the cathedral office further evolved, newer elements from there also found their way into some urban monastic traditions, and in this way the hybrid varieties of offices to which Taft has drawn attention were produced.

For example, some communities apparently had prayer at midnight, in the morning, at the third, sixth, and ninth hours, in the evening and again before

---

18 'Daily Prayer in the *Apostolic Tradition* of Hippolytus', *JTS* 40 (1989), pp. 389–400. See also Bradshaw, Johnson, and Phillips, *Apostolic Tradition: A Commentary* on chapter 41.
19 'Cathedral vs. Monastery: The Only Alternatives for the Liturgy of the Hours?', in Alexander, ed., *Time and Community*, pp. 123–36.

bed, but extended the midnight hour into a longer vigil of consecutive psalmody after the Egyptian pattern. Others began their day with an Egyptian-style office at cock-crow, culminating in Psalms 148–50 (the original core of the cathedral morning office), and prayed at the third, sixth, and ninth hours, in the evening, and again before bed, but later added a further morning office containing newer cathedral elements.[20] While some communities probably had a cathedral-style evening prayer, others appear to have had either an Egyptian-style service with consecutive psalmody or a combination of the two. To complicate matters further, some monastic traditions, among them Jerusalem, seem to have added to their own version of evening prayer another one shared with the secular church around them, and so eventually produced a composite office which contained a number of elements in duplicate.[21]

This hybrid character of urban monastic prayer *practice* also led to a blurring of the distinction between cathedral and monastic *understandings* of the nature of psalmody and prayer, not only within those communities but also in the wider Church. It led to what James McKinnon has described as a 'psalmodic movement' in Christianity: on the one hand, 'an unprecedented wave of enthusiasm' for the psalms among leading fourth-century ecclesiastical figures, virtually all of whom had lived as a monk at one time or another, leading to the use of a wider range of psalms within the cathedral tradition; and on the other hand, a greater cognizance of the hymnic character of the psalms within urban monastic communities, leading to the introduction of more elaborate forms of their performance. 'Monasticism made a quantitive contribution to the song of the fourth-century church, and received in exchange the gift of musicality.'[22] However, the defence mounted by certain patristic writers with regard to these innovations suggests that at first not everyone welcomed them.[23]

The distinction between the two traditions was further obscured from the early fifth century onwards when communities of monks were given responsibility for maintaining the prayer and sacramental life of basilicas in the city of Rome. Even though the external *form* of their daily offices of psalmody may have remained unchanged, yet in this new context their *function* was effectively transformed from the spiritual advancement of the individual members of the community to the celebration of the praise of the Church. Moreover,

---

20 See Taft, *The Liturgy of the Hours in East and West*, pp. 75–91.
21 See Bradshaw, *Daily Prayer in the Early Church*, pp. 80–1, 105–6; Jeffery, 'The Sunday Office of Seventh-Century Jerusalem', pp. 62–3.
22 James W. McKinnon, 'Desert Monasticism and the Later Fourth-Century Psalmodic Movement', *Music and Letters* 75 (1994), pp. 505–21, here at p. 519 = idem, *The Temple, the Church Fathers and Early Western Chant*, XI.
23 See especially Basil, *Ep.* 207.3; Niceta of Remesiana, *De psalmodiae bono* 2.

this Roman institution provided a model that was imitated by others, including the establishment by the Franks of similar foundations in connection with sanctuaries dedicated to specially venerated saints.[24]

The Liturgical Year

Sunday

The New Testament contains only three texts (Acts 20.7–12; 1 Corinthians 16.2; and Revelation 1.10) which may allude to the Christian observance of Sunday, and even their meaning is a matter of some dispute.[25] Nevertheless, scholars have not generally accepted the thesis of the Seventh-Day Adventist Samuele Bacchiochi that Sunday observance only began among Christians in the second century.[26] Instead, many have tended to believe that the first Christians chose Sunday as their Sabbath day in order to differentiate themselves from other Jews, and furthermore that during the first century the Christian Eucharist was usually celebrated on Saturday evening, after the Sabbath was over and as Sunday began according to the Jewish reckoning of the day.

In 1962, however, Willy Rordorf made a significant contribution to the matter, arguing that Jesus had deliberately challenged not just an over-zealous interpretation of the Sabbath commandment by the Pharisees, but the very keeping of the Sabbath itself. Moreover, while the early Christians certainly retained the eschatological image of the Sabbath rest, and while Jewish-Christians may have gone on observing the actual weekly Sabbath, Gentile Christians who adhered to the Pauline view of the Law would not have done so, and would therefore have had no interest in transferring the Sabbath to Sunday. Taking up an idea first put forward by Oscar Cullmann, Rordorf suggested that instead the Christian celebration of Sunday probably arose out of the post-resurrection meal appearances of Jesus, many of which seem to have taken place on the first day of the week. He also argued that the weekly eucharistic assemblies were held at first on Sunday evening rather than Saturday evening, and only later transferred to Sunday morning.[27]

Though warmly welcomed by many, Rordorf's explanation has not met with universal approbation. Some conservative scholars have defended the

---

24 See Angelus Haüssling, *Mönchskonvent und Eucharistiefeier* (Liturgiewissenschaft Quellen und Forschungen 58; Münster 1973), pp. 123–42.
25 See Rordorf, *Sunday*, pp. 193–215.
26 *From Sabbath to Sunday*, esp. pp. 90–131.
27 *Der Sonntag = Sunday*, esp. pp. 54–153, 215–73. See also his later studies, 'Ursprung und Bedeutung der Sonntagsfeier im frühen Christentum', *Liturgisches Jahrbuch* 31 (1981), pp. 145–58; 'Sunday: The Fullness of Christian Liturgical Time', *SL* 14 (1982), pp. 90–6. For Cullmann, see above, p. 66.

traditional view of the origins of the day, insisting that the Sabbath command-ment was not abrogated either by Jesus or by the early Christians.[28] Others have challenged the assumption that the Eucharist emerged out of the post-resurrection meals shared by Jesus with his disciples, and argued that on the contrary, the meal-stories emerged out of the eucharistic celebrations of the early Christians.[29] But support for Rordorf's general position came from a perhaps rather surprising quarter: a collection of essays by a group of conser-vative scholars in 1982 agreed that Christians first began to observe Sunday not as a substitute for the Sabbath but as their day for corporate worship.[30]

Wednesday and Friday

Didache 8.1 directed Christians not to fast on Mondays and Thursdays (the regular Jewish fast-days) but on Wednesdays and Fridays, and this custom continued to be widely observed in later centuries, with regular services of the word also taking place at the ninth hour on these days. It was traditionally assumed that Christians made this change in order to differentiate their practices more clearly from those of the Jews and merely picked these days at random. In 1960 Annie Jaubert argued, however, that this assumption did not take account of how deep-rooted liturgical customs were, and pointed to the solar calendar in use among the Jewish community at Qumran, in which Wednesday and Friday had a certain prominence.[31] Scholars have subse-quently concluded, therefore, that, while they were apparently not marked by fasting or by any special liturgical assemblies at Qumran so far as we are aware, the Christian choice of these particular days in place of the traditional Jewish ones was probably influenced by the familiarity of some early converts with the solar calendar of Qumran.[32]

Easter

There are two major questions concerning the celebration of Easter (or *Pascha*, as it was called) in primitive Christianity: How early in the history of the Church did it begin? and Which came first – its observance on the Sunday closest to the date of the Jewish Passover or its observance on the actual day of the Passover (the fourteenth day of the Jewish month Nisan) found in some churches in Asia Minor, a practice consequently termed Quartodeci-manism? Many scholars have taken the view that the Christian festival of

28 See in particular Roger Beckwith and William Stott, *This is the Day* (London 1978) = *The Christian Sunday. A Biblical and Historical Study* (Grand Rapids 1980).
29 See above, p. 66, n. 97.
30 D. A. Carson, ed., *From Sabbath to Lord's Day* (Grand Rapids 1982).
31 'Jésus et le calendrier de Qumrân', *NTS* 7 (1960), pp. 1–30. See also Rordorf, *Sunday*, pp. 183–6.
32 See Bradshaw, *Daily Prayer in the Early Church*, pp. 40–1.

Easter goes back to the apostolic age, even though explicit testimony to its observance only appears in the second century, and that its celebration on a Sunday was normative from the first, with the Quartodeciman practice being merely a local aberration from this, part of a general Judaizing tendency observable in early Christianity.[33] A few have even suggested that the annual celebration of Easter on a Sunday is older than the weekly observance of Sunday.[34]

On the other hand, some scholars have claimed that the Quartodeciman practice originated in Palestine as the early Jewish-Christian adaptation of the Passover festival.[35] Yet others have gone further still and argued that the celebration of Easter on a Sunday was a considerably later development than is often supposed, and that it was not established at Rome until around 165, though it may have been adopted at Alexandria and Jerusalem somewhat earlier.[36] Prior to this, these churches would have known no annual paschal observance at all. If this is true, it effectively reverses the usual conclusions reached by the majority of earlier scholars: Quartodecimanism is not some local aberration from an apostolic norm but is instead the oldest form of Easter celebration, with the Sunday version – although it was eventually to achieve dominance – being a secondary adaptation of the original practice.

Because it was often difficult for Christians to calculate the Jewish date, the Quartodecimans in Asia Minor appear to have settled for the compromise of celebrating Easter on the fourteenth day of the first spring month according to the version of the Julian calendar in use in their culture, which was the equivalent of 6 April. Elsewhere, by the third century, especially in the West, attempts were being made to compute what would have been the exact date of the death of Jesus according to the Julian calendar. This was generally agreed to have been 25 March, and August Strobel has suggested that some communities in Asia Minor, Syria, Spain, Gaul, and northern Italy celebrated Easter annually on that date.[37]

---

33 See, for example, A. A. McArthur, *The Evolution of the Christian Year* (London 1953), pp. 98–107; Jungmann, *The Early Liturgy*, pp. 25–6.

34 See Kenneth Strand, 'Sunday Easter and Quartodecimanism in the Early Christian Church', *Andrews University Seminary Studies* 28 (1990), pp. 127–36, and especially n. 1 for other studies adopting a similar stance.

35 See, for example, B. Lohse, *Das Passafest der Quartadecimaner* (Gütersloh 1953); Jeremias, *Eucharistic Words of Jesus*, pp. 122–3.

36 Karl Holl, *Gesammelte Aufsätze zur Kirchengeschichte. II: Der Osten* (Tübingen 1927), pp. 204–24; Marcel Richard, 'La question pascal au IIe siècle', *L'Orient syrien* 6 (1961), pp. 212–21; Talley, *The Origins of the Liturgical Year*, pp. 13-27. See also Robert Cabié, 'A propos de la "Question pascale": quelle pratique opposait-on à celles des Quartodecimans?', *EO* 11 (1994), pp. 101–6.

37 *Ursprung und Geschichte des frühchristlichen Osterkalenders* (TU 121, 977), pp. 370–2. See also Talley, *The Origins of the Liturgical Year*, pp. 5–13; Philipp Harnoncourt, 'Kalendarische Fragen und ihre theologische Bedeutung nach den Studien von August Strobel', *ALW* 27 (1985), pp. 263–72.

The evidence suggests that the early Christian version of the Passover was preceded by a period of fasting and vigil during the Jewish festivities of the 14 Nisan, and only began at cock-crow on 15 Nisan.[38] When Easter started to be celebrated on a Sunday, therefore, the preceding Saturday was also kept as a fast-day (even though primitive Christian tradition seems to have generally regarded all other Saturdays, like Sundays, as inappropriate for fasting), but since this followed directly after the normal weekly Friday fast, it led to the establishment in many places of a continuous pre-paschal fast of two days. By the third century in some places, notably Syria and Egypt, this was further extended back to the beginning of the week, resulting in a full six days of fasting before the feast.

The theory of the primacy of the celebration on 14 Nisan helps to explain the otherwise somewhat puzzling fact that the principal focus of the feast in all early Christian writings, and not just those arising from Quartodeciman circles, was on 'Christ, the paschal lamb, sacrificed for us' (cf. 1 Corinthians 5.7) rather than upon the resurrection. However, by the end of the second century in Alexandria the beginning of a shift in understanding of the feast can be seen, one that focused upon 'passage' rather than 'passion' – the passage from death to life. Clement of Alexandria describes the Passover as humanity's passage 'from all trouble and all objects of sense' (*Stromata* 2.11.51.2); Origen in the middle of the third century explains the word as referring to the exodus from Egypt (*Peri Pascha* 1); and later writers combine the themes of Christ's passion and his passage from death to life in their exegesis of the feast.

Although this change of focus may be in part simply the result of a more accurate exegesis of the Hebrew Scriptures, it is also in line with the general tendency among Alexandrian theologians to de-historicize and allegorize the Christian mysteries. To this should also be added the influence that would have been exercised by the day of the week on which the feast now occurred: Sunday was primarily associated with the resurrection of Christ to new life rather than with his death. Moreover, the fact that Easter was now preceded by a continuous two-day fast on Friday and Saturday nearly everywhere encouraged the beginnings of a trend to view the whole observance as a *triduum*, a three-day commemoration of Christ's transition from death to resurrection. The first signs of this occur in third-century evidence from both Egypt and Syria. Thus Origen viewed the paschal events as fulfilling the prophecy of Hosea 6:2: 'Now listen to what the prophet says: "God will revive

38 Talley, *Origins of the Liturgical Year*, p. 6. But cf. Gerard Rouwhorst, 'The Quartodeciman Passover and the Jewish Pesach', *QL* 77 (1996), pp. 152–73, who argues that the Quartodeciman celebration originally began at midnight and ended at cock-crow, and that too much prominence should not be given to its alleged eschatological character.

us after two days, and on the third day we shall rise and live in his sight." For us the first day is the passion of the Saviour; the second on which he descended into hell; and the third, the day of resurrection' (*Hom. in Exod.* 5.2). Although there is no hint that the first two days were as yet liturgically celebrated in any special way, the seeds were being sown for that development in the fourth century, which we shall consider further in the final chapter.[39]

Pentecost

The Christian observance of the 50-day period following Easter as a festal season is first attested in a number of sources from a variety of regions at the end of the second century. It was regarded as a time of rejoicing, and every day was treated in the same way as Sunday; that is, with no kneeling for prayer or fasting.[40]

On the other hand, there are signs that the observance of this season may not have been quite as universal as is generally supposed, and it is interesting to note that for many ancient writers the term 'Pascha' refers to the days beginning with the fast preceding the feast and ending with the feast itself, rather than to any period following it. Furthermore, Canon 20 of the Council of Nicea refers to some who kneel on Sundays and in the days of Pentecost, ordering them to desist; and neither Aphraates nor Ephrem in East Syria in the first half of the fourth century make mention of anything other than a single week of celebration following the feast.[41] Elsewhere too, the first week after Easter receives special emphasis within the 50-day season, which may perhaps be an indication that this shorter period was at one time the only extension of the Easter festival in some places. In addition, Canon 43 of the Spanish Council of Elvira (305) seeks to correct what it describes as a corrupt practice and insists that all should celebrate 'the day of Pentecost'. On the basis of a variant reading in two manuscripts, Robert Cabié interprets the corrupt practice as being a recent innovation of prematurely terminating the Easter season on the fortieth day,[42] but it is not impossible that the canon is

39 On the whole subject of Easter, see further, Paul F. Bradshaw, 'The Origins of Easter', in Bradshaw and Hoffman, eds, *Passover and Easter: Origin and History to Modern Times*, pp. 81–98; and for the ET of many of the relevant primary texts, see Raniero Cantalamessa, *Easter in the Early Church* (Collegeville 1993).

40 For details see Robert Cabié, *La Pentecôte: L'évolution de la Cinquantaine pascale au cours des cinq premiers siècles* (Paris 1965), pp. 35–45.

41 ibid., pp. 153, n. 1, and 154, n. 3. Talley (*The Origins of the Liturgical Year*, pp. 56–7) cites similar testimony from the homilies of Asterius the Sophist, a Cappadocian writing between 335 and 341, but they are now thought to be the work of an otherwise unknown Asterius writing later in the fourth or early in the fifth century. See Wolfram Kinzig, *In Search of Asterius. Studies on the Authorship of the Homilies on the Psalms* (Göttingen 1990).

42 *La Pentecôte*, pp. 181–2.

seeking to introduce the celebration of Pentecost to churches which had not previously known it.

In any case, the integrity of the 50 days does not seem to have been so deep-rooted that it was able to resist erosion in the course of the fourth century. We have already mentioned the existence in many places of a special emphasis on the first week of the season. In addition to that, in Constantinople, Rome, Milan, and Spain the fiftieth day itself came to be celebrated as a commemoration of the gift of the Spirit, while in other places – including Jerusalem – both the Ascension and the gift of the Spirit were celebrated together on that day. Towards the end of the century a separate feast of the Ascension on the fortieth day emerged in a number of places, including Antioch, Nyssa, and northern Italy, and became almost universal early in the fifth century. There are also traces of the existence in some places of a 'mid-Pentecost' festival. Although some churches still continued to observe the whole 50 days as a festal season, even when punctuated in this way, others resumed the regular weekly fasts after the fortieth day, while still others (at least according to Filastrius, Bishop of Brescia in northern Italy in the late fourth century) fasted even before the Ascension.[43]

Lent

Evidence for the existence of the season of Lent emerges rather suddenly in the early part of the fourth century. As Thomas Talley has commented, 'Prior to Nicea, no record exists of such a forty-day fast before Easter. Only a few years after the council, however, we encounter it in most of the Church as either a well-established custom or one that has become so nearly universal as to impinge on those churches that have not yet adopted it.'[44] Before Talley's work, scholars assumed that the association of this season of fasting with Jesus' fast in the wilderness was a secondary development, a piece of historicizing which took place only after the period of baptismal preparation before Easter (from which Lent was thought to take its origin) had been extended to six weeks for purely practical reasons. Similarly, both its focus on fasting by the whole Christian community, rather than primarily by the baptismal candidates, and its adoption as the usual period for penance for those who had committed grave sins, were also thought of as having arisen later.[45]

Talley has presented a strong case, however, for a quite different under-

---

43 See Cabié, *La Pentecôte*, passim; Martin F. Connell, 'From Easter to Pentecost', in Paul F. Bradshaw and Lawrence A. Hoffman, eds, *Passover and Easter: The Symbolic Structuring of Sacred Seasons* (Notre Dame 1999), pp. 94–106; Talley, *The Origins of the Liturgical Year*, pp. 54–70.
44 *The Origins of the Liturgical Year*, p. 168.
45 See, for example, Dix, *The Shape of the Liturgy*, p. 354.

standing of the emergence of the season. Building upon a suggestion originally made by Baumstark[46] and upon research done by René-Georges
Coquin,[47] Talley assembled the evidence for the existence in Egypt from early
times of a 40-day fast in commemoration of Jesus' fasting in the wilderness.
This did not take place immediately before Easter, but began on the day after
6 January, which the Alexandrian church observed as the celebration of the
baptism of Jesus,[48] and thus was situated in the correct chronological
sequence of the Gospel accounts. Furthermore, it seems also to have functioned as the final period of preparation for baptism, with the rite itself being
celebrated at the end of the 40 days, and may have been associated with the
restoration of penitent apostates.[49] The Lenten season which emerges as a
universal phenomenon in the fourth century, therefore, appears to be the
result of the fusion of two quite distinct earlier traditions – the Alexandrian
post-Epiphany fast of 40 days, which had culminated in the baptism of new
converts, and the shorter (perhaps three-week[50]) period of baptismal preparation which had existed in other churches, in some cases (North Africa and
Rome) already being situated immediately before Easter. Coquin suggested
that this fusion came about as part of the settlement of the paschal question
at the Council of Nicea.[51]

When the different churches attached the 40-day fast to the paschal
season, however, they did so in varying ways, to a large extent depending
upon the shape of their own pre-existent fasting arrangements.[52] Rome, which
had previously known only a two-day general fast before Easter, situated the
40 days immediately before this, resulting in a composite 42-day season
beginning on the Sunday which fell six weeks before Easter. Since there was
never any fasting on Sundays, this meant that there were 36 days of actual
fasting here, before it was later extended backwards by four days to begin on
what then became known as Ash Wednesday. Milan did the same as Rome,
but adhered to the custom found in the East of excluding Saturdays (apart
from the day before Easter itself) as well as Sundays from fasting and so to
begin with had only 31 days of actual fasting.

---

46 *Comparative Liturgy*, p. 194.
47 'Les origines de l'Épiphanie en Égypte', in Bernard Botte *et al.*, *Noël, Épiphanie: retour
    du Christ* (Paris 1967), pp. 139–70.
48 For this, see further below, p. 189.
49 Talley, 'The Origin of Lent at Alexandria', *SP* 18 (1982), pp. 594–612 = idem, *Worship:
    Reforming Tradition* (Washington, DC 1990), pp. 87–112; idem, *The Origins of the Litur-
    gical Year*, pp. 189–214.
50 See above, p. 169, n. 100.
51 'Une réforme liturgique du concile de Nicée (325)?', *Comptes Rendus, Académie des
    Inscriptions et Belles-lettres* (Paris 1967), pp. 178–92.
52 For further details, see Talley, *The Origins of the Liturgical Year*, pp. 168–74, and the
    sources there cited.

Churches in the East, on the other hand, which had already extended the pre-paschal fast to six days, usually began the 40-day fast on the Monday after the Sunday seven weeks before Easter and ended it on the Friday nine days before Easter, thus retaining the six-day fast in the following week as a separate entity. Because these churches did not fast on either Saturday or Sunday, this resulted in 30 days of fasting, together with six more days in the final week, as Saturday was included in that week's fast. Alexandria was an exception to the Eastern rule. It adopted the pre-paschal location of the fast rather more slowly than other places, but when it did make the move, it placed the season immediately before Easter, thus overlapping the six-day fast which it had previously observed, and resulting in a total of only six weeks like Rome, but in this case with fasting on only five days in each of the weeks, except for the last. Eventually, here and elsewhere, the duration was increased in order that a full 40 days of actual fasting might be kept: in the Byzantine tradition, for example, although Lent proper continued to begin seven weeks before Easter, an extra week of partial fasting was inserted before it.

The pilgrim Egeria appears to imply that some such a development had already taken place at Jerusalem in the late fourth century, for she speaks of the existence of a total of eight weeks of Lent there, including the final week before Easter (*Peregrinatio* 27.1),[53] but because it was hard to reconcile her testimony with other evidence (at a later period Jerusalem had a total of only seven weeks), scholars usually dismissed it as a mistake on her part or regarded it as a local experiment that did not last.[54] Recently, however, some support for Egeria's statement has come from Frans van de Paverd's argument that there was also a similar eight-week Lent at Antioch in the late fourth century. He suggests that the seven-week Lent found in Constantinople was derived from Cappadocian rather than Antiochene practice, and that it was the influence of Constantinople which later brought Jerusalem back to seven weeks.[55]

Holy Week

The emergence of what Western Christians came to call Holy Week and Eastern Christians Great Week – the attempt to commemorate liturgically

53 See above, p. 116.
54 See A. A. Stephenson, 'The Lenten Catechetical Syllabus in Fourth-Century Jerusalem', *Theological Studies* 15 (1954), p. 116; Baldovin, *The Urban Character of Christian Worship*, p. 92, n. 37.
55 *St John Chrysostom, the Homilies on the Statues: An Introduction* (OCA 239, 1991), pp. 210–16, 250–4; see also ibid., pp. 161–201, for Antiochene liturgical services in Lent.

the detailed events of the last week of Jesus' life on the particular days on which they were thought to have occurred – was believed by earlier generations of liturgical scholars to have been a fourth-century creation which began in Jerusalem, and was often attributed to 'its liturgically-minded bishop' Cyril.[56]

Once again, the true story seems rather more complex. It is highly likely that much of what later became standard Holy Week liturgy in many parts of the Church does owe its origin to the desire of pilgrims who flocked to the Holy Land in the new religious climate of the fourth century to commemorate Gospel events in the very places and on the very days that they were said to have happened. But Robert Taft has shown that such 'historicizing' tendencies existed among Christians long before the fourth century, and that the degree of historicization in the fourth-century Jerusalem liturgy can be overstated: no attempt was made, for example, to locate the Holy Thursday liturgy at the supposed site of the Last Supper, nor did the procession through the city early on Good Friday seek to replicate exactly the route taken by Jesus, with detours to the house of Caiaphas or Pilate, but went directly to Golgotha.[57]

Moreover, the research done by Talley suggests that Jerusalem may have been as much an importer of liturgical practices as an exporter at this period, with different groups of pilgrims bringing their own local customs and traditions with them and introducing them into the liturgical cycle of the city, as well as carrying back with them ideas for innovations in the worship of their home churches. For example, the double celebration of the Eucharist on Holy Thursday, which appears to have been a feature of the Jerusalem liturgy in the late fourth century, has previously been inexplicable, but Talley has put forward the hypothesis that the second celebration may have been a concession to pilgrims who came from a tradition which liturgically followed the Johannine chronology of the Passion and associated the death of the Lord with the hour of the slaying of the lambs.[58]

More significantly still, Talley has argued that the celebration of Lazarus Saturday and Palm Sunday did not belong to indigenous Jerusalem practice but were brought there from Constantinople, which in turn derived the observances from Alexandria, where they had originally formed the festal conclusion of the 40-day fast, as they continued to do at Constantinople, thus suggesting a relationship between Alexandria and Constantinople to which, as Talley comments, 'liturgiology has given little attention'.[59] While accepting

56 See especially Dix, *The Shape of the Liturgy*, pp. 334, 348–53.
57 'Historicism Revisited', *SL* 14 (1982), pp. 97–109 = *Beyond East and West*, pp. 15–30, 2nd edn, pp. 31–49; see also Baldovin, *The Urban Character of Christian Worship*, pp. 87–8.
58 *The Origins of the Liturgical Year*, pp. 44–5.
59 ibid., pp. 176–89, 203–14.

the general outline of Talley's thesis, John Baldovin has proposed instead that Jerusalem may have inherited the Lazarus Saturday/Palm Sunday tradition directly from Alexandria rather than via Constantinople, and indeed that Constantinople itself may have received it from Jerusalem.[60] Whichever of these theories is correct, the implication is that Holy Week did not develop as a single integrated whole, but as the result of the fusion of two previously distinct traditions, the commemoration in Jerusalem of the final events in the life of Jesus according to the chronology of Matthew's Gospel, and the celebration elsewhere of the raising of Lazarus and of the entry of Jesus into Jerusalem (which is given a precise chronological connection to the death of Jesus only in the Fourth Gospel, being said to take place five days before the Passover).

Christmas and Epiphany

It seems clear that by the middle of the fourth century 25 December had emerged as a Christian festival at Rome and in North Africa, while elsewhere in the East and West, including North Italy,[61] a similar festival existed instead on 6 January. It also seems clear that through a process of interchange the two eventually spread to become virtually universal observances throughout the Church. However, the reason for the choice of the particular dates is not so obvious, and there have been two main theories concerning the origin of these feasts.[62]

One theory – often termed the computation hypothesis and first advanced by Louis Duchesne[63] – attributed the festivals to the results of attempts to calculate the exact day in the year on which Jesus had actually been born. These particular dates had been arrived at, it was thought, by inference from the alleged date of the death of Jesus, since early Christians were convinced that he must have lived upon earth for an exact number of years and therefore the date on which he died would also have been the same as the date of his conception. Thus, those who regarded 25 March as the date of the crucifixion and conception would have placed the nativity nine months later, on 25 December, while those who believed the date of his death to have been 6 April would have assigned the birth to 6 January.

Later scholars generally rejected this explanation and preferred an older

---

60 'A Lenten Sunday Lectionary in Fourth Century Jerusalem', in Alexander, ed., *Time and Community*, pp. 115–22.

61 See Martin F. Connell, 'Did Ambrose's Sister Become a Virgin on December 25 or January 6? The Earliest Western Evidence for Christmas and Epiphany Outside Rome', *SL* 29 (1999), pp. 145–58.

62 For an account of the debate, see Susan K. Roll, *Toward the Origins of Christmas*, (Kampen, The Netherlands 1995), pp. 87–96, 127–49.

63 *Christian Worship*, pp. 257–65.

theory, known as the 'history of religions' hypothesis, according to which 25 December was chosen at Rome because it was also the date of the winter solstice in the Julian calendar and a popular pagan feast, the *dies natalis solis invicti*, the birthday of the invincible sun, established by the emperor Aurelian in 274. After the Peace of Constantine the Christians, it was said, wanted to draw people away from these pagan festivities and point to Christ as the true Sun of Righteousness, and so instituted at Rome the feast of the Nativity on the same date. The Eastern provinces of the Roman Empire, on the other hand, were said to have observed 6 January as the date of the winter solstice according to the ancient calendar of Amenemhet I of Thebes (*c.* 1996 BCE), and so the Christian feast too was established on that date there. The roots of this explanation can be traced back as far as the seventeenth century, but it received its chief impetus from Hermann Usener in 1889.[64]

Thomas Talley, however, has challenged the dominance attained by this theory and revived the Duchesne's hypothesis. He has pointed out that Augustine in one of his sermons alluded to the fact that the Donatists in North Africa, unlike the Catholics, had not adopted the celebration of the feast of the Epiphany on 6 January, which seemed to imply that they did celebrate 25 December. This in turn suggested that Christmas must already have existed prior to the Donatist schism in 311, and hence at a date when it would have been unlikely that the Christians would have wanted any 'accommodation to less than friendly imperial religious sentiment'. On the basis of other evidence supporting the computation hypothesis (from Augustine and from an anonymous work known as *De Solstitiis* which was apparently also of North African provenance), Talley tentatively suggested the possibility that Christmas may have first appeared in that region rather than at Rome, as is usually supposed.[65]

Talley presented even stronger grounds for preferring the computation hypothesis for 6 January. He demonstrated that there never was a calendar of Amenemhet I, nor any clear evidence of a widespread pagan festival on 6 January, while Roland Bainton had shown that Clement of Alexandria as early as the end of the second century believed 6 January in the year 2 BCE to have been the date of the birth of Christ. What Bainton had not known, however, was that 6 April constituted the solar equivalent of 14 Nisan in Asia Minor, and so the choice of 6 January could therefore have been dependent upon that.[66]

---

64 *Das Weihnachtsfest* (Bonn 1889; 2nd edn 1911; 3rd edn 1969). For later exponents, see for example Baumstark, *Comparative Liturgy*, p. 152–64; Bernard Botte, *Les origines de la Noël et de l'Épiphanie* (Louvain 1932); idem, ed., *Noël, Épiphanie: retour du Christ*; John Gunstone, *Christmas and Epiphany* (London 1967).

65 *The Origins of the Liturgical Year*, pp. 85–103.

66 Roland Bainton, 'The Origins of the Epiphany', *Early and Medieval Christianity. The Collected Papers in Church History*, Series One (Boston 1962), pp. 22–38; Talley, *The Origins of the Liturgical Year*, pp. 103–21.

Talley then drew attention to the evidence of the *Canons of Athanasius*, a document probably composed in Egypt in the second half of the fourth century. Here the focus of the feast of the Epiphany is clearly the baptism of Jesus; the nativity is not mentioned; and a considerable point is made of Epiphany being the beginning of the year. From this Talley argued that, as a result of 6 January being regarded as the birth of Christ, it came to be treated as the beginning of the liturgical year in Egypt, just as 25 December seems to have been viewed in the Roman Chronograph of 354, and hence the course reading of the Gospel of Mark – the evangelist especially associated with Alexandria – was begun upon that date. Since that particular Gospel began with the baptism of Jesus, the focus of the festival there was consequently directed towards the baptism and not the nativity. He went on to propose that something similar may have happened in other places too. Because of the strong connection of John's Gospel with Asia Minor, its reading may have been begun there on 6 January, and so given to that feast the association with the miracle at Cana in John 2.1–11. In Jerusalem, according to Egeria and the Armenian lectionary, the focus of the festival was on the nativity, and there are signs that the course reading of Matthew's Gospel, in which an account of the nativity is included, may originally have been begun at this season.[67] More recently Gabriele Winkler has pursued Talley's hypothesis further and in a detailed examination of the theme of the appearance of light in connection with the baptism of Jesus has shown how the original focus of the feast on the baptism was gradually widened to embrace all the manifestation themes found in the fourth century.[68] In the absence of a more compelling theory, this remains the most likely hypothesis, although not without its difficulties. A recent alternative proposal by Merja Merras, that it was a Christianization of the Jewish feast of Tabernacles, has not so far won acceptance.[69]

There is somewhat similar uncertainty over the origins of the later Western season of Advent. This seems to have some possible precursors in the shape of pre-Christmas (or pre-Epiphany) prescriptions with regard to preparatory fasting and appropriate readings from the late fourth century

---

67 *The Origins of the Liturgical Year*, pp. 121–34.
68 'Die Licht-Erscheinung bei der Taufe Jesu und der Ursprung des Epiphaniefestes. Eine Untersuchung griechischer, syrischer, armenischer und lateinischer Quellen', *Oriens Christianus* 78 (1994), pp. 177–229 = 'The Appearance of the Light at the Baptism of Jesus and the Origins of the Feast of the Epiphany: An Investigation of Greek, Syriac, Armenian, and Latin Sources', in Maxwell E. Johnson, ed., *Between Memory and Hope: Readings on the Liturgical Year* (Collegeville 2000), pp. 291–347.
69 *The Origins of the Celebration of the Christian Feast of Epiphany* (Joensuu, Finland 1995).

onwards, but none of these show incontrovertible links with what emerged subsequently.[70]

Saints' Days

Finally, reference needs to be made to one other very significant feature of the earliest Christian calendars – the emergence of saints' days. Reverence accorded towards the mortal remains of Christian martyrs can be traced back to at least the middle of the second century, and was focused in a regular celebration at the place of burial of the anniversary of the date of the death, which was viewed as being the martyr's *natalia*, day of birth to eternal life. Such commemorations were therefore essentially local in character, and hence each church's calendar of saints would be quite different from that of its neighbours. They were also quite modest in the pre-Constantinian era, especially during periods of persecution when it would have been dangerous to do otherwise, and took the form of a celebration of the Eucharist at, or close to, the grave. In the fourth century, however, although still limited to the place of burial itself, these celebrations became more elaborate, and buildings known as *martyria* were gradually erected over or close to the tombs in order to house them. In this period when martyrdom became a memory rather than a current reality, the remains of other holy men and women also began to be venerated in the same way.

In the West until the seventh century the Roman law which forbade the opening or re-siting of a grave in order to protect the peace of the dead was generally (though not totally) obeyed, and so hindered the spread of the cult of a saint beyond his or her immediate locality. In the East, on the other hand, there was no objection either to *translatio*, the re-housing of remains, or to *dismemberatio*, taking them to pieces and distributing them to several churches. Thus, for example, in 365–6 the emperor Constantius ordered the relics of Timothy, the apostle Andrew, and the evangelist Luke to be brought to Constantinople, which was done with considerable ceremony. In this way, the cult of saints began to spread beyond the merely local, and churches increasingly traded between one another both relics and the annual observance that accompanied them.[71]

---

70 See further, J. Neil Alexander, *Waiting for the Coming: The Liturgical Meaning of Advent, Christmas, and Epiphany* (Washington, DC 1993); Martin F. Connell, 'The Origins and Evolution of Advent in the West', in Johnson, ed., *Between Memory and Hope*, pp. 349–71; Talley, *The Origins of the Liturgical Year*, pp. 150–2.

71 For further details, see Victor Saxer, *Morts, martyrs, reliques en Afrique chrétienne aux premiers siècles* (Paris 1980); G. J. C. Snoek, *Medieval Piety from Relics to the Eucharist* (Leiden 1995), pp. 9–16. See also John Crook, *The Architectural Setting of the Cult of the Saints in the Early Christian West, c. 300–1200* (Oxford 2000).

Conclusion

Many lessons can be drawn from the shifts in scholarship that we have observed in this chapter, but perhaps three are particularly significant. First, once again, as in the cases of baptism and Eucharist, the further one digs into the primary sources, the more it is diversity rather than uniformity which is encountered in the first few centuries. Second, what has been perceived as the mainstream practice of the early Church is in many instances often a later development or adaptation of earlier traditions, and what were dismissed as seemingly local aberrations are frequently in reality ancient practices that exerted a much more powerful influence on the rest of Christian antiquity than was formerly supposed. Third, the traditional assumption that it was the calendar which gave rise to the lectionary cannot be sustained in every case. On the contrary, as Talley has argued, it may sometimes have been the tradition of reading certain biblical passages at particular times of the year that led to the institution of some feasts and seasons in the annual cycle.

9

Ministry and Ordination

Older Scholarship

The origins and development of Christian ministry has been an even more hotly debated topic than the evolution of Christian liturgy, and for much longer. At first, and especially from the Reformation onwards, the debate focused principally upon whether the offices of bishop and elder/presbyter were quite different from the very beginning, or alternatively were indistinguishable in New Testament times, and monarchical episcopacy therefore a later development. Subsequently, the argument of the Dutch Protestant theologian Vitringa[1] at the end of the seventeenth century, that the Church modelled its presbyterate after the pattern of the Jewish synagogue, influenced the thinking of many nineteenth-century scholars. But that was not the only theory advanced in that period. Some acknowledged the existence of a charismatic ordering of ministry in the Pauline churches, which they believed was only gradually replaced by the institutional structure derived from the synagogue;[2] while others argued that the model for the ministry adopted by the early Church was that of the leadership patterns of the pagan *collegia*. Perhaps the most notable exponent of this last position was Edwin Hatch in his Bampton Lectures at Oxford in 1880,[3] although he did also admit to some influence from the synagogue.

After the publication of the text of the *Didache* in 1883, with its apparent provision for apostles, prophets, and teachers as well as bishops and deacons, alternative theories began to emerge. Adolf Harnack postulated the existence of two forms of leadership alongside one another in early Christianity: itinerant apostles, prophets, and teachers on the one hand; and congregation-

---

1 See above, p. 23.
2 H. J. Holtzmann of the 'history-of-religions school' (above, p. 21) appears to have been an early advocate of this position: *Die Pastoralbriefe, kritisch und exegetisch behandelt* (Leipzig 1880), pp. 194ff.
3 Published as *The Organization of the Early Christian Churches* (London 1881).

ally elected bishops and deacons with administrative duties on the other, the latter eventually taking over the role of the former when that charismatic ministry disappeared, and a distinction then emerging between bishops and presbyters.[4] Rudolph Sohm, however, challenged Harnack's twofold pattern and argued instead for the apostolic Church having had a purely charismatic ministry, which eventually gave way to the threefold ordained ministry,[5] a view that met with heavy criticism in his lifetime but later exerted a profound influence on a large number of twentieth-century German Protestant scholars, including Rudolf Bultmann, Hans von Campenhausen, Eduard Schweizer, and Ernst Käsemann, at least as regards the Pauline churches, if not more universally.[6]

In England, on the other hand, Hatch's view that monarchical episcopacy did not emerge fully until the third century (even though it began to develop from the time of Ignatius of Antioch onwards), met with criticism from a number of leading Anglican theologians anxious to defend the apostolic origin of the office of bishop, among them Charles Gore and the contributors to the volume of essays edited by H. B. Swete, *Essays on the Early History of the Church and the Ministry*. Whatever their views on this particular matter, however, what emerged as the dominant English consensus was that it was from the synagogue that the early Christians had derived the pattern for the shape of their ministry. This opinion was expounded, among others, by J. B. Lightfoot towards the end of the nineteenth century[7] and by Gregory Dix and other contributors to Kenneth Kirk's volume, *The Apostolic Ministry*, in the middle of the twentieth century.[8]

More Recent Studies

As Harry Maier has pointed out in a recent study of early Christian ministry,[9] all of the above theories presumed a considerable degree of uniformity in primitive Christian practice,[10] a view which has increasingly been called into

---

4 See his works, *Die Lehre der zwölf Apostel* (TU 2/1–2, 1884 = 1991), pp. 88–151; *Die Quellen der sog. apostolischen Kirchenordnung*, pp. 31ff.

5 *Kirchenrecht I. Des geschichtlichen Grundlagen* (Leipzig 1892); *Wesen und Ursprung des Katholizmus* (Leipzig 1910).

6 See Bengt Holmberg, 'Sociological versus Theological Analysis of the Question Concerning a Pauline Church Order', in Sigfred Petersen, ed., *Die Paulinische Literatur und Theologie* (Århus/Göttingen 1980), pp. 187–200.

7 *Saint Paul's Epistle to the Philippians* (8th edn, London 1888), pp. 191ff.

8 London 1946.

9 *The Social Setting of the Ministry as Reflected in the Writings of Hermas, Clement and Ignatius* (Waterloo, Ontario 1991), p. 3.

10 But there were some earlier exceptions to the rule: for example, B. H. Streeter, *The Primitive Church* (London 1929) pp. 50ff., argued for varying forms of ministry in

question in recent decades and largely been supplanted in contemporary scholarship by a prevailing vision of early Christianity as constituted by relatively independent trajectories. Maier himself argues that one such trajectory is the adoption of Graeco–Roman household structures of leadership in certain early Christian communities, beginning before or with Paul and extending to Rome (as evidenced by the *Shepherd of Hermas*), Corinth (as evidenced in *1 Clement*), and the Asia Minor communities addressed by Ignatius of Antioch. Maier claims that the typical leaders of the early Christian communities in these places would have been the wealthier members of the Church, with homes large enough to accommodate meetings there, who as the patrons and hosts of the community would have been accorded the position of *patres-familias*. It has, of course, long been recognized that the early Christians generally met in houses, but connections have not often been made between patterns of hospitality and leadership. Although some studies in the last 40 years have begun to assess the importance of the household for leadership in Pauline churches and to abandon the conviction that those churches were under the sole leadership of charismatic ministers,[11] the trajectory has hardly ever been extended beyond that to encompass later, non-canonical sources.[12] In addition to the texts that Maier has studied, Chapters 27–8 of the *Apostolic Tradition* might also be included as an instance of a situation where an older pattern of leadership by the patron was giving way to one exercised by the bishop.[13]

Rather than trying to force the New Testament and post-apostolic testimony to fit into one single mould, therefore, the evidence is better served by the presumption of the probable existence of varied patterns of leadership in different early Christian communities, and also of a variety of influences in bringing those patterns about. In some cases, the disposition of officers in the pagan *collegia* may have played a part in shaping Christian practice, as Hatch

---

different areas of the Roman Empire; and Walter Bauer, *Rechtgläubigkeit und Ketzerei im ältesten Christentum* (Tübingen 1934; ET: *Orthodoxy and Heresy in Earliest Christianity*, Philadelphia 1971) pioneered the idea of a primitive diversity and claimed that it was more appropriate to speak of ministries and developments in the plural rather than in the singular in this period.

11 See Maier, *The Social Setting of the Ministry*, pp. 32–54.

12 Maier cites Ernst Dassmann as one who envisaged a house-church setting for Ignatius' letters: 'Hausgemeinde und Bischofsamt', in *Vivarium: Festschrift Theodor Klauser* (Jahrbuch für Antike und Christentum Ergänzungsband 11; Münster 1984), pp. 82–97; 'Haus', *Reallexikon für Antike und Christentum* 13 (1985), pp. 886–901.

13 See Bradshaw, Johnson, and Phillips, *Apostolic Tradition: A Commentary* on chapters 27–8; Charles Bobertz, 'The Role of Patron in the Cena Dominica of Hippolytus' Apostolic Tradition', *JTS* 44 (1993), pp. 170–84; Alistair Stewart-Sykes, 'The Integrity of the Hippolytean Ordination Rites', *Augustinianum* 39 (1999), pp. 97–127, here at 114–15.

and others formerly argued;[14] in others the Graeco–Roman household may have been more determinative of the arrangement adopted; and in others the patterns of the Jewish synagogue may have been the model, although present-day scholars have begun to be considerably more reserved about this latter influence than those of previous times, as certainty about just what the organizational structure of the synagogue was in the first century has receded.

The variety of forms of Christian leadership would have included in some cases persons who were recognized as leaders because of their possession of particular *charismata*, especially those of prophecy and teaching; in others they may have been those who offered hospitality to the house-churches; and in others they may have been elected to that office by the local congregation, especially where those with obvious charismatic gifts were lacking or there was dissension within the community over who should lead it. Those elected in this way might well have continued to number among them the patrons of the house-church. Sometimes leadership may have been shared between those from two or more of the above groups, for example, the patron and several prophets, rather than being concentrated in one form alone. Similarly, in some cases leadership may have been exercised by a corporate body for a considerable period of time, while in other churches a single individual may have emerged as the principal leader at quite an early stage, with others functioning only in an advisory capacity.

Whether leadership was always restricted to men or at least sometimes included women has also been a much debated topic in recent years. The difficulty here is the lack of decisive evidence. So, for example, Bernadette Brooten made a detailed examination of evidence from inscriptions and other sources in order to try to demonstrate that there were female rulers of synagogues in antiquity,[15] but in the end it is difficult to determine conclusively whether those to whom that title is ascribed were rulers in their own right or merely the wives of rulers. Similarly, much has been made by some of the New Testament testimony that some of the houses where churches met were owned by women (Acts 12.12; Colossians 4.15) and hence the probability that they would have exercised leadership roles there; of the description by Paul of Priscilla/Prisca as a 'fellow-worker' (Romans 16.3–5; cf. Acts

14 Among modern scholars who have pointed to *collegia* as having had a greater or lesser effect, see Robert Wilken, 'Collegia, Philosophical Schools, and Theology', in Stephen Benko and John J. O'Rourke, eds, *The Catacombs and the Colosseum* (Valley Forge, PA 1971/London 1972), pp. 268–91; William Countryman, 'Patrons and Officers in Club and Church', in Paul J. Achtemeier, ed., *Society of Biblical Literature 1977 Seminar Papers* (Missoula, MT 1977), pp. 135–43; Wayne Meeks, *The First Urban Christians* (New Haven, CT 1983), pp. 77–80; Abraham J. Malherbe, *Social Aspects of Early Christianity* (Baton Rouge, LA 1977), pp. 87–91. All these, however, attribute more influence to the household.

15 *Women Leaders in the Ancient Synagogue* (BJS 36, 1982).

18.1–3, 18, 25; 1 Corinthians 16.19); of the possibility that the apostle Junia(s) was a woman (Romans 16.7); and of the mention of Phoebe as a deacon (Romans 16.1); but again these references are not unambiguous. And it is equally difficult to determine whether the exercise of liturgical presidency by women among the Montanists and within some Gnostic groups during the second century represents a deliberate deviation from mainstream tradition or alternatively the survival of a once more widespread Christian practice from earlier times before the ministries of women became restricted.[16]

The original debate about the relationship between *episkopoi* and *presbyteroi* in the New Testament era has taken a new turn in some scholarly writings in recent years. Although the dominant consensus for some time has been that the two titles were at first synonyms for the same office – with perhaps one being preferred in some places and the other in other localities – and only became distinguished later, several scholars have suggested that presbyters originally may not have been church officers in the same sense that an *episkopos* was. Just as the term *diakonos* and *diakonia* can be used both in a general, seemingly non-technical sense to refer to 'minister' and 'ministry' in the New Testament and other early sources (e.g., 1 Timothy 4.6), and also at the same time more specifically to denote a particular official called a 'deacon' and the 'diaconate', so too *presbyteroi* seems to be capable of several meanings: its normal Greek sense of 'older people', to whom societal norms would expect respect to be paid because of their age; perhaps also a more specifically Christian sense of 'those senior in the faith', i.e., those who had been converted longer and therefore deserving of respect for that reason; and a third, more specific, technical sense of 'elders' as a council whose opinion and judgement were respected in the Christian community, probably composed of persons drawn from both of the earlier categories, which would in any case have overlapped.

Thus Frances Young has proposed that in the Pastoral Epistles the *episkopos* (singular) and the *diakonoi* were the only appointed officers of a congregation in a pattern modelled on the household (1 Timothy 3.15) – the *episkopos* being the equivalent of the steward of the household (Titus 1.7) and the *diakonoi* of the servants – while *presbyteros* is used in a non-technical sense (1 Timothy 5.1; Titus 2.2) but *presbyterion* appears with reference to a council of seniors (1 Timothy 4.14).[17] A similar pattern can also be seen both

16 On these matters see, among other works: Ute E. Eisen, *Women Officeholders in Early Christianity: Epigraphical and Literary Studies* (Collegeville 2000); Elisabeth Schüssler Fiorenza, *In Memory of Her: A Feminist Theological Reconstruction of Christian Origins* (New York 1984); Karen Jo Torjesen, *When Women Were Priests: Women's Leadership in the Early Church and the Scandal of Their Subordination in the Rise of Christianity* (San Francisco 1993).

17 However, while in this letter the presbyters seem to have appointed the recipient (as *episkopos*?) with the imposition of hands, in Titus 1.5 the recipient is instructed to appoint the elders, who are then described as *episkopoi*, which suggests that a somewhat different arrangement was operative in this case.

in the letters of Ignatius of Antioch and in the third-century *Didascalia*, where the bishop and the deacons are the ministers of the congregation and the presbyters an advisory council. Frances Young tentatively suggests that increasing conformity to the model of the synagogue may have encouraged this development, with its ruler (*archisynagogos*), attendants, and council of elders, a movement from being God's household to being God's people.[18] It also seems to be confirmed to some extent by later practice, where a candidate for the episcopate might be elevated directly from the diaconate, without the presbyterate being viewed as a necessary intervening step.[19]

Disputed Leadership

It would be natural to expect that the transition from the older patterns of leadership to the later standard model was not always accomplished smoothly and without controversy within individual communities, and also that earlier situations of shared leadership might themselves produce tensions and conflict. Indeed, such disputes do appear to have left their mark upon some early Christian literature.

The general consensus with regard to ministry in the *Didache* essentially follows Harnack in seeing it as evidence for a situation where charismatic leaders were gradually being replaced by elected bishops and deacons (no mention being made of presbyters) because of a decline in both the quality and number of the former, and where this transition involved something of a struggle. André de Halleux, however, has argued against this conclusion and claimed that: prophets and teachers in the *Didache* constitute one category and not two; they were usually resident and not itinerant; they existed alongside bishops and deacons rather than being replaced by them; and there is no need to view Chapter 15 as a later addition to the rest of the text, as many scholars do.[20] While this may go a little too far, it is possible that the *Didache* does reflect a situation where both charismatic and elected officials had formerly shared together in the leadership of the community, with different responsibilities, but that with the decline of the former, the latter were now being called upon to fulfil a wider role and take upon themselves functions once exercised by the charismatic leaders. This would explain why *Didache* 15.2 finds it necessary to exhort its readers not to 'despise them, for

---

18 'On Episkopos and Presbyteros', *JTS* 45 (1994), pp. 142–8. On the household setting of the Pastoral Epistles, see also David C. Verner, *The Household of God: The Social World of the Pastoral Epistles* (Chico, CA 1983).

19 See John St H. Gibaut, *The Cursus Honorum: A Study of the Origins and Evolution of Sequential Ordination* (New York 2000).

20 'Les ministères dans la Didachè', *Irénikon* 53 (1980), pp. 5–29 = 'Ministers in the Didache', in Draper, ed., *The Didache in Modern Research*, pp. 300–20.

they are those who are to be honoured by you with the prophets and teachers': there would have been a not unnatural reluctance on the part of congregations to accept them as the equals of those more obviously gifted. It would also explain the existence of prayer-texts in *Didache* 9–10, an unusual feature in Christianity as in early Judaism, where prayers were not normally written down. While prophets were to be free to use their own words (10.7), less gifted worship leaders might need some written help to prevent them appearing liturgically incompetent.

The *Shepherd of Hermas* is believed to have originated in Rome and is usually dated around the middle of the second century, although several recent scholars have contended that it was written much earlier, near the end of the first century.[21] Whatever the truth of this claim, the document certainly reflects a very primitive stage of development of ministry. It is not entirely clear whether the term *diakonoi* here (*Sim.* 9.26.2) refers to 'deacons' as such or is being used in a more general sense, as *diakonia* is (*Sim.* 9.27.2). The author addresses his remarks to 'those who are leaders (*proegoumenoi*) of the church' and to 'those in the first seats (*protokathedritais*)' (*Vis.* 2.2.6; 3.9.7). Elsewhere there is mention of 'the presbyters who preside in the church' (*Vis.* 2.4.3) and *episkopoi* who have a ministry (*diakonia*) of hospitality (*Sim.* 9.27.2). The question which arises, therefore, is whether all of these refer to a single group of people, or whether distinctions should be made between them. Maier believes that certain elders out of a larger presbyteral body acted as bishops, each one representing a house-church, although there was not as yet a full distinction between *episkopoi* and *presbyteroi*.[22] This is certainly a plausible explanation, but not the only possible one.

It is also apparent that prophets exercised some authority within this community, for the author is told to communicate his prophetic visions to the elders (*Vis.* 2.4.2–3). Although there is no explicit evidence for the existence of specific conflict between prophetic and presbyteral authority, yet there are many references to divisions between members, at least some of which were over prominence and involved leaders (*Vis.* 3.9.9–10; *Sim.* 8.7.4; 9.31.4–6), and in one place a false prophet is described as 'coveting the first seat (*protokathedria*)' (*Man.* 11.12), which certainly suggests a lack of harmonious leadership within the church. A further possibility, both here and in the *Didache*, is that every house-church did not possess the full diversity of ministers mentioned, but that, for example, some might have been under the leadership of a prophet and others under that of an *episkopos*, and standardization was yet to come.

---

21 Among them, James S. Jeffers, *Conflict at Rome: Social Order and Hierarchy in Early Christianity* (Minneapolis 1991), pp. 106–12; Maier, *The Social Setting of the Ministry*, pp. 55–8.
22 *The Social Setting of the Ministry*, pp. 63–4.

On the other hand, dispute over leadership is clearly manifested in the *First Epistle of Clement*, written from the church at Rome to the Christians in Corinth and usually dated *c.* 96 CE, although both earlier and later dates have occasionally been suggested instead.[23] The whole letter is a denunciation of those in Corinth who have removed from office some who have fulfilled their ministry blamelessly (44.6). Attempts have been made by various scholars to determine the cause of the dispute, whether it was, for example, charismatic or gnostic Christians who were rejecting the authority structures, a rebellion by the young against the old, a theological dispute, or merely a personality clash; but there is simply not enough evidence to draw any firm conclusions,[24] and in any case the letter may reveal more about the situation in the Roman church than it does about the church at Corinth. Maier concluded that there had been 'a division within one or two of the Corinthian house churches which has resulted in the creation of an alternative meeting place, the exodus of members who are sympathetic with these persons and, presumably, the exclusion of members who are opposed to them'.[25] On the other hand, the author of the letter could have been trying to play down the seriousness and extent of the disruption, which may have involved more than just 'a few reckless and arrogant individuals' (1.1; see also 47.6).

Unlike the *Shepherd of Hermas*, explicit mention is made here of an office of deacon, but references to bishops and presbyters in the letter have been treated by most scholars as denoting the same office, the corporate leadership of the church. However, it may perhaps be better to see those called bishops as emerging out of a larger group of elders within the community, and this would certainly provide a better fit for the analogy of the threefold minister-ial structure of the Old Testament – high-priest, priests, Levites – that the author uses (40.5) as one of his major arguments to defend the divinely intended permanence of appointment of office. The author not only cites scriptural precedent in defence of his position, but also claims apostolic insti-tution. His assertion that the apostles themselves originally appointed their first converts as bishops and deacons – an arrangement which was no novelty but already prophesied in Isaiah 60.17 (42.4–5) – may perhaps contain a kernel of genuine historical truth, but it is interesting to note that when it comes to maintaining that they intended these offices to be held for life, he seems to speak somewhat more cautiously, saying that they 'afterwards added the codicil that if they should fall asleep, other approved men should succeed

---

23 See, for example, A. E. W. Hooijbergh, 'A Different View of Clement Romanus', *Heythrop Journal* 16 (1975), pp. 266–8; John A. T. Robinson, *Redating the New Testament* (London/Philadelphia 1976), pp. 327–35; Lawrence Wellborn, 'On the date of First Clement', *Biblical Research* 29 (1984), pp. 35–54.

24 *The Social Setting of the Ministry*, pp. 87–94.

25 ibid., p. 93.

to their ministry' (44.2). Was this because he knew that the recipients of the letter would have been cognizant of some churches which were not governed in this way? For it is interesting that in the whole of this lengthy and impassioned plea for obedience to God's will, the author never once plays what would surely have been a trump card – a reference to the fact that the expulsion of presbyters is unheard of, and contrary to the practice of all churches. Later Christian writers had no hesitation in making universalistic claims for various liturgical practices which were in reality far from being generally observed. Why then did our author draw back from using such an argument? Could it have been because he was well aware that such an assertion could easily be disproved?

The letters of Ignatius of Antioch, conventionally dated early in the second century, provide the earliest clear evidence for a threefold order of bishop, presbyters, and deacons, at least in some churches. In them, the bishop's presidential role was compared to that of either God the Father or of Jesus Christ, the presbyterate to the college of the apostles, and the deacons were seen as entrusted with the ministry, *diakonia*, of Jesus.[26] Yet even here episcopal leadership was apparently not accepted without question, and Ignatius has repeatedly to insist on the necessity of obedience to the bishop, presbyters, and deacons. While both these letters and *1 Clement* have traditionally been understood as merely expressing what was the established practice in the Church at the time, that ministers were always appointed for life and that episcopal government was the norm, more recent study has suggested that, since they were both apparently having to argue the case at considerable length and with great vigour against opponents who seemingly did not share their conclusions, they actually represent only one view among others at the time, a view which ultimately came to triumph but which did not achieve supremacy without a considerable struggle against alternative positions and practices. Thus Christine Trevett has argued that Ignatius' opponents, who were continuing to hold their own liturgical assemblies, were being led by those displaying prophetic gifts, with the result that Ignatius himself is forced into the rather odd position of claiming that he too has received a charismatic revelation – that the people should respect episcopal rather than charismatic authority![27]

By the end of the second century, however, the threefold ministry of

---

26 See Ignatius, *Magn.* 6.1; *Smyrn.* 8; *Trall.* 2–3.1. Irenaeus late in the second century (*Adv. haer.* 3.12.10; 4.15.1) is the first writer to make a connection between the diaconate and Stephen and his companions in Acts 6, but the older typology still persists in the third-century *Didascalia* (2.26.5; 2.28.4; 2.34.3), *Apostolic Tradition* 8, and some other later writings.

27 'Prophecy and Anti-episcopal Activity: A Third Error Combatted by Ignatius?', *JEH* 34 (1983), pp. 1–18.

bishops, presbyters, and deacons does seem to have gained pre-eminence everywhere in mainstream Christianity, and the episcopate had either subsumed into itself other ministries, especially those formerly exercised by teachers and prophets (and with that the right to extemporize the eucharistic prayer as those charismatic figures had done), or at least brought them under episcopal control.[28] Yet this may not have been quite as firm a grasp as is often portrayed. For it has been claimed that even the *Didascalia* in the third century reflects an attempt to impose episcopal structure on the church and restrict the activity and authority of women;[29] *Apostolic Tradition* 9 refers to an otherwise unknown provision that those who had confessed the faith had the 'honour of the presbyterate' without the need for ordination (and hence their appointment was not subject to episcopal regulation); and in the writings of Cyprian we can observe his need to resist attempts by presbyters to act independently of him in permitting the reconciliation of the lapsed to the church. Indeed, this experience seems to have brought about a change in his policy, in ceasing to treat presbyters as his counsellors, whom he made a point of consulting on all matters, and instead regarding them as his subordinates[30] – a practice which thereafter increasingly became the norm everywhere. The situation in North Africa, however, is complicated by the existence of a further group of *seniores*, who seem to be some sort of lay advisory body and thus closer in character to the original form of the presbyterate elsewhere than are the local presbyters themselves.[31]

Priesthood

Prior to the beginning of the third century, no Christian text uses the title 'priest' (*hiereus* in Greek, *sacerdos* in Latin) directly to designate a particular individual or group of ministers within the Church. Instead, sacerdotal terminology is applied both to Christ – usually as 'high-priest', following the language of the Letter to the Hebrews (e.g., Justin, *Dialogue with Trypho* 116.1; Irenaeus, *Adv. haer.* 4.8.2) – and also to Christians in general, following 1 Peter 2.9; Revelation 1.6; 5.10; 20.6. Christians constituted 'the true

---

28 With regard to the way in which the ministry of the word was exercised, see Bradshaw, *Liturgical Presidency in the Early Church*, pp. 16–19.

29 C. Methuen, 'Widows, Bishops and the Struggle for Authority in the *Didascalia Apostolorum*', *JEH* 46 (1995), pp. 197–213. But cf. Georg Schöllgen, *Die Anfänge der Professionalisierung des Klerus und das kirchliche Amt in der Syrischen Didaskalie* (Münster 1998).

30 See Albano Vilela, *La condition collégiale des prêtres au IIIe siècle* (Paris 1971), pp. 273–303.

31 See W. H. C. Frend, 'The *seniores laici* and the origins of the Church in North Africa', *JTS* 12 (1961), pp. 280–4; Brent D. Shaw, 'The elders of Christian Africa', *Mélanges offerts en hommage au Révérend Père Étienne Gareau* (Quebec 1982), pp. 207–26.

high-priestly race of God' (Justin, *Dialogue with Trypho* 116.3; see also Irenaeus, *Adv. haer.* 4.8.3; 5.34.3), whose principal sacrifice was the oblation of their lives (see Romans 12.1) but also included the offering of worship, both eucharistic and non-eucharistic (e.g., *Didache* 14.1; Justin, *Dialogue with Trypho* 117.1ff.; Irenaeus, *Adv. haer.* 4.17.5–6).

This imagery was continued in the centuries that followed. Thus, for example, the baptismal anointing of a Christian was often interpreted in a priestly sense, as we have seen, and the eucharistic prayer in the *Apostolic Tradition* speaks of Christians as having been made worthy to stand before God and serve as priests. Moreover, both widowhood (Tertullian, *Ad uxorem* 1.7) and martyrdom (Cyprian, *Ep.* 76.3) could also be described as special forms of priestly consecration. Alongside this, however, began to develop a different usage, the seeds of which can already be seen at the end of the first century: *Didache* 13.3 compares Christian prophets to high-priests when speaking of the offering of firstfruits; and *1 Clement* cites the example of the assignment of different cultic roles to different ministers in the Old Testament Law as an argument against Christians transgressing the appointed limits of their respective ranks (40–41), and also uses the cultic expression 'offered the gifts' in relation to Christian presbyter-bishops rather than the Christian community as a whole (44.4). These passages, however, are unique within Christian literature of the first two centuries, and in any case do not go as far as explicitly saying that Christian ministers are priests. It is not until the beginning of the third century that sacerdotal terminology starts to be used regularly and in a more literal manner to refer to ordained ministers.

The episcopal office was naturally the first to be described in priestly terms. Tertullian uses the term 'high-priest' (*summus sacerdos*) to denote the bishop only once in his writings, and then in a context which suggests that it may perhaps have been a metaphor occasioned by the particular argument rather than a regular term for the office (*De bapt.* 17.1); but he implies elsewhere that priest, *sacerdos*, may have become a commonly used designation for the bishop in the North African church;[32] and Cyprian, half a century later, regularly calls the bishop *sacerdos*, reserving *summus sacerdos* for Christ alone (e.g., *Ep.* 63.14). This development was by no means restricted to North Africa. In Alexandria, Origen consistently described bishops as priests (e.g., *De oratione* 28); and as we shall see, the *Apostolic Tradition* also viewed the episcopal office as sacerdotal. In this latter case, however, there is a significant difference in the terminology employed, the bishop being seen in his ordination prayer not merely as 'priest' but as exercising the high-priesthood (*archierateuein*) and as possessing authority 'through the high-priestly spirit'. The same is true of the *Didascalia*: while acknowledging that Christ is the true

32 *De exhort. cast.* 11.1–2; *De monog.* 12; *De pud.* 20.10; 21.17.

high-priest, at the same time it does not hesitate to call the bishop 'the levitical high-priest' (2.26.4). Thereafter sacerdotal terminology became standard in theological discourse about the bishop in both East and West, although there are still vestiges in certain later sources of some hesitation over the appropriateness of its adoption. Augustine, for instance, uses *sacerdos* more cautiously than his contemporaries, at least in part because of his need to insist on the unique priesthood of Christ in his debate with the Donatists (e.g., *Parm.* 2.8.15–16).

Because of their close association with the bishop, presbyters were also naturally thought of as sharing in his priesthood, but it is not clear whether third-century theologians would have understood them individually to possess a priesthood that was independent of the priesthood of the bishop. Indeed, some scholars have maintained that presbyters were not called priests unequivocally until the fifth century. Thus, although Tertullian on one occasion does say that presbyters belong to the *ordo sacerdotalis* (*De exhort. cast.* 7), the passages where he might seem to call them *sacerdotes* are all ambiguous (e.g., *De pud.* 20.7).[33] A similar doubt also exists in the case of Cyprian. Like Tertullian, he certainly understood presbyters to share in the priesthood exercised by the bishop (e.g., *Ep.* 1.1.1; 61.3.1), but scholars have disputed whether he regarded them as priests in their own right (see, e.g., *Ep.* 40.1.2; 67.4.3).[34] The *Didascalia* sees presbyters as corresponding to Old Testament priests, but in a passage which concerns the offering of tithes and extends the image to include both orphans and widows (2.26.3); the comparison may therefore be intended more to justify their financial support than to ascribe cultic status, as also seems to be the case in *Didache* 13.3 mentioned above. On the other hand, Origen does speak of presbyters as exercising an inferior priesthood (*Hom. in Exod.* 11.6; *Hom. in Lev.* 6.6).[35] This concept was probably inspired by 2 Kings 23.4 and is one which recurs in later writings, including the classic Roman ordination prayer for presbyters, which equates them with the 'men of a lesser order and secondary dignity' (*sequentis ordinis viros et secundae dignitatis*) chosen by God as assistants to the high-priests in the Old Testament.[36]

While the *Apostolic Tradition* does not regard deacons as forming part of

33 See, for example, Maurice Bevénot, 'Tertullian's Thoughts about the Christian "Priesthood"', in *Corona Gratiarum I. Miscellanea Patristica, Historica et Liturgica, Eligio Dekkers OSB XII Lustra Complenti Oblata* (Bruges 1975), pp. 125–37.
34 See Maurice Bevénot, '"Sacerdos" as Understood by Cyprian', *JTS* 30 (1979), pp. 413–29; John D. Laurance, *'Priest' as Type of Christ. The Leader of the Eucharist in Salvation History According to Cyprian of Carthage* (New York 1984); Vilela, *La condition collégiale des prêtres au IIIe siècle*, pp. 281–5.
35 See Vilela, *La condition collégiale des prêtres au IIIe siècle*, pp. 83–98.
36 See also Innocent I, *Ep. ad Decentium* 3; Leo I, *Serm.* 48.1; Gregory I, *Hom. in Ezek.* 10.13.

the priesthood, arguing that this was why the bishop alone – and not the bishop and presbyters together – laid hands on a candidate for the diaconate, its ordination prayer for a deacon described his duties as being 'to present in your holy of holies that which is offered to you by your appointed high-priest', thus implying that he was the equivalent of the Levite. The *Didascalia* explicitly compared the deacon to the Levite (2.26.3), as did Origen (*Hom. in Jos.* 2.1), and this typology later became common. A few ancient writers, however, were willing to extend this image further and speak of the diaconate as constituting a third order *within* the priesthood. The earliest extant instance of this view is in Optatus of Milevis in the fourth century (*Adv. Don.* 1.13), and it became standard in later Eastern, but not Western, thought. The Syrian church order, the *Testamentum Domini*, goes even further than this and calls widows, readers, and subdeacons 'priests' as well (1.23), but like the passage from the *Didascalia* referred to above in relation to presbyters, this may possibly have more to do with their right to financial support from the Christian community than with their cultic status as such.

A similar diversity of opinion can be seen in the early Church with regard to the limits of the term 'clergy' (*kleros* in Greek, *clerus* in Latin). The word originally meant a 'lot', both in the sense of the token used in a lottery and in the sense of an allotment of land, but it was adopted by Christian writers from Clement of Alexandria onwards (*Quis dives salvetur* 42) as a designation for ordained ministers. The reasons for this are not entirely clear, but it may well be derived from the allocation of priestly duties by lot in the Old Testament (e.g., 1 Chronicles 24.5; 25.8), especially as the *Apostolic Tradition* uses the expression 'to give lots' in its ordination prayer for a bishop apparently to mean 'to assign ecclesiastical duties' (3; see also *Apostolic Tradition* 30, and cf. 1 Peter 5.3). Later, however, Augustine related it to the election of Matthias by lot in Acts 1.26 (*Psal.* 67.16), while Jerome (*Ep.* 52.5) connected it with the Levites who possessed no land because the Lord was their lot (Numbers 18.20), an interpretation derived from Philo (*De spec. leg.* 1.131,156). This explanation became enormously popular in later centuries, and was used to justify the special status, privileges, and rights of the clergy. At first, however, it was not clear which of the ordained ministers were to be accounted as 'clergy'. The *Apostolic Tradition* seems to exclude deacons from 'the council of the clergy' because they lack the 'common and similar spirit of the clergy' (8), but some passages in ancient authors seem to use the term clergy inclusively of all ordained ministers, while others include deacons but exclude bishops from the designation (e.g., Tertullian, *De monog.* 12.1). Later writers tended to adopt this last usage and speak of 'bishops and clergy'.

From the above it can be seen that the application of sacerdotal language and imagery to Christian ministers evolved only slowly. Some conservative scholars would understand this to be merely the gradual unfolding of a reality which was already present in the priesthood of Christ and shared from the outset by bishops and presbyters, who acted in the place of Christ (*vice Christi*), even though Cyprian was the first to articulate this idea explicitly (*Ep.* 63.14). Others would understand it to be a genuinely new development at the end of the second century, marking the inception of a major change in the relationship between the people and their ministers within the Church: bishops and presbyters would eventually cease to be seen as the presiders within a priestly people, and become instead a priesthood acting on behalf of 'the laity' – a term already used in this sense in *1 Clement* 40.5. Although thereafter liturgical texts themselves might still carry the more ancient image of the common priesthood in which all Christians participated, both theological discourse and ecclesiastical practice instead viewed ordination rather than baptism as the decisive point of entry into the priestly life.

Scholars who adopt this latter view often interpret the development largely as the result of social pressures on the Church, because in the ancient world a religion needed a priesthood. But this explanation does not seem sufficient to account for it. At the period when sacerdotal language first emerged, Christian apologists were still insisting that Christianity was not a religion like others in the ancient world. Moreover, Judaism, which survived the loss of the Temple by viewing synagogue worship as a surrogate for the cult, did not find it necessary to take this step at all. It is perhaps more likely, therefore, that what caused Christianity to begin to regard its ministers as priests was the increasing importance which came to be attached to authoritative leadership in the Church's struggle against heresy and schism during the course of the second century. In this situation the sense of the unity of the whole Christian community became less significant than the part played by the ordained ministers within it, and so in turn the pattern of Old Testament sacrificial worship gradually came to be seen as fulfilled in a more literal fashion in the persons of those ministers rather than in a more spiritual way by the body as a whole.

It is vitally important to recognize, however, that while the source of the image of priesthood for Christianity may be the cultic practices of the Old Testament, the concept of the sacerdotal office in the early Church went far beyond merely the offering of sacrifice. Praxis shaped theory, and not the other way around. Thus, priestly service was not simply focused on the Eucharist but also included the celebration of other sacramental rites, and even more significantly was understood to extend to both preaching and teaching. So, for example, John Chrysostom in his homily on the day of his presbyteral ordination proclaimed that he had been placed among the priests and that the word was his sacrifice.[37]

---

37 Migne, *Patrologia Graeca* 48.694,699; see also Cyprian, *Ep.* 63.18.3; and one of the Byzantine ordination prayers for presbyters, which incorporates the phrase 'exercise the sacred ministry of the word'.

Evidence for Ordination: The *Apostolic Tradition*

Although certain early sources offer evidence that some ministers were elected to their office, they provide no details of the process, nor any indication of what else besides election might have been involved. Thus, *Didache* 15.1 instructs its readers to 'elect for yourselves therefore bishops and deacons worthy of the Lord'; and *1 Clement* 44.3 speaks of ministers having been appointed by the apostles 'or afterwards by other eminent men with the consent of the whole church'. Some further evidence of election procedures is provided by Cyprian and others in the third century,[38] but no source before the fourth century, with the possible exception of the so-called *Apostolic Tradition*, refers to anything resembling an ordination rite such as we find in later evidence. For that reason this church order has assumed an even more crucial role in establishing ancient ordination practice than it has in other areas of liturgy. Unfortunately, however, the uncertainties surrounding its true origin and provenance make it a very unreliable witness, and its ordination prescriptions themselves show signs of having undergone considerable modification.

The rite for the episcopate confronts us with two distinct difficulties in accepting the extant text as its oldest form. First, the various linguistic versions in which the church order has been preserved differ markedly with regard to their mention of the participation of other bishops in the whole procedure. While both the Latin text and the version in *Apostolic Constitutions* 8 include 'those bishops who are present' in the list of those who are to assemble for the ordination, the Sahidic, Arabic, and Ethiopic versions have 'deacons' instead, and insert a somewhat clumsy reference to bishops in the next sentence: 'all the bishops who have laid their hands on him shall give consent . . . ' On the other hand, the *Canons of Hippolytus* does not refer to the presence of bishops at all until the final sentence of the instructions, when it suddenly and rather oddly says: 'they choose one of the bishops and presbyters; he lays his hand . . . ' Dix thought that this was a sign of what he called 'theoretical presbyterianism' on the part of the redactor of the *Canons of Hippolytus*,[39] but in the light of the variations in the other versions, it seems more likely that Ratcliff was correct when he claimed that 'discernible between the lines of the several versions of *Apostolic Tradition* there are signs which can be taken as indicating that, in its original form, the direction instructed the presbyters to conduct the proceedings.'[40]

38 See Roger Gryson, 'Les élections ecclésiastiques au IIIe siècle', *Revue d'histoire ecclésiastique* 68 (1973), pp. 353–404.
39 *The Treatise on the Apostolic Tradition of St Hippolytus*, pp. lxxviii–lxxix.
40 'Apostolic Tradition: Questions concerning the Appointment of the Bishop', *SP* 8 (1966), pp. 266–70, here at 269 = *Liturgical Studies*, pp. 156–60.

If this was so, then the various references to the involvement of other bishops would have been supplied later by the individual redactors of the versions in order to bring the text into line with what had by their day become the standard contemporary practice.[41] The earliest reference to the involvement of other bishops appears in the letters of Cyprian in North Africa in the middle of the third century,[42] but this does not prove that the practice was universal by this date. There is at least some evidence to suggest that in Alexandria the older custom of presbyters presiding at the ordination of their new bishop persisted at least until the middle of the third century, if not later,[43] and the same may well also have been the case elsewhere. Indeed, the fact that the Council of Nicea (canons 4 and 6) found it necessary to legislate for the participation of other bishops suggests that it was not even accepted everywhere by the early fourth century.[44]

Second, the rite looks as if it is a composite one, formed by the combination of two originally distinct texts. This is suggested particularly by the apparent double imposition of hands and by the rather strange use of the conjunction *ex quibus* in the Latin version at what seems to be the point at which the two texts are joined.[45] In the first of the two rites the presbyters originally laid hands together on the candidate and all prayed in silence for the descent of the Holy Spirit; in the second it was one of the presbyters (or was it one of the bishops?) who acted on behalf of the others, laying hands alone on the candidate and saying an ordination prayer. It thus reveals two quite different ways of conducting an ordination. The former has otherwise disappeared almost without trace in later traditions, where silent prayer occurs only as a preliminary to an ordination prayer proper, and a collective imposition of hands appears only in texts which are derived from the *Apostolic Tradition* itself.[46]

In addition, the ordination prayer is so very different from most later ordination prayers that it seems unlikely to have been typical of those of the pre-fourth-century period. (Indeed, Eric Segelberg has attempted to discern an original text beneath what he regards as later strata, but his reconstruction is not entirely convincing.[47]) Not only, as we noted earlier, does the prayer use

41 See Paul F. Bradshaw, 'The Participation of Other Bishops in the Ordination of a Bishop in the *Apostolic Tradition* of Hippolytus', *SP* 18/2 (1989), pp. 335–8.
42 *Ep.* 55.8; 67.5. See T. Osawa, *Das Bischofseinsetzungsverfahren bei Cyprian* (Frankfurt/Bern 1983).
43 See Vilela, *La condition collégiale des prêtres au IIIe siècle*, pp. 173–9, and the works cited in n. 5 there.
44 See C. W. Griggs, *Early Egyptian Christianity: From its Origins to 451 C.E.* (Leiden 1990), pp. 132–3.
45 On both the points, see further Bradshaw, Johnson, and Phillips, *Apostolic Tradition: A Commentary* on chapter 2.
46 See Bradshaw, *Ordination Rites of the Ancient Churches of East and West*, pp. 30–2, 44–6.
47 'The Ordination Prayers in Hippolytus', *SP* 13 (1975), pp. 397–408.

'high-priest' rather than the more common 'priest' to designate the bishop, but its overall strongly sacerdotal character and its detailed listing of the powers of the episcopate is unlike most ancient ordination prayers for a bishop. While it is true that most of these prayers do have some reference to the priestly character of the episcopal office, in nearly every case this is peripheral to the main imagery of the prayer, and so appears to be a secondary addition, and even the ordination prayer for a bishop in the fourth-century *Canons of Hippolytus* excises all the high-priestly language from the version found in the *Apostolic Tradition*. Only the classic Roman ordination prayer has as its central theme the priestly character of the episcopate, and even this does not enumerate the individual functions belonging to the order, as that in the *Apostolic Tradition* does, but concentrates instead on the inner qualities requisite in a true bishop as the spiritual counterpart of the Old Testament high-priest. Similarly, no other extant prayer from ancient times lists in its primary stratum the powers and functions of the episcopate in the way that this one does. In other prayers, the fundamental images are generally those of shepherd and teacher, with either the precise liturgical and pastoral functions associated with the office left largely unspecified (as, for example, in the case of the Byzantine rite) or with their being added in what are obviously secondary strata in the prayer originating in later centuries (as in the East and West Syrian rites).[48]

The rite for the ordination of a presbyter also raises questions. The direction that the presbyters as well as the bishop are to lay their hands on the ordinand is unparalleled in ancient ordination rites, except for those directly dependent on this text.[49] Does it therefore represent a very old tradition, one that may ante-date the existence of a distinct episcopate when presbyters collectively laid hands on a new member of their order? Did the emergence of the episcopal office lead to the need to include in *Apostolic Tradition* 8 the explanation that the presbyters' touching did not mean that they were doing what the bishop did? And was it the possibility of misinterpretation that caused the practice subsequently to disappear from virtually all other ecclesiastical traditions? Or was the practice merely a local custom that did not survive later standardization, or even merely the invention of the compiler?

Several scholars have claimed to see a strongly Jewish background to the prayer for a presbyter. Thus, Gregory Dix was of the opinion that its substance might go back to the earliest Jewish–Christian synagogues governed by a college of presbyters, or even to pre-Christian Jewish practice,[50] and a similar view was put forward by

---

48 Bradshaw, *Ordination Rites of the Ancient Churches of East and West*, pp. 46–56.
49 ibid., pp. 59–60.
50 'The Ministry in the Early Church', in Kirk, ed., *The Apostolic Ministry*, pp. 183–303, here at p. 218.

Albano Vilela.[51] Pierre-Marie Gy, however, was more cautious, admitting that 'one could suspect some rabbinic background, especially in connection with the typology of the seventy elders and Moses', but adding the warning that 'for the ordination of rabbis, as for the berakah, one should not give excessive value to rather late texts'.[52] This caution seems very wise in the light of Lawrence Hoffman's conclusions that the term 'rabbi' did not come into use until after the destruction of the Jerusalem Temple, and that although individual rabbis subsequently did appoint disciples, if ever there was any liturgical ceremony associated with this act, we do not know anything about it.[53]

However, this prayer certainly has a more ancient feel to it than the prayer for the bishop, especially as the text has only the briefest reference to Christ at the beginning and a total absence of any clear New Testament allusions. Its central focus is on the typology of the 70 elders appointed by Moses (Numbers 11.16f.) and on the presbyterate's role in governing the Christian community. Allen Brent has argued that because of this different vision of the role of the ordained ministry from the more sacerdotal picture of the episcopate, both prayers cannot have been 'part of an original single rite of the Roman community',[54] and Alistair Stewart-Sykes has taken Brent's line of argument further still and claimed, very improbably, that the prayer for the bishop is the older of the two and that for the presbyter a third-century interpolation, but from within the same school as that in which the bishop's prayer arose.[55]

The rite for the deacon seems to imply an election by the community, in contrast to both the *Didascalia* and the letters of Cyprian, which state that the bishop appointed deacons,[56] although the latter observed that he usually consulted the clergy and people before acting, and remnants of a popular approbation can also be seen in a number of later ordination rites.[57] As noted above, the prayer combines the typology of the *diakonia* of Christ, found from Ignatius of Antioch onwards, with that of the Old Testament Levite, found in the *Didascalia*, Origen, and other later writings, whose duty is to serve the 'high-priest', suggesting that it belongs to the same stratum of material as the ordination prayer for the bishop.

---

51 *La condition collégiale des prêtres au IIIe siècle*, p. 354.
52 'Ancient Ordination Prayers', *SL* 13 (1979), p. 82. See also Georg Kretschmar, 'Die Ordination im frühen Christentum', *Freiburger Zeitschrift für Philosophie und Theologie* 22 (1975), pp. 46–55.
53 'Jewish Ordination on the Eve of Christianity', *SL* 13 (1979), pp. 11–41.
54 *Hippolytus and the Roman Church in the Third Century*, p. 305; see also ibid., pp. 465–91.
55 'The Integrity of the Hippolytean Ordination Rites'.
56 Cyprian *Ep.* 32.1; 64.3; 67.4–5; *Didascalia* 3.12.1.
57 Bradshaw, *Ordination Rites of the Ancient Churches of East and West*, pp. 21–5.

The Fourth Century

The *Apostolic Tradition*, therefore, does not provide much of a basis on which to make generalizations about ordination practice before the fourth century, and even that century offers relatively little additional evidence. There is some further information concerning the conduct of episcopal elections,[58] but there is only one collection of ordination prayers for bishop, presbyter, and deacon which is not directly derived from those in the *Apostolic Tradition*, and that is in the *Sacramentary of Sarapion*.[59] This consists simply of the prayers themselves, without any directions at all to indicate the rest of the rite. Maxwell Johnson has argued that these three prayers reflect two different strata of material, those for the bishop and deacon belonging to one and that for the presbyter to another, as also seems to be the case in the *Apostolic Tradition*, with which the prayer for a presbyter in this collection also shares the typology of the 70 elders appointed by Moses and the presbyterate's role in governing the Christian community.[60] In addition to this source there are a few references to details of ordination practices in some late-fourth-century writings, especially with regard to the custom of imposing the book of gospels on the head of a bishop at his ordination,[61] but all these together are not sufficient to paint a clear and complete picture of ordination rites at this time. On the other hand, a comparative examination of the texts of later ordination rites does reveal at their core the existence of a fairly consistent pattern throughout East and West, including the main themes of the prayers,[62] which strongly suggests that this common shape had emerged no later than the end of the fourth century, and so helps us to fill out our deficient picture. However, because of the general problems associated with reading back fourth-century liturgical evidence into earlier times which have been delineated in the rest of this book, we cannot go on to argue that all these practices must also have existed in the third or the second century, and so must be content to remain ignorant of many of the details of the ways in which ministers were appointed in these earlier periods.

58 See Roger Gryson, 'Les élections episcopales en Orient au IVe siècle', *Revue d'histoire ecclésiastique* 74 (1979), pp. 301–45.
59 See above, p. 104.
60 *The Prayers of Sarapion of Thmuis*, pp. 92–5, 148–62.
61 See Bradshaw, *Ordination Rites of the Ancient Churches of East and West*, pp. 39–40.
62 ibid., pp. 20–36.

10

The Effects of the Coming of
Christendom in the Fourth Century

A Turning-point?

The apparent conversion to Christianity of the emperor Constantine early in
the fourth century is usually portrayed as marking a crucial turning-point in
the evolution of forms of Christian worship; and it is undoubtedly true that a
very clear contrast can be observed between the form and character of liturgical practices in the pre- and post-Constantinian eras. However, scholars
have begun to realize that one must be careful not to overstate this distinction
between the two periods of ecclesiastical history.[1] A number of developments,
the genesis of which has traditionally been ascribed to the changed situation
of the Church after the Peace of Constantine, can be shown as having roots
that reach back into the third century, and in some cases even earlier still.
Similarly, many of the differences that really do seem to be new creations in
the fourth century first come to our attention in the second half of that
century, and in some cases its final quarter, suggesting that they were not so
much the immediate consequences of Constantine's conversion but rather
part of a process that had certainly begun well before that momentous event,
was intensified by it, but only issued forth in radical changes of practice
through the interaction of a complex series of cultural and doctrinal shifts in
the course of the succeeding decades.

For example, as we have seen in a previous chapter, the pattern of daily
worship practised in the urban monastic communities which began to emerge
in the early fourth century was not entirely a new creation of this movement.
In some respects it was simply a conservative preservation of a very tradi-

---

1 See, for example, Alexander Schmemann, *Introduction to Liturgical Theology* (London
1966), p. 76: 'It is really impossible to speak of a "liturgical revolution" in the fourth
century, if by this we mean the appearance of a type of worship differing radically from
that which had gone before. It is also difficult, however, to deny the profound change
which after all did mark the Church's liturgical life beginning with the epoch of Constantine.'

tional style of prayer and spirituality. There are certainly some new features – such as the regular recitation of the Book of Psalms in its entirety and in its biblical order as the cornerstone of the spiritual life – but in other ways the monks and nuns of the fourth century were simply continuing to do what ordinary Christians of earlier centuries had once done. Their customs only appear peculiarly monastic because they had by now been abandoned by other Christians, who, in the more relaxed atmosphere of the Constantinian era, tended to be more lukewarm about their religious commitment than their predecessors in the age of persecution.

Similarly, the interest in time and history that comes to the fore during this period is not something to which the Constantinian world gave birth, though it certainly suckled and nurtured it. It is simply not true, as earlier generations of liturgical scholars tended to conclude, that the first Christians could not possibly have been concerned to discover and commemorate the precise dates and times of the events of the life of Jesus or establish a rhythmical pattern of hours of prayer because they expected the end of this world to come at any moment with the return of their Lord.[2] On the contrary, an interest in time and eternity, history and eschatology, can coexist, and indeed the one can be an expression of the other. The early Christians established regular patterns of daily prayer-times not because they thought that the Church was here to stay for a long while, but precisely so that they might practise eschatological vigilance and be ready and watchful in prayer for the return of Christ and the consummation of God's kingdom.[3] Hence, the interest in eschatology, which certainly declined when it appeared less and less likely that the world was going to end soon, was not simply replaced by a new concern for time and history. Rather, a pre-existent interest took on a new vigour in a new situation, and a multiplicity of feasts and commemorations began to emerge in the fourth century in a way they had not done earlier.

Thus, in instances like these, the so-called Constantinian revolution did not so much inaugurate new liturgical practices and attitudes as create conditions in which some pre-existent customs could achieve a greater measure of pre-eminence than others which were no longer considered appropriate to the changed situation of the Church.

The Golden Age?

Traditional scholarship has also tended to paint a picture of post-Constantinian forms of worship as constituting the classic expression of the

2 See, for example, Dix, *The Shape of the Liturgy*, chapter XI: 'The Sanctification of Time'.

3 See Bradshaw, *Daily Prayer in the Early Church*, pp. 37–9.

Christian faith. Liturgy is viewed as gradually evolving from its inchoate roots in the New Testament through the refining processes of the second and third centuries and finally bursting into full bloom in the light of the Constantinian era. It then threw off the shackles that persecution and poverty had put upon it, and became what it was always intended to be, reaching the zenith of form and articulation in this 'Golden Age', before beginning its long period of slow decline, disintegration, and obfuscation in the course of the Middle Ages. Once again, while there is some truth to this perspective, it tends to be wildly overstated. On the contrary, many of the fourth-century liturgical developments were the responses of a Church which had already passed its peak, was experiencing the beginnings of decline, and was trying to do something to stem the tide. Unfortunately, all too often the 'something' that was then done unwittingly carried within it the seeds of further destruction rather than the solution that would preserve the glories of the past.

This chapter, therefore, seeks to offer some illustrations of these two fourth-century trends – the gradual and complex evolution of liturgical practice rather than its sudden switch of focus, and the inbuilt tendency towards disintegration of that evolution rather than the full flowering of the Christian vision – by focusing upon two principal causes: paganism and the formulation of doctrine.

Paganism

It is often said that early Christian worship felt little effect from the pagan world around because Christians were anxious to keep their practices separate and distinct from what went on in the contemporary culture. They wanted to show that they were not a religion like other religions, that they had no altars, sacrifices, temples, or feasts in the sense in which others did; and the periodic accusations of atheism that came from their critics suggest that they were generally successful in this attempt. Thus, it is claimed, it was only when paganism ceased to be a threat to the integrity of the Christian faith in the fourth century that its adherents felt free to borrow and absorb the vocabulary and images of other religions to enhance the expression of its own liturgical worship.

Although there are certainly some elements of truth in this account, the real story is by no means as simple as that. First, Christianity's differences from other cults in the first three centuries should not be exaggerated. As Wayne Meeks has observed, 'it is hard to see why not only Pliny, but also Tacitus and Suetonius would apply the term *superstitio* to an ethical debating society that had no ritual. One uses such a term to characterize someone else's rituals that one does not like. If they had not been "perverse and uncon-

trolled" . . . they could have been called *religio*.[4] Second, while the predomi-
nant external influence on the shape of Christian worship in the early centuries
certainly came from Judaism (both in terms of elements that had been
preserved from its roots in that tradition and also in the form of its subsequent
reaction against continuing practices that made it appear to be dependent upon
Judaism), yet as we indicated above in Chapter 2, neither Judaism nor Christianity existed in strict isolation from the Graeco–Roman world surrounding
them. Thus, liturgical historians have more recently begun to look once again
for possible pagan religious and cultural influences on the Christian worship of
the second and third centuries. Anscar Chupungco, for example, has suggested
that a number of elements in the Christian baptismal rites of this period were
drawn from the surrounding pagan culture, although he has not developed this
line of argument in detail;[5] and Alistair Stewart-Sykes has recently claimed that
the manumission of slaves was the source of the post-baptismal imposition of
the hand in the baptismal rite described by Tertullian.[6]

Hence the effects of paganism prior to the Peace of Constantine must not
be discounted. But conversely, the Christian Church after the Peace of Constantine did not immediately open its arms to embrace paganism fully.
Instead we see a persisting ambivalence of attitude towards it revealed by the
pursuit of two parallel – and seemingly contradictory – trajectories. On the
one hand, pagan practices were still viewed as a threat to the integrity of the
Christian faith, and ecclesiastical authorities felt it necessary to try to draw
the faithful away from the temptation to participate in them. We can see this
exemplified best with regard to pagan winter solstice celebrations. There are a
number of signs that Christians were being encouraged to intensify their
regular practice of fasting around this period of the year, apparently in an
attempt to keep them from indulging in the excesses of the pagan feasting
during this season; 1 January, for instance, was designated as a day of fasting
by the church at Rome.[7] It soon became clear to the ecclesiastical authorities,
however, that Christian *feasts* rather than *fasts* would provide more effective
counter-attractions to the pagan delights, and hence 1 January was later
changed into a feast in honour of the Virgin Mary.[8] Similarly, even though

---

4 *The First Urban Christians*, p.140.
5 'Baptism in the Early Church and its Cultural Settings', in Stauffer, ed., *Worship and
   Culture in Dialogue*, pp. 39–56, reproduced in expanded form in idem, *Worship: Beyond
   Inculturation* (Washington, DC 1994), pp. 1–18.
6 'Manumission and Baptism in Tertullian's Africa'.
7 See Talley, *The Origins of the Liturgical Year*, pp. 149–51; Alexander, *Waiting for the
   Coming*, pp. 8–23.
8 See Bernard Botte, 'La première fête mariale de la liturgie romaine', *EL* 47 (1933), pp.
   425–30; also J.-M. Guilmard, 'Une antique fête mariale au 1er janvier dans la ville de
   Rome?' *EO* 11 (1994), pp. 25–67.

scholars may still debate why 25 December was originally selected as the feast of the Nativity of Christ at Rome, as we have seen,[9] yet its subsequent adoption in northern Italy (and very likely in other places too) was undoubtedly motivated by a desire to rival the pagan solstice celebrations held on that date in the Julian calendar.[10]

On the other hand, at the same time as this was going on, the Church was appropriating language, images, and ceremonies from pagan practice in order to serve its liturgical purposes. A good example of this trend is the major shift that the whole style of initiation practice underwent everywhere in the fourth century in imitation of pagan mystery rites. Edward Yarnold attributes the prime responsibility for this development to the Emperor Constantine himself.[11] The ceremonies surrounding baptism became highly elaborate, much more dramatic – one might even say theatrical – in character, and cloaked in such great secrecy that candidates would have no idea in advance what was going to happen to them. Often it was only after they had experienced the celebration of baptism and the Eucharist that an explanation of the meaning of the sacred mysteries in which they had partaken was given to them in what was called mystagogy – post-baptismal instruction, usually during the week following their initiation, and apparently replacing the 'restricted' pre-baptismal instruction in doctrine which had been a feature of earlier rites.[12] The baptismal homilies of the period use expressions such as 'awe-inspiring' and 'hair-raising' to describe the sensational style of the ceremonial now used in the rites, which included such things as frequent dramatic exorcisms and other purificatory elements within the catechumenal process.[13] Apart from references of uncertain date and provenance in the *Apostolic Tradition*, the only evidence from an earlier period for a Christian practice of regular pre-baptismal exorcism for all (as distinct from individuals thought to be particularly possessed of evil spirits) comes from mid-third-century Africa,[14] and this seems to have spread elsewhere in the course of the fourth century, as part of the attempt to heighten the dramatic character of the process and thus to communicate to candidates the intensity of the life-changing nature of Christian initiation. It was apparently not directly copied from paganism, where it was not a regular religious practice, but probably

9 See above, pp. 187–8.
10 See Martin Connell, 'The Liturgical Year in Northern Italy (365–450)' (unpublished PhD dissertation, University of Notre Dame 1995), pp. 169–233.
11 *The Awe-Inspiring Rites of Initiation,* pp. 55–62; 'Baptism and the Pagan Mysteries in the Fourth Century', *Heythrop Journal* 13 (1972), pp. 247–67; 'Who planned the churches at the Christian holy places in the Holy Land?' *SP* 18/1 (1989), pp. 105–9.
12 See above, p. 166, n. 87.
13 See further, Yarnold, *The Awe-Inspiring Rites of Initiation*; Riley, *Christian Initiation*.
14 See above, pp. 157–8.

came from Gnostic circles, as there is some evidence for its use in this context there.[15]

A similar shift in the style of celebrations of the Eucharist can also be observed at the same period. They became much more formal and elaborate; they used such things as ceremonial actions, vesture, processions, and music to an extent previously unknown; and in both word and action they stressed the majesty and transcendence of God and the divinity of Christ present in the eucharistic mystery.[16] At first, these notes were struck more in preaching and teaching about the Eucharist than in the liturgical rites themselves. Thus John Chrysostom repeatedly speaks of the 'dreadful sacrifice', of the 'fearful moment' when the mysteries are accomplished, and of the 'terrible and awful table' that should only be approached with fear and trembling.[17] But gradually the style of celebration began to reflect this attitude too. The directions given in the *Mystagogical Catecheses* attributed to Cyril of Jerusalem on how the newly baptized are to receive communion, for instance, illustrate the extent of the reverential gestures now expected:

So when you come forward, do not come with arm extended or fingers parted. Make your left hand a throne for your right, since your right hand is about to welcome a king. Cup your palm and receive in it Christ's body, saying in response *Amen*. Then carefully bless your eyes with a touch of the holy body, and consume it, being careful to drop not a particle of it. For to lose any of it is clearly like losing part of your own body . . . After partaking of Christ's body, go to the chalice of his blood. Do not stretch out your hands for it. Bow your head and say *Amen* to show your homage and reverence, and sanctify yourself by partaking also of Christ's blood. While your lips are still moist with his blood, touch it with your hands and bless your eyes, forehead, and other organs of sense.[18]

15 See Kelly, *The Devil at Baptism*, pp. 57–77. Elizabeth Leeper, 'From Alexandria to Rome: The Valentinian Connection to the Incorporation of Exorcism as a Prebaptismal Rite', *VC* 44 (1990), pp. 6–24, argued that the rites of pre-baptismal exorcism in Rome came directly from Valentinian Gnostic rituals of initiation, but her case is weakened by an over-optimistic reading of the sources and the assumption that the rites in the so-called *Apostolic Tradition* reliably reflect third-century Roman practice.

16 See Jungmann, *The Early Liturgy*, pp. 122–74.

17 See Edmund Bishop, 'Fear and Awe attaching to the Eucharistic Service', in Connolly, *The Liturgical Homilies of Narsai*, pp. 92–7; Josef A. Jungmann, *The Place of Christ in Liturgical Prayer* (London 1965), pp. 245–55; J. G. Davies, 'The Introduction of the Numinous into the Liturgy: An Historical Note', *SL* 8 (1971/72), pp. 216–23.

18 *Mystagogical Catechesis* 5.21–2; ET from Yarnold, *The Awe-Inspiring Rites of Inititation*, pp. 94–5.

Many other examples could be cited of the tension between, on the one hand, the desire to make a clear distinction between pagan and Christian practices and ideas, and on the other hand, the desire to use the images and vocabulary of paganism. For instance, Christians were deeply sensitive to charges made against them by Manichaeans and others that because the disposition of their annual feasts was made in connection with the movement of the moon and the sun, they were worshipping those heavenly bodies; and various leading figures, among them Ambrose of Milan and Leo the Great, mounted staunch defences against these attacks.[19] Yet, when Constantine embarked upon his ambitious program of church building, Christians were quite willing to employ the language of 'temples' and 'sanctuaries' in relation to these edifices. Even the Church's extensive use of public space in the cities for processions and other ceremonial acts ('worship on the town', as Aidan Kavanagh has termed it), can be seen both as an anti-pagan demonstration that it had conquered what was formerly pagan territory and also at the same time as an adoption of the very forms and practices of paganism itself.[20]

Causes and Effects (i): Initiation

If we ask why the Church was willing, even eager, to adopt elements from pagan worship in its liturgies at the very same period when it was apparently still viewing pagan religion as a rival against which it had to mount a defence, the answer lies in part in the changed situation in which the Church found itself. Now that its liturgy was functioning as a *cultus publicus*, seeking the divine favour to secure the well-being of the state, it needed to have more of the appearance of a conventional religion; it had to employ the language and symbolism of its rivals to enable it to communicate more effectively with the surrounding culture; and it wanted to portray itself as the fulfilment of that to which those other religions had dimly pointed. Thus, for example, the rapid expansion of the liturgical year at this time was generated at least in part by apologetic factors. Since the Church now needed to present the tenets of its faith to a barbarian world which was willing to listen, and to defend its doctrinal positions against a variety of heretical attacks, what better means could be found than the promotion of occasions that publicly celebrated aspects of what it believed?[21]

19 See Charles Pietri, 'Le temps de la semaine à Rome et dans l'Italie chrétienne (IV–VI s.)', in Jean-Marie Leroux, ed., *Le temps chrétien de la fin de l'antiquité au Moyen Age (IIIe-XIII siècles)* (Colloques internationaux du Centre Nationale de la Recherche Scientifique 604; Paris 1984), pp. 72–3.

20 Aidan Kavanagh, *On Liturgical Theology* (New York 1984), p. 65; see also Baldovin, *The Urban Character of Christian Worship*; Charles Pietri, 'Liturgy, Culture, and Society: The Example of Rome at the End of the Ancient World (Fourth–Fifth Centuries)', *Concilium* 162 (1983), pp. 38–46.

21 See further, Taft, 'Historicism Revisited'.

But for a more complete answer to the question, we must turn to my second thesis: that fourth-century liturgical developments were often part of the process of disintegration of Christian worship rather than its full flowering. While it has been usual to view the elaborations of liturgical practice such as we have just noted as manifesting the classic or golden age of liturgical evolution, in reality many of them are symptoms of a Church that was already losing the battle for the hearts and minds of its followers and was desperately attempting to remedy the situation by whatever means lay to hand.

Prior to the fourth century, one could reasonably assume that those who sought admission to the Church and were prepared to take upon themselves the attendant risks of social ostracism, if not actual, though sporadic, persecution, were generally motivated by some genuine conversion experience that they were undergoing in their lives. In such a context, the initiatory rituals of Christianity served to give symbolic expression to a reality which already existed for the candidates. In the changed circumstances of the fourth century, however, not all those who sought admission to the Church took the step because they had experienced an inner conversion: some did so from less worthy motives, such as the desire to marry a Christian or to please a master or friend, or because it promised to be advantageous to their career or political ambitions. Moreover, once having become catechumens, many people were in no hurry to complete the process of initiation. Since they were already regarded as Christians, they saw no need to proceed to baptism itself, especially as that would leave no second chance to obtain the forgiveness of sins that baptism was believed to convey. It seemed preferable, therefore, to delay the actual baptism as long as possible so as to be sure of having all one's sins forgiven and so of gaining salvation. Consequently, many parents enrolled their children as catechumens early in their life but delayed presenting them for baptism at least until after the passions of youth had subsided and there was less chance of them succumbing to temptation; and many adults deferred their own baptism until they became seriously ill and feared that they might die unbaptized.[22]

All of this had a profound effect on the nature of the baptismal process itself. The reluctance of candidates to proceed to baptism led to a tendency among the clergy to 'lower the hurdles' as far as possible to encourage them to come in. In their enthusiasm to win more members, they tended to welcome baptismal candidates without such a rigorous examination of the genuineness of their conversion and of their lifestyle as had earlier been customary. Consequently, rather than being the outward expression of an

22 See further, Dujarier, *A History of the Catechumenate*, pp. 78–111.

inner conversion that had already taken place, the rites now became instead the means of producing a powerful emotional and psychological impression upon the candidates in the hope of bringing about their conversion. The greater formalization of the time of the catechumenate, for example, with its periodic punctuation with ritual moments that might involve such things as exorcism or the tasting of salt, is not an advance upon the less formalized preparation for baptism of earlier centuries, but a sign that the process was no longer working properly and needed shoring up. Similarly, the subsequent transmutation of the pre-baptismal 'scrutinies' into a driving out of the devil instead of an examination of the candidates' moral conduct reflects the shift that was occurring in the understanding of baptism, as effecting a metaphysical transformation of the inner person rather than testifying to an outward change of behaviour that had taken place.

Causes and Effects (ii): Eucharist

Similar factors were also at work in the changes that were happening in the style of eucharistic celebration. Since many members of the Church could be described as at best only half-converted and half-instructed, their behaviour both in their daily lives and at public worship often left a great deal to be desired. According to John Chrysostom, for example, they pushed and pulled one another in an unruly manner during the services; they gossiped with one another; young people engaged in various kinds of mischief; and pickpockets preyed upon the crowd.[23] Thus, the regular liturgies had to assume more of an instructional and formational role than heretofore. It was necessary to try to communicate through the style of liturgical celebration itself something of the majesty of God and the reality of Christ's sacramental presence, as well as of the appropriate attitude of reverence required before that divinity. Even the introduction of the narrative of institution into eucharistic prayers at this period may well have been in order that it might serve a catechetical purpose within the liturgy rather than outside it, as in previous centuries, especially as it then tended to function parenthetically within those prayers.

Unfortunately, however, once again the cures chosen for these particular ills carried within themselves unintended consequences: the seeds of further liturgical destruction. Thus, for example, while the ultimate aim was to secure the worthy participation of all in the Christian mysteries, the measure chosen towards this end was to exclude the unworthy. Fourth-century preachers regularly warned their congregations against coming to communion while still leading sinful lives. John Chrysostom again was particularly vigilant in this regard, frequently emphasizing the sincerity and purity of soul necessary

---

23 For references, see Davies, 'The Introduction of the Numinous into the Liturgy', p. 222.

to approach the supper of the Lord: 'With this, approach at all times; without it, never!' He advised those who were guilty of sin to leave the service before the eucharistic action itself began.[24]

The purpose of preaching such as this was of course not to *dis*courage the reception of communion, but rather to *en*courage higher standards of Christian living and of behaviour in church. But, as so often happens, the results were exactly the opposite of the intentions of the preachers. Many people preferred to give up the reception of communion rather than amend their lives. Thus began the practice of non-communicating attendance at the Eucharist. Contrary to Chrysostom's advice, many people apparently stayed until the time for communion and then left the church. The ecclesiastical authorities were eventually forced to accept this practice, and they began to make provision in the rites at the time of the communion for a formal blessing and dismissal of non-communicants in order to encourage a more orderly departure.[25]

This development had a significant effect upon people's understanding of the Eucharist, since it severed the act of communion from the rest of the eucharistic action. It made it possible for them to think of the Eucharist as complete and effective without the need for them to participate in the reception of the bread and wine, and thus helped to further the idea that liturgy was something that the clergy did on their behalf, which ultimately did not even require their presence. This notion, too, had roots that went back well before the age of Constantine. Already by the middle of the third century, the idea that the bishops with their clergy constituted a priesthood which would act on behalf of the rest had already made an appearance, and was beginning to break down the older concept that the whole people – ordained ministers and laity together – composed a royal priesthood func-tioning before God in their worship and offering the sacrifice of praise.[26] Thus, clericalism was not a novelty of the fourth century. But it certainly took a sig-nificant step forward then. The more professionalized clergy of this period increasingly dominated public worship, and the people were content to let them do it, the pure acting for the impure, the experts for the ignorant. Even Chrysostom's very assertion that there were some moments when there was no difference at all between the roles of priest and people in the Eucharist is itself a tacit admission that there were other times when there most definitely was a difference:

---

24 John Chrysostom, *Hom. in Eph.* 3.4.
25 See Robert F. Taft, 'The Inclination Prayer before Communion in the Byzantine Liturgy of St John Chrysostom: A Study in Comparative Liturgy', *EO* 3 (1986), pp. 29-60.
26 See above, pp. 201–5.

But there are occasions when there is no difference at all between the priest and those under him; for instance, when we are to partake of the awful mysteries . . . And in the prayers also, one may observe the people contributing much . . . Again, in the most awful mysteries them- selves, the priest prays for the people and the people also pray for the priest; for the words 'with thy spirit' are nothing else than this. The offering of thanksgiving again is common: for neither doth he give thanks alone, but also for all the people . . . [27]

Yet a further problem with the incorporation of certain pagan symbols and language into Christian worship was that it brought with it the uncritical adoption of other alien devotional practices. Thus Augustine reports that even his devotedly Christian mother Monica still continued the pagan practice of providing food for the departed (*Confessions* 6.2.2). Nor was this an isolated instance. In the passage quoted above from the *Mystagogical Cat- echeses*[28] we can see that not only were the eucharistic elements to be treated with great reverence when they were consumed, but they were also regarded as objects of power which could be used to confer blessing on a person's body and protect it against evil and sickness. Similarly, Ambrose in the sermon at the funeral of his brother Satyrus relates how Satyrus once wrapped up the eucharistic bread in a cloth and fastened it round his neck for protection before casting himself into the sea when the ship on which he was travelling was wrecked, and so came safely to land (*De exitu fratris* 1.43). While from earliest times Christian rites had certainly been understood as conferring pro- tection from sickness and healing power upon their recipients,[29] the idea of the material elements themselves being able to convey such effects divorced from their intrinsic ritual use does seem to be a new development. Preachers also accorded similar powers to sacred relics and to items of clothing that had belonged to saints. Thus the life of Macrina mentions her carrying a particle of the true cross around her neck (*Vita Macrinae* 30); John Chrysystom refers to both men and women valuing this protective adornment (*Contra Judeaos et Gentiles* 10); and Augustine also speaks favourably of a widow and her daughter wearing relics of St Stephen (*Ep.* 212).

---

27 *Hom. in 2 Corinthians* 18.3.
28 p. 216.
29 e.g., the use of oil for the sick in James 5.14; Ignatius of Antioch's description of the Eucharist as 'the medicine of immortality' (*Ephes.* 20); and the healing power ascribed to the baptismal waters in Tertullian, *De baptismo* 4.4.

The Movement Towards Conformity in Liturgical Practice

We must not assume, however, that the challenge posed by paganism was the only thing responsible for the changing character of Christian worship in the fourth century. As well as pressures from without, there were fears from within. The drive towards greater precision in the formulation of doctrine played a significant part in reshaping liturgical practice in a more uniform direction in the Constantinian age. Although earlier generations of scholars tended towards the view that there had always been a large measure of homogeneity in the liturgical traditions stemming from the apostolic age, more recent research – as we have seen – has pointed towards the conclusion that liturgical variety generally diminished rather than increased as the Church developed. Thus, the large measure of agreement in liturgical practice that can be seen in later sources is more often the result of a conscious movement towards standardization that did not take place until the fourth century – and frequently only in the second half of that century – rather than the survival of an ancient way of doing things that all Christians shared from the beginning. This is not to say that there were no attempts at all to imitate or adopt what others were dong liturgically prior to this time – one has only to look at either the composite character exhibited by initiation rites or the fusion of parallel patterns of daily prayer in the third century to see that this process had begun earlier[30] – but that it only truly began to gather momentum under the pressures towards conformity that the fourth century brought.

Causes

The causes of this transformation are not hard to find. The fourth century was a time when Christians travelled to other parts of the world much more than they had tended to do before, and consequently were more aware of the existence of other ways of worshipping than they had formerly been. There were pilgrims to the Holy Land, who not only saw what was done in that liturgical centre and carried the news back home, but also came into contact with the liturgical practices of other Christians arriving there from different parts of the world, as well as those through whose regions they passed on the way.[31] One might say that Jerusalem became an important hub of the liturgical import–export business, a clearing-house for attractive ideas and practices with regard to worship. In addition to pilgrims, there were also those at this

---

30 See above, pp. 169–70, 175–6.
31 Among recent studies of the phenomenon of pilgrimage, see Joan E. Taylor, *Christians and the Holy Places: The Myth of Jewish–Christian Origins* (Oxford 1993); Robert L. Wilken, *The Land Called Holy: Palestine in Christian History and Thought* (New Haven 1992).

time who visited the major centres of monastic life, and brought back novel liturgical customs to their home countries, and there were now frequent councils of bishops and other church leaders that extended far beyond the local region and so exposed their participants to what was going on in distant lands.

However, experience of other liturgical customs was alone not sufficient to account for the extent of the fusion of practice that took place in the late fourth century. Just because other places did things differently did not of itself mean that a particular church thought that it always had to come into line with them. It was the challenge posed by heretical movements that added further pressure towards liturgical conformity. Heresy was of course not a new problem for the Church: it had been there ever since the first Christians tried to define their faith. But the problem of heresy was now posed far more acutely, as much for political and practical reasons as for theological ones: it was, for example, essential to be able to decide who were the rightful owners of ecclesiastical property. Thus the fourth century brought to the boil doctrinal issues that had been simmering for some time, and through the successive ecumenical councils of the period required all local churches to declare themselves clearly on one side or another of the various debates. In such a situation, therefore, any tendency to persist in what appeared to be idiosyncratic liturgical observances was likely to have been interpreted as a mark of heterodoxy,[32] and hence this gave rise to a movement towards greater uniformity of practice.

Examples

This can be illustrated from many aspects of liturgical practice. In the area of Christian initiation the widespread adoption of Easter as the preferred baptismal season seems to have been a development of the mid-fourth century, and prior to that time the custom was restricted to North Africa and Rome.[33] Along with this change in practice went a shift in theology (although whether as cause or effect is unclear), as churches adopted as their central concept the Pauline image of baptism as participation in the death and resurrection of Christ, and a consequent decline in other local baptismal theologies, especially the Jordan motif of the earlier Syrian tradition. Similarly, while the use of a declaratory baptismal formula to accompany the

32 See, for example, Rowan Williams, 'Baptism and the Arian Controversy', in Michael R. Barnes and Daniel H. Williams, eds, *Arianism after Arius: Essays on the Development of the Fourth-century Trinitarian Conflicts* (Edinburgh 1993), pp. 149–80; Maurice Wiles, 'Triple and Single Immersion: Baptism in the Arian Controversy', *SP* 30 (1997), pp. 337–49.
33 See Paul F. Bradshaw, '"Diem baptismo sollemniorem": Initiation and Easter in Christian Antiquity', in Ephrem Carr *et al.*, eds, *Eulogêma*, pp. 41–51 = Johnson, ed., *Living Water, Sealing Spirit*, pp. 137–47.

act of immersion was beginning to make a journey from its Syrian home, appearing in Egypt in the early fourth century, and later in Spain, Gaul, and Rome,[34] and a pre-baptismal anointing was starting to make an appearance in traditions that do not seem to have formerly had one, at the same time Western elements were being carried eastwards, among them the use of credal interrogations and a post-baptismal unction in the rite, generally turning up first – not surprisingly – in Jerusalem, where pilgrimages brought East and West face to face. The result was certainly not uniformity of baptismal practice throughout Christendom, as the Eastern versions were often markedly different in detail from their Western counterparts, but there did emerge a broad similarity which largely masked the earlier diversity.

In the area of eucharistic worship, there is a similar convergence of practice. This can be most clearly seen with regard to eucharistic prayer itself. The apparently relatively simple local patterns of earlier centuries were expanded with new features, many of which – like the Sanctus, the narrative of institution, and epiclesis – were simply borrowed from the practice of other places and inserted into the native structures. Sometimes large portions of two prayers from different regions were combined to form a complex and composite anaphora, and sometimes whole prayers were exported from one ecclesiastical centre to become the standard liturgical fare of other localities.[35]

Again, in the area of the liturgical year, as we have seen in an earlier chapter, the adoption of Lent as a universal pre-paschal phenomenon appears to date only from the middle of the fourth century. Prior to that, the season seems have been unique to Egypt, and to have been located immediately after the celebration of the baptism of Jesus on 6 January.[36] What is even more clear is that before the late fourth century no church included both 25 December and 6 January in its liturgical calendar. Indeed, the celebration of 25 December now appears to have originally been a peculiarity of Rome, and perhaps North Africa too.[37] Yet within the space of less than half a century, both feasts became established features of all major centres of Christianity.[38]

---

34 See further, E. C. Whitaker, 'The Baptismal Formula in the Syrian Rite', *Church Quarterly Review* 161 (1960), pp. 346–52; idem, 'The History of the Baptismal Formula', *JEH* 16 (1965), pp. 1–12; P-M. Gy, 'La formule "Je te baptise" (Et ego te baptizo)', in *Communio Sanctorum: Mélanges offerts à Jean-Jacques von Allmen* (Geneva 1982), pp. 65–72; Paul de Clerck, 'Les origines de la formule baptismale', in Paul de Clerck and Eric Palazzo, eds, *Rituels: Mélanges offerts à Pierre-Marie Gy, O.P.* (Paris 1990), pp. 199–213.

35 See further, Fenwick, *Fourth Century Anaphoral Construction Techniques* and the various contributions to Bradshaw, ed., *Essays in Early Eastern Eucharistic Prayers.*

36 See above, pp. 183–4. The attempt by Charles Renoux, 'La quarantaine pré-pascale au 3e siècle à Jerusalem', *La Maison-Dieu* 196 (1993), pp. 111–29, to posit the existence of a 40-day Lent in Jerusalem as early as the third century is not convincing.

37 See above, pp. 187–8.

38 See Talley, *The Origins of the Liturgical Year*, pp. 134–47.

Above all, in spite of the Quartodeciman disputes of the second century, a common date for the celebration of Easter itself only became more of a reality as part of the Nicean settlement, and even after that some variation still persisted.[39]

Fear of heresy also began to place limitations around the practice of extemporizing public prayer. The almost total absence of extant liturgical texts prior to the fourth century is not because they were all destroyed by later generations, but because they did not exist in the first place. It was not part of the early Jewish and Christian traditions that liturgical prayers should be written down. Instead, they were passed on orally, and subject to development and modification in response to changing circumstances. But this freedom meant that individual bishops and other clergy might introduce unorthodox ideas into their prayers, whether consciously or unwittingly. In the more doctrinally sensitive climate of the fourth century, therefore, we see fences gradually being erected around such liberty. Not only do written eucharistic prayers now begin to appear,[40] but in some places steps are taken to censor the contents of all forms of public prayer. The earliest instances of this are in North Africa, where local ecclesiastical councils enacted legislation requiring the liturgical texts used by bishops and presbyters to be submitted to the scrutiny and approval of their colleagues.[41] The virtual disappearance of early Christian hymns and their replacement in liturgical worship by the canonical psalms at this period is another symptom of the desire to control doctrine. The Arian use of hymns to promote their beliefs caused a reaction against all non-canonical compositions among their opponents, and a strong preference for biblical psalms and canticles, the orthodoxy of which could be safely guaranteed.[42]

These represent just some of the many examples that could be cited to demonstrate that what we tend to regard as the classical pattern of Christian liturgy is in reality a construct of the second half of the fourth century, and not something that is rooted in the customs of the apostolic age, which appear on the contrary to have been much more diverse in character. We should also note that this process applied not just to liturgies themselves but also to the buildings in which they were celebrated: L. Michael White has suggested that 'the basilica may be seen as a further adaptation, monumentalization, and ultimately a standardization of diverse pre-Constantinian patterns of development'.[43]

39 See Anscar J. Chupungco, *Shaping the Easter Feast* (Washington, DC 1992), pp. 43–50, 69–73.
40 See further, Bouley, *From Freedom to Formula*.
41 See Kilmartin, 'Early African Legislation Concerning Liturgical Prayer'.
42 See Bradshaw, *Daily Prayer in the Early Church*, pp. 90, 94, 113, 118.
43 *Building God's House in the Roman World: Architectural adaptation among pagans, Jews, and Christians* (Baltimore 1990), p. 139.

Doctrine Shaping Liturgy

Doctrinal debate not only encouraged churches to adopt a similar liturgical appearance to one another, but also appears to have been responsible for determining the particular form that at least some of these shared expressions then took.

We have noted earlier that the initial concept of a paschal *triduum* seems to have its roots in a third-century shift in the Alexandrian theological interpretation of the feast from *passio* to *transitus*.[44] Its earliest liturgical expression, on the other hand, appears to have been at Jerusalem in the fourth century primarily as a response to popular piety – pilgrims seeking appropriate liturgical celebrations of the events connected with the passion and resurrection at the sacred sites themselves and on the days and at the times when they had occurred.[45] While that same piety was no doubt partly responsible for its spread from Jerusalem to other parts of the world, its dissemination in the West seems to have been somewhat slower than in the East[46] and its adoption there not unrelated to the continuing christological controversies of the period. Homiletic material from northern Italy, for example, demonstrates the assistance that was given to attempts to define the divine/human nature of Christ by the emerging separation of the commemoration of Christ's death on Good Friday from the celebration of his resurrection on Easter Day.[47] In the same way, anti-Arian concerns seem to have strongly influenced the content of the new feast of Christmas as a celebration of the incarnation of the pre-existent Son of God rather than merely a historical commemoration of Jesus' nativity. For it is not without significance that readings from both the Gospel of Luke and that of John are included in the earliest stratum of the lectionary tradition for this feast at Rome.[48]

Similarly, the fourth-century pneumatological debates appear to have affected the specific shape of liturgy in several ways, especially in the wording of doxological formulae,[49] the development of the epicletic element in

---

44 See above, pp. 181–2.

45 See Egeria, *Peregrinatio* 29–37.

46 For the East see, for example, Basil of Caesarea, *Hom.* 13; Gregory of Nazianzus, *Or.* 1. The earliest firm evidence for the liturgical observance of Holy Saturday as the burial/descent into hell is in Amphilochius, Bishop of Iconium from 373 to 394, *Or.* 5. On Christ's descent into hell, see Aloys Grillmeier, 'Der Gottesohn im Totenreich: soteriologische und christologische Motivierung der Descensuslehre in der alteren christlichen Überlieferung', *ZKTh* 71 (1949), pp. 1–53, 184–203.

47 See Martin F. Connell, 'Heresy and Heortology in the Early Church: Arianism and the Emergence of the Triduum', *Worship* 72 (1998), pp. 117–40.

48 See Lester Ruth, 'The Early Roman Christmas Gospel: Magi, Manger, or Verbum Factum?', *SL* 24 (1994), pp. 214–21.

49 See Jungmann, *The Place of Christ in Liturgical Prayer*, pp. 172-90.

eucharistic prayers,[50] and the spread of a post-baptismal anointing related to the Holy Spirit. A variety of competing theories has been advanced to account for the introduction of this post-baptismal anointing in the East. Ratcliff regarded it as the result of the influence of Jerusalem, and its adoption there as the consequence of the celebration of Christian initiation at Easter in close proximity to the actual sites of the death and resurrection of Jesus, which thus led to a revival of the Pauline doctrine of baptism,[51] while Botte linked its emergence with the practice adopted at the reconciliation of heretics.[52] Winkler and Brock, however, seem closer to the truth. Winkler thought that the change came about through:

> the inner change of dynamics within the ritual itself. Once baptism moved away from its original essence, being the *mimesis* of the event at the Jordan, and shifted at the same time toward a cathartic principle, it was inevitable that all rites that preceded baptism proper became subordinated to a process of thorough cleansing. The catharsis slowly became an indispensable condition for the coming of the Spirit. Consequently, only after intensive purification and the washing away of sins could the Spirit enter the heart of the baptized.[53]

Sebastian Brock thought that it came about in part because the baptism of Christ, where the Holy Spirit appears after Jesus emerges from the water, became increasingly seen as the model for Christian baptismal practice.[54]

Yet, surprisingly, neither of them paid much attention to two other factors that seem to be of significance: the influence that would have been exercised by the existence of a precedent for a post-baptismal anointing in Western rites, knowledge of which would have been carried by pilgrims to Jerusalem – which is where we first encounter such an anointing in the East; and the effect that the doctrinal debates about the Holy Spirit would have had on the rites, in encouraging the emergence of a distinct ceremony conveying the Spirit rather than its mere association with immersion itself, as we find in Chrysostom.[55] On the other hand, while the Jerusalem church may have been stimulated to introduce a post-baptismal anointing partly in imitation of

---

50 See the studies cited above, p. 137, nn. 92, 93.
51 'The Old Syrian Baptismal Tradition'.
52 'L'onction postbaptismale dans l'ancien patriarchat d'Antioche', in *Miscellanea Liturgica in onore di sua Em. il Card. G. Lercaro* 2 (Rome 1967), pp. 795–808 = 'Post-baptismal Anointing in the Ancient Patriarchate of Antioch', in Jacob Vellian, ed., *Studies on Syrian Baptismal Rites* (Syrian Churches Series 6; Kottayam, India 1973), pp. 63–71.
53 'The Original Meaning of the Prebaptismal Anointing', p. 42 (= 78), n. 63.
54 'The Transition to a Post-Baptismal Anointing in the Antiochene Rite', pp. 220–5.
55 *Baptismal Homily* 2.25.

Western practice, the precise form that the anointing took did not copy the Western model. In place of a single anointing of the head, the Jerusalem and later universal Eastern custom was to anoint the forehead, ears, nostrils, and chest[56] – not a particularly obvious choice for a ceremony associated with the bestowal of the Spirit. This suggests the possibility of yet a further influence behind the Eastern practice. One conceivable root could be Gnosticism: it has been conjectured that there existed a Gnostic initiation practice involving both water and the anointing of the five senses (in that order).[57] If that is true, and if there were still Christian Gnostic groups around which practised this ritual, then it might not have seemed so radical a step to incorporate something like it into the mainstream liturgy at Jerusalem. Alternatively, there are some parallels of form with the 'opening' ritual of Western rites.[58] Although in the West this is always pre-baptismal, there may still be some connection between the two that is hidden from our view by the paucity of evidence.

Liturgy Shaping Doctrine

On the other hand, while it may often have been changes in doctrine that brought about some modification in the structure of a rite or the wording of its prayers – on the principle of form following function – it also appears that sometimes the reverse may have been the case, that the form that a rite took was responsible for altering the way in which it was understood. In particular, this may be true of the emergence of the belief that the Eucharist was a propitiatory sacrifice. Scholars have usually taken the statement in the *Mystagogical Catecheses* attributed to Cyril of Jerusalem that 'we believe that [the souls of the departed] will obtain the greatest help if we make our prayers for them while the holy and most awesome sacrifice is being offered'[59] as the explanation as to how eucharistic prayers came to include a wide range of objects of intercession, for the living and the departed, rather than just petition for the communicants, which is all that is found in some ancient texts. It was the idea of the Eucharist as a sacrifice, it was thought, that led to the idea that it could be offered for others, which in turn led to the introduction of intercessions into the eucharistic prayer itself rather than at the earlier point in the rite after the ministry of the word that had been their original home.

---

56 *Mystagogical Catechesis* 3.3–4.
57 Logan, 'The Mystery of the Five Seals'. However, as indicated above, p. 154, the rest of his argument does not stand up to close scrutiny. But see also *Acts of Thomas* 5, where the apostle after a meal signs his forehead, nostrils, ears, and chest with oil, apparently in preparation for a wedding.
58 See above, pp. 165–6.
59 *Mystagogical Catechesis* 5.9. ET from Yarnold, *The Awe-Inspiring Rites of Initiation*, p. 92.

The Strasbourg Papyrus, however, suggests an alternative hypothesis. We have proposed earlier that the complete absence of any specific eucharistic reference in this prayer implies that it was originally used in a non-eucharistic context and only much later drafted into eucharistic usage.[60] It may well be, therefore, that it was the adoption of prayers like this, already containing a substantial block of intercessory material, that helped to give rise to the idea of the Eucharist as a propitiatory sacrifice, and not the other way around.

Conclusion

Those responsible for shaping Christian liturgy in the fourth century thus found themselves caught between two opposing forces. One was the desire to remain counter-cultural, to draw a sharp dividing line between what was pagan and what was Christian, for fear of the dilution of distinctively Christian beliefs and of the confusion and misunderstanding that the adoption of practices resembling those of other religions might cause. The other was the need to communicate with the pagan world around in its own terms, to inculturate the Church's liturgy in the context in which it was situated, to clothe its worship in the language and symbols that converts and potential converts would more easily understand, and by this means to lead them to full and right participation in the Christian mysteries.

After something of a struggle, the second force won the day, for the Church did not know how otherwise to handle the growing flood of new members who lacked the understanding of the biblical background possessed by the earliest Jewish converts and the deep commitment to Christian discipleship possessed by the adherents of former, and less comfortable, centuries. But such a step was not only a tacit admission of defeat in the process of the full conversion of all its followers; it also carried with it the seeds of further destruction. While in one sense the process of liturgical evolution that then ensued helped to save the Church from even worse consequences, it also led to the disappearance or transformation of many worship practices that had safeguarded and given expression to important aspects of the primitive Christian faith, which were consequently lost to later generations of believers.

A similar story can be told with regard to the effects of the crystallization of Christian doctrine. Once again, there was something of a struggle between traditional liturgical forms on the one hand and the demands of the new orthodoxy on the other. But eventually doctrinal correctness won; variety was reined in, and a more homogenized pattern of liturgy began to emerge, displacing many ancient local traditions. Some of the consequences of this process of liturgical convergence cannot but be regarded as positive effects

60 See above, p. 143, n. 105

on Christianity. The Church undoubtedly gained a greater sense of its own internal cohesion and was also strengthened in its defence of orthodoxy by the united liturgical front that it was thus able to present to its opponents and to the pagan world. Moreover, the adoption of different customs from other Christian traditions was for the most part a real enrichment of the liturgical life of the various local churches, and it enlarged their earlier limited and often one-sided vision of the Christian faith.

On the other hand, this fourth-century development also had consequences which perhaps should not be viewed in such a positive light. The amalgamation of liturgical customs from different regions did not result in the preservation of everything from former times, but more often led to the dominance of certain ways of saying and doing things over others. Thus enrichment brought with it some impoverishment, as various local traditions were either subordinated to others, reduced to a mere shadow of their former selves, or even entirely eliminated from contemporary practice. Furthermore, what emerged in the fourth century, although containing elements from a number of earlier Christian traditions, was itself identical to none of them. Local churches gave up their indigenous liturgical tradition and received back a mixed bag of native and foreign practices that did not fully reflect their own particular heritage and culture, but instead a more generic regional or universal concept of worship. Although, as we have said, this development succeeded in strengthening the unity and catholicity of the Church, the price paid was a loss of some sense of local self-identity.

Postscript

In 1981 the late Geoffrey Cuming concluded a valuable survey of recent scholarship concerning early eucharistic liturgies with the remark: 'The time has come to rewrite the textbooks.'[1] Now, two decades later, still further rewriting is required, as yet more advances have taken place not merely in the study of the evolution of the Eucharist (in which, as we have seen, Cuming himself played an important part) but also in the investigation of many other aspects of early liturgical history. We need to take note not only of new sources which may have come to light but more importantly of the methods of interpretation which are to be employed in relation to all the sources. For, as Robert Taft has frequently stated, 'Knowledge is not the accumulation of data, not even new data, but the perception of relationships in the data, the creation of hypothetical frameworks to explain new data, or to explain in new ways the old.'[2]

What this particular contribution to research has tried to do, therefore, is to help construct just such a new matrix for the search for the origins of Christian worship, one which takes seriously the altered face of Jewish liturgical scholarship, the basic pluriformity of New Testament Christianity and the inherent ambiguity of its witness to primitive liturgical practice, the real character of the source-documents of the early centuries and the extent of the gaps in our knowledge of the period, and above all the clues which point to the essentially variegated nature of ancient Christian worship. The resultant shape formed within this matrix may be less satisfying than the picture painted by earlier scholarship – but a much better representation of the truth.

1 'The Early Eucharistic Liturgies in Recent Research', in Spinks, ed., *The Sacrifice of Praise*, pp. 65–9.
2 e.g., 'Comparative Liturgy Fifty Years after Anton Baumstark', p. 523.

Index of Modern Authors

Subject Index